T0330783

Routledge Revivals

On the Economic Identification of Social Classes

First published in 1977, *On the Economic Identification of Social Classes* centres around the economic identification – the definition in terms of production relations – of social classes, focussing on the developed capitalist countries. The basic stages of capitalist development are considered, with special emphasis on monopoly capitalism. The book includes a detailed analysis of the functional element of the capitalist production relations; the identification, in terms of production and distribution relations, of the new middle class under monopoly capitalism; and the analysis of the process of proletarianism of this class. New theoretical concepts – of position, devaluation of labour power through dequalification of positions, and of capitalist and non-capitalist state activities – are developed to further the discussions, which, although fresh in approach, are immersed in the complex texture of Marxist thought. This book will be of interest to students of economics and sociology.

On the Economic Identification
of Social Classes

G. Carchedi

Routledge
Taylor & Francis Group

First published in 1977
By Routledge & Kegan Paul

This edition first published in 2022 by Routledge
4 Park Square, Milton Park, Abingdon, Oxon, OX14 4RN
and by Routledge
605 Third Avenue, New York, NY 10017

Routledge is an imprint of the Taylor & Francis Group, an informa business

Publisher's Note
The publisher has gone to great lengths to ensure the quality of this reprint but points
out that some imperfections in the original copies may be apparent.

Disclaimer
The publisher has made every effort to trace copyright holders and welcomes
correspondence from those they have been unable to contact.

A Library of Congress record exists under ISBN: 0710086482

ISBN: 978-1-032-39880-8 (hbk)
ISBN: 978-1-003-35533-5 (ebk)
ISBN: 978-1-032-40920-7 (pbk)

Book DOI 10.4324/9781003355335

ON THE ECONOMIC IDENTIFICATION OF SOCIAL CLASSES

GUGLIELMO CARCHEDI
Instituut voor Economische Sociologie
University of Amsterdam

ROUTLEDGE DIRECT EDITIONS

ROUTLEDGE & KEGAN PAUL
London, Henley and Boston

First published in 1977
by Routledge & Kegan Paul Ltd
39 Store Street,
London WC1E 7DD,
Broadway House,
Newtown Road,
Henley-on-Thames,
Oxon RG9 1EN and
9 Park Street,
Boston, Mass. 02108, USA
Printed by Thomson Litho Ltd
East Kilbride, Scotland

British Library Cataloguing in Publication Data

Carchedi, Guglielmo
On the economic identification of social classes,
1. Social classes - Economic aspects
I. Title
301.44   HT675   77-30143

ISBN 0-7100-8648-2

CONTENTS

ACKNOWLEDGMENTS

The author and publishers are grateful for permission to reproduce the articles which have previously appeared in journals as follows: chapter 1: 'Economy and Society', vol. 4, no. 1; chapter 2: 'Social Praxis', vol. 2, no. 3; chapter 3: 'Amsterdams Sociologisch Tijdschrift', vol. 2, no. 2; chapter 4: 'Economy and Society', vol. 4, no. 4.

INTRODUCTION
SUMMARY OF CONCLUSIONS AND
EXPLANATORY REMARKS

The articles collected in this volume centre around the economic identification, i.e. the definition in terms of production relations, of the major social classes in the developed capitalist countries or, to be more precise, in those countries where capitalism has reached the monopolistic stage. All the four articles have already appeared in different magazines and are reproduced in this book in their original form, exceptions being made for some additions and modifications which do not alter their substance but are only meant to clarify or substantiate some points. Faced with the choice between re-writing the material (in order to improve the presentation, to make some substantial modifications, and to provide a more complete and systematic exposition) and presenting it with only minor alterations of either its form or its substance, I have chosen the latter solution, basically for two reasons. First, the articles in their original form give an idea of the development of the theory submitted, i.e. they allow the reader to see what has been added, modified, further developed, etc., and thus to compare the initial with the final results. It is for this reason that the articles are presented in chronological order, in their order of writing. Second, a more systematic (and, whenever necessary, revised) reformulation of the material would have been perhaps a better didactical and more attractive solution. However, this would have required not only re-writing the already existing material but also the addition of some chapters, since what is missing here is a complete and detailed analysis of the structure of the economy under monopoly capitalism.(1) In other words, this solution would have amounted to the writing of another book. While it is my intention to carry out this project in the near future, I feel that the theory which emerges from these four articles, the methodology followed, the theoretical hypotheses, as well as their practical and political implications deserve to be discussed and criticized already at this stage of the research. Clearly, I am very well aware that many of the hypotheses and results might have to be re-formulated or substantially modified. I mention this not to elicit the sympathy of the reader or to try to prevent criticism, but on the contrary to encourage a debate over the issues dealt with in these papers, issues which in my opinion are of considerable theoretical and

1

practical importance.

In order to allow the reader to get acquainted with some of the basic propositions of this book, I will proceed first of all to describe briefly the content of each of the four chapters. Moreover, by doing so, both a basis of comparison with other authors' approaches and the opportunity to introduce some revisions will be provided.

To engage in theoretical work means also to abstract relevant from less relevant phenomena. The choice of the phenomena considered is determined, within a broad theoretical framework, by the level of abstraction on which the social scientist collocates himself. The study of classes is of course no exception to this general rule. Classes can and should be studied at different levels of abstraction, as a way to approach, by steps, a more and more detailed analysis of the concrete. The first chapter (On the economic identification of the new middle class) focuses exclusively on the two highest levels of abstraction, i.e. on the pure capitalist structure level and on the socio-economic system level. In the first section, I make clear what I include in, and exclude from, the study of classes at these two levels.(2) In short, on the former level I examine only the production process typical of the capitalist economic system (as analysed in detail by Marx) and the production (and distribution) relation corresponding to it. Therefore, the production agents are subdivided into the two classes typical of the capitalist system, the capitalist class and the working class. On the latter level of abstraction I consider how the definition of classes is modified when the relation between production and distribution relations and the relation between the economic structure on the one hand and the superstructure and class struggle on the other hand are examined. On this level one must consider the middle classes, both old and new. But to place oneself on the socio-economic system level of abstraction implies necessarily also facing the question of what is the nature of the above-mentioned relations among the several parts of the socio-economic system. It is a dialectical relation, a relation of determination and overdetermination, as explained in detail in chapter 3. Basically, the concept of dialectical determination submitted can be put concisely as follows.(3) First of all, the determinant instance (e.g. the economic structure) determines the determined instance (e.g. the superstructure) in the sense that the former calls into existence the latter as a condition of the determinant instance's own existence. To take an example within the economic structure, capitalist production determines capitalist distribution in the sense that without a certain type of distribution (e.g. of the social product into wages and profit) a certain type of production would not be possible (e.g. production for profit). Production determines distribution, yet without the latter the former would not be possible. Second, the determined instance modifies, reacts upon the determinant instance, i.e. the determinant instance is overdetermined by the determined instance. For example, a change in the distribution of the social product into wages and profits in favour of the former, implies also an increased production of wage goods and a decreased production of luxury and/or production goods. Implied in this concept of overdetermination are at least three other points, i.e.:

1   the determined instance has a relative autonomy vis-à-vis
    the determinant instance;
2   the determined instance can have a dominant role;
3   the determined instance can be either in correspondence
    or in contradiction with the determinant instance.
Examples illustrating these three propositions will be provided in
chapter 3. Third, the determinant instance sets the limits of variation to its own overdetermination. These limits of variation can
be exploded when both the objective and the subjective conditions
for revolutionary change are present. Among the factors creating
these conditions, class struggle is of paramount importance.
    Having thus decided how to delimit the field of inquiry, i.e.
having decided what elements to include in the study of classes and
what is the relation between these elements, I choose a definition
of classes suitable for the levels of abstraction to which I limit
myself. This definition, first given by Lenin, is discussed in
chapter 1, section I. In this section, beside slightly modifying
the fourth element of the definition, i.e. the element having to do
with distribution relations, I discuss the three elements making up
the production relations and the three-fold nature of the relation
binding them together. Lenin's definition has been slightly modified as follows. Classes are defined as large groups of agents differing from each other:
1   by the place they occupy in a historically determined system of
    social production;
2   by their relation (in most cases fixed and formulated in law) to
    the means of production;
3   by their role in the social organization of labour; and
4   consequently, (a) by the share of social wealth going to a class,
                   (b) by the mode of acquiring this wealth,
                   (c) by the wealth's origin.
In my opinion, the importance of this definition resides in the fact
that emphasis is placed not only on the place occupied by the production agents in the process of production (e.g., under capitalism,
whether they are productive or unproductive labourers) and on the
ownership of the means of production. These two aspects have been
repeatedly stressed in the Marxist literature. This definition also
brings into sharp relief the third element making up the production
relations, i.e. the social function performed by the production
agents within the production process. As far as the capitalist production process is concerned, Marx has shown that it can be regarded
as the unity in domination of the labour process and of the surplus
value producing process. This is only a concise way of expressing
the fact that, under conditions of capitalist production, use values
are produced only as a means to produce exchange values, i.e. to
produce surplus value. This means that, *in terms of the function*
reverting to each of the two classes of agents, in the capitalist
production process participate both those agents performing the
function of labour (the labourer) and those performing the function
of capital (the non-labourer).
    Therefore, the capitalist production relations are defined as
those relations which bind together the three elements of the capitalist production process - i.e. the two types of agents of production and the means of production - and which are regarded from a

three-fold point of view. From the point of view of the ownership
of the means of production, they bind together the owner, the non-
owner, and the means of production. From the point of view of productiveness, they bind together the producer (exploited), the non-
producer (exploiter), and the means of production. From the point
of view of the function performed within the production process,
they bind together the labourer (i.e. the agent who performs the
function of labour), the non-labourer (i.e. the agent who performs
the function of capital) and the means of production. In other
words, the agents of production take on a different connotation
according to which aspect of the production relations is considered.
The agents of production can thus be either the owner or the non-
owner of the means of production, either the producer (and thus,
under capitalism, typically but not exclusively, the exploited) or
the non-producer (and thus typically the exploiter), and either the
labourer or the non-labourer. Thus the element of the function performed within the capitalist production process is explicitly introduced within the capitalist production relations. This of course has
nothing to do with marrying Marxism and functionalism. The functional aspect of the capitalist production relations is not introduced ex novo since it is already present in Marxist theory. Rather,
this aspect has been given greater emphasis here than in other Marxist works and a considerable part of this chapter is devoted to an
analysis of the function of labour and of the function of capital,
both in general under capitalism, and in the several stages of capitalist development.

    If it is true that the functional element is important in defining
the capitalist production relations, it follows that one should be
absolutely clear. as to the meaning of performing the function of
capital and performing the function of labour. This is what I
attempt to do in section III. To the best of my knowledge, no detailed analysis has been carried out in the Marxist literature in
order to find out what is the meaning of performing one function
rather than the other, and how this meaning has undergone modifications in shifting from one stage of capitalism to another. While
Marx analysed the shift from the individual to the collective labourer, he did not (and could not have done so) analyse the shift from
the individual to what I call the global capitalist within the capitalist production process. Thus, section III attempts to define the
function of the individual labourer, the function of the collective
labourer, the function of the individual capitalist, and that of the
global capitalist. To summarize schematically:

(a) the capitalist production process is the unity in domination of
     the labour process and the surplus value producing process, i.e.
     it is a process in which the production of surplus value domi-
     nates the production of use values;

(b) to perform the function of labour means to take part in the
     labour process and thus, under capitalism, to the surplus value
     producing process; with the real subordination of labour to
     capital, the function of labour is performed by a large body of
     agents, by what Marx calls the collective worker; each of these
     agents, then, performs the function of the collective worker;

(c) to perform the function of capital means to take part exclu-
     sively in the surplus value producing process, i.e. to carry out

the work of control and surveillance. Under monopoly capitalism this function is not performed any more by the individual
capitalist but by a large number of agents, i.e. by what I
call the global capitalist. All agents performing this function perform thus the global function of capital.
Since there are three aspects to the capitalist production relations, the problem now arises as to the relative importance of each
of these aspects vis-à-vis the others. In my opinion, these three
aspects are bound together by a relationship of determination, where
the determinant role reverts to the ownership element. In other
words, to be the owner of the means of production implies also being
the non-producer (exploiter) and the non-labourer. Since a relationship of determination implies either correspondence or contradiction
between the determinant and the determined elements, we can define
the two fundamental classes, the working class and the capitalist
class, in terms of correspondence among the three aspects of the
capitalist production relations. I.e. the capitalist class is defined as the owner/exploiter/non-producer/non-labourer, while the
working class is defined as the non-owner/exploited/producer/
labourer.
The rest of section III is an application of all the concepts
worked out so far, to the economic identification of the proletariat
and the bourgeoisie at the socio-economic system level of abstraction and considering three stages of capitalist development: the
stage of private capitalism characterized by formal subordination of
labour to capital, the stage of private capitalism characterized by
real subordination of labour to capital, and the stage of monopoly
capitalism. For example, in the stage of monopoly capitalism the
bourgeoisie is economically identifiable as all those agents who, 1,
either exploit or economically oppress;(4) 2, have the real, economic ownership (not to be confused with the legal ownership) of the
means of production; 3, are the non-labourers in the sense that they
perform the global function of capital; and 4, derive their income
from surplus value, whose income is limited by the extent of surplus
value, and whose surplus value is either produced in their own
enterprise or acquired through participation in the sharing of surplus value produced elsewhere. The proletariat is identifiable as
all those agents who, 1, are exploited or economically oppressed;
2, do not own the means of production; 3, perform the function of
the collective worker; and 4, consequently (a) are paid a wage the
amount of which is tendentially determined by the value of their
labour power, (b) are paid their income by the capitalist, and (c)
either are paid back a part of the value they themselves produced or
are paid out of the surplus value produced in the productive spheres.
But on the socio-economic system level of abstraction we consider
not only the two primary classes but also the middle classes, i.e.
those classes which in terms of production relations are a sort of
'hybrid', a mixture of the two 'pure' classes. In fact, a relationship of determination implies not only correspondence but also contradiction between the determinant and the determined instances.
Thus, the middle classes are defined in terms of non-correspondence
between the ownership aspect (determinant aspect) on the one hand
and the productiveness and functional aspect (determined aspects)
on the other. For example, there are agents who, while not owning

the means of production (and we speak here of real, economic ownership and not of legal ownership), are expropriated of surplus labour
and perform the function of capital, thus being either the exploiter
or the economic oppressor. This is approximately the definition of
one of the two sections of the new middle class in terms of production relations. This section will be examined in detail in chapter 4.
The other section, which performs in a varying balance both the
function of labour and the function of capital, will be summarily
discussed further down in this Introduction and analysed in detail
in chapter 1.

   However, before we can provide an exact definition of the new
middle class (as well as of the capitalist class and of the working
class) under monopoly capitalism, we must analyse the changes undergone by the two functions in the several stages of capitalist development. The conclusion reached in this chapter is that under
monopoly capitalism the function of labour is performed by the collective worker while the function of capital (here defined as the
work of control and surveillance) is performed by what I call the
global capitalist, i.e. by a hierarchical and bureaucratic structure
which replaces the individual capitalist in carrying out the work of
control and surveillance. Therefore, since the rise of the new
middle class is a phenomenon typical of monopoly capitalism, a precise definition of this class must be given, as far as the functional
aspect is concerned, in terms of function of the *collective* labourer
and of *global* function of capital. It should be clear by now why
the functional aspect should be dealt with explicitly and at length.
First of all, since there are three aspects to the capitalist production relations and since there can be contradiction between them, an
identification of classes must take place in terms of all three
aspects (thus including the functional one). Second, the function
of capital, which in the stage of individual capitalism was a prerogative of the capitalist, undergoes, under monopoly capitalism,
important modifications. Only by focusing on, and analysing, the
functional aspect can we study these modifications and identify
classes in terms of production relations in an exact and unambiguous
way.

   Let us now elaborate further on the concept of function. Since
the capitalist production process is always both a technical process
and a process which rests on definite production relations (the relations in which the agents of production and the means of production
engage in participating in the production process), it follows that
a function has always a double content, i.e. a technical and a social
content. The latter is given by the performing of either the (global) function of capital or of the function of the (collective)
worker. The former, on the other hand, is given by the technical
nature of the production process, by the fact that such a process is
subdivided in a number of 'jobs', of tasks with a certain definite
technical nature. A 'job account', then, i.e. technical description
of a function, if sufficiently specified, should always provide us
with enough information to judge about not only that function's
technical content but also that function's social nature. For sake
of concreteness, let us provide a few examples drawn from a recent
field research.(5) For example, it was found out that the technical
nature of a chemical supervisor's function was, in his own words:

'laboratory supervision which means that I have to supply ...
chemical analyses or spectrographical analyses which we need on
site. The main job is metal analyses since we produce metal.'

It is clear that here, in spite of the use of the word 'supervision', which in my terminology refers to the (global) function of
capital, the function of this agent is typically that of the collective worker. The same social nature must be attributed also to the
following function, that of a production assistant, who describes
his tasks as follows:(6)

'well we in this case [i.e. in case of repairs to be done on a
machine, G.C.] tell the actual foremen to get the maintenance
people in. The foremen are more concerned with the actual minute
to minute, the day to day running.... If I am not satisfied with
the way they are getting on with it you know I'll go and see the
maintenance people but generally the foremen ... can deal with
it.'

And finally, this is the picture of a metallurgical technician's
'job', as it emerges from his own account, the social content of
which is again the same as that of the two functions mentioned
above:(7)

'I work with a senior extrusion metallurgist. The thing is we
keep the standard practices and press practices up to date - on
the presses, what temperature they have to extrude at, the speed
they extrude at, container temperature, we check them. We go
around in the morning and we look at all the presses. Any problems that's arisen on the presses we then have to sort out.'

As an example of an agent performing the global function of capital,
i.e. the work of control and surveillance as carried out not any
longer by an individual capitalist but by a large number of agents
hierarchically and bureaucratically organized in a complex structure, we mention a production supervisor. This agent, in the words
of Fairbrother, 'is a person who performs the tasks of control and
surveillance at a level above that of the foreman....' For example,
one young production supervisor described his job in the following
way:(8)

'Here at the moment I got three foremen and about ninety odd men
in my area that I supervise.'

To facilitate an insight in the nature of the function of capital
let us, following Fairbrother, compare the function just described
with that of another production supervisor:(9)

' ... although I am a production supervisor ... I don't have
control of men. I don't schedule the work through the mill. I
don't push the job through.... I am more of an industrial engineer. I evolve new techniques, recommend new processes and new
equipment.'

As Fairbrother correctly remarks, 'each job description was presented in terms of work actually done by these two production supervisors, the significance of them being that two entirely different
experiences were associated with each job. For the first supervisor, his job consisted primarily of the performance of the tasks
of control and surveillance. The second supervisor, however, gained
little or no experience in this aspect of the job. He performed
tasks associated with the maintenance and development of the technology of the production process itself. In his work he did not

control or supervise the work of others in the plant, although his
formal job title indicated the performance of such tasks.'(10)
     One more point should be added in discussing the functional ele-
ment of the capitalist production relations: the fact that an agent
can perform both functions even though not at the same time.   This
point will be dealt with at greater length in chapter 1.   Here I
only want to provide an example of an agent performing both the function of the collective worker and the global function of capital.
Let us, once more, draw on Fairbrother's field study:(11)

> But, of course, the performance of a job may involve more or
> less of the control and surveillance function or the production
> function.   For example, an administration supervisor described
> his job in the following way.   He began with a description of
> his department's activities.
>
> > 'Supplies Department comprises two sections - the store stock
> > control section and the purchasing section.   Purchasing func-
> > tion speaks for itself.   I suppose we are responsible for
> > ordering all materials used in the factory other than metal....
> > Stock control section is responsible for controlling all store
> > stock items, that is items which we keep in stores.'
>
> About his job he said:
>
> > 'I am responsible for discipline and methods.'
>
> Methods meant:
>
> > '... I suppose it's true to say that up to a point the work
> > I am doing is work that is the same type of work that is done
> > by people in either purchases or stock control but I come in
> > on a higher level - when it's vital.'

This last is an example of an agent who, in terms of production
relations falls into that part of the new middle class analysed in
detail in section IV.   In this section, in fact, I focus basically
on one part of the new middle class (which encompasses technicians,
employees, middle and lower managers, etc. and thus is directly
relevant for the discussion about the class collocation of these
agents) i.e. on those agents who 1, do not own, either legally or
economically, the means of production; 2, perform, *but not at the
same time,* both the function of the collective worker and the global
function of capital; 3, are therefore both the labourer (either productive or unproductive) and the non-labourer; and 4, are both exploiters (or economic oppressors) and exploited (or economically
oppressed).(12)
     The economic definition of this part of the new middle class is
directly relevant for a discussion of the *distribution* relations
characterizing it.   If the production relations identifying the new
middle class are a sort of mixture of the relations identifying the
two basic classes (proletariat and bourgeoisie), it follows that the
income of the new middle class, as shown in section V, must be made
up both of *revenue,* inasmuch as it performs the global function of
capital, and of *wages,* inasmuch as it performs the function of the
collective labourer.   In this section I compare the new middle class
to the labour aristocracies to emphasize the fact that only the
former is middle class already at the level of production relations.
The latter, on the other hand, while members of the working class on
the level of production relations, become middle class (or better
said, petty bourgeoisie) when distribution relations, superstructure,

and class struggle are considered.

This chapter closes with section VI, a discussion of the process of proletarianization of the new middle class. Such a process hinges on two basic points. First of all, the new middle class is subjected to the same law to which all skilled labour is subjected under capitalism: the constant tendency to the devaluation of the labour power of the new middle class in relation to the average value of the labour power. This is a tendency typical of capitalism in all its stages, i.e. the reduction of skilled to unskilled labour. For the new middle class, however, the process of devaluation of labour power is coupled with the process of progressive decreasing of the time dedicated to the global function of capital and thus with a progressive increase of the time during which the function of the collective worker is performed. Strictly speaking, then, we can speak of proletarianization of the new middle class only when this process (in its double aspect) has reached its conclusion. 'Proletarianization is the limit of the process of devaluation of the new middle class's labour power, i.e. the reduction of this labour power to an average, unskilled level coupled with the elimination of the global function of capital.' The reduction of the time spent performing the global function of capital vis-à-vis the function of the collective worker is the particular way through which monopoly capital reduces the time spent unproductively by its wage-earners.(13)

Clearly, then, proletarianization is explained in terms of capital accumulation, i.e. in dynamic terms, rather than in broadly descriptive economic and sociological terms. The proletarianization of the new middle class is here considered from a double aspect: the reduction of the value of the labour power, i.e. reduction of necessary labour, and thus increase of surplus value or of surplus labour, and on the other hand the increase of the time spent on performing the function of labour and thus also on performing productive or unproductive labour. Both aspects of the process of proletarianization reflect thus the same aim: the increase in surplus labour or surplus value. All the other aspects usually referred to as aspects of the proletarianization of the new middle class, as e.g. lower wages, loss of positions of privilege, loss of prestige, etc., are only consequences of the double phenomenon of devaluation of labour power and tendencial disappearance of the global function of capital.

Confusion might arise around the concept of unproductiveness and therefore on who is productive and who is not. Due to the importance of these concepts for the identification of classes, we will have to deal at some length with 1, the unproductive *labourer* and, 2, the *non-labourer*, who by definition is non-productive.

In chapter 1, besides the capitalist production process which I define as the unity in domination of the labour process and of the surplus value producing process, I analyse also what I call the *unproductive capitalist production process*. In the unproductive capitalist production process the labourer (either the individual or the collective labourer) does not produce surplus value and yet is expropriated of surplus labour.(14) He produces a certain use value (e.g. a service) while, at the same time, being expropriated of surplus labour. This means that he takes part both in a labour process

and in what I call the *surplus labour* producing process, where the
latter dominates the former. Since this worker is unproductive, he
cannot be exploited. Since, however, he provides surplus labour, we
can say that he is *economically oppressed*. As a general rule, all
labour employed in the circulation sphere, i.e. in the formal transformation of money-capital into commodity-capital and vice-versa, is
unproductive labour and thus is economically oppressed.(15)

Now the concept of unproductiveness, and thus of economic oppression, takes on a different meaning according to whether we refer to
the unproductive labourer or to the non-labourer. To understand
better what follows, let us simplify the discussion by focusing only
on those agents who, while not owning the means of production, perform only the global function of capital, e.g. the foremen. The time
spent performing the global function of capital is neither productive
nor unproductive, in the sense given to these terms within the discussion about productive and unproductive labour. From the point of
view of capital there is a basic difference between the unproductiveness of the unproductive *labourer* and the unproductiveness of the
non-labourer. The former is the channel through whom the unproductive (e.g. commercial) capitalist participates in the redistribution
of the surplus value produced in the productive spheres of the
economy. Even though this labourer is not directly productive, the
difference between the value of his labour power (in hours of
socially necessary labour time) and the hours he works every day is
the way the unproductive capitalist appropriates the surplus value
produced in other, productive branches of the economy. The more the
unproductive labourers employed by a certain capitalist, the more
the surplus value he can take for himself, ceteris paribus. The non-
labourer, on the other hand, is non-productive in quite a different
way.· His wage (or salary) is a *faux frais* of capitalist production,
it is a *deduction* from the surplus value produced or appropriated, it
does not serve either to create or to appropriate surplus value from
other branches of the economy, but it serves to expropriate surplus
value or surplus labour on behalf of the capitalist. To clarify
further this point, let us draw a comparison between the 'variable'
capital spent in the circulation sphere and the capital spent for the
wages of the non-labourers (i.e. simply to maintain and re-produce
the despotic organization of the enterprise). They are both 'as far
as the entire capitalist is concerned, a deduction from the surplus
value or surplus product'.(16) However, the former type of expenditure (wages spent for unproductive labourers) allows the commercial
capitalist to participate in the distribution of surplus value, while
the latter type of expenditure (wages for the non-labourers) is
simply deductions from his profits; it is simply money the capitalist
must spend without any direct effect on the creation or appropriation
of surplus value. This money must be spent because the function of
capital is a necessary aspect of the capitalist production relations,
i.e. because in the capitalist production process must take part also
agents who perform the function of capital (or the global function of
capital, if we consider classes under monopoly capitalism). In this
sense this expenditure is not useless, but necessary. However, from
the point of view of surplus value creation or redistribution it is
only a negative element. To make a somewhat paradoxical example, a
commercial enterprise employing 100 unproductive labourers and one

supervisor is certainly better off than a similar enterprise employing one unproductive labourer and 100 supervisors (agents performing
the global function of capital), even though from the point of view
of the creation of surplus value they both make no direct contribution. Since both the unproductive labourer (e.g. the commercial
worker) and his supervisor are expropriated of surplus labour, we
can extend the concept of economic oppression also to the second
category of agents. However, when the functional element is considered as well, the concepts of unproductiveness and of economic
oppression take on quite a different meaning according to whether
the agents expropriated of surplus labour perform one or the other
function.

To get a better grip on the meaning of the non-labourer's unproductiveness, it is useful to distinguish between the capitalist production process and the capitalist production relations.(17) When
we consider the *capitalist production process,* the type of unproductiveness under consideration implies a *faux frais* for the capitalist, a necessary expenditure which, however, has no direct relevance for either the creation or the transfer of surplus value.
This is why the capitalist tends to eliminate the part of the working day devoted to the global function of capital for all those
agents who perform this function either exclusively or in combination with the function of the collective worker. When we consider
the *capitalist production relations* this type of unproductiveness
means that an agent, while being economically oppressed (inasmuch
as he is paid, in terms of hours of labour, less than the hours he
works), performs himself a function the content of which is either
exploitation or economic oppression. To repeat, only the capitalist
can be *just* the exploiter or the oppressor - i.e. the agent who not
only expropriates but also appropriates, has the power to dispose of,
surplus value - because he has the economic ownership of the means
of production. On the other hand, the agent who does not own the
means of production and yet performs the global function of capital
is *at the same time both* 1, oppressed (he cannot be exploited since,
being a non-labourer, he cannot produce surplus value), because, not
having the ownership of the means of production, he is paid less
than the hours he works *and,* 2, either oppressor or exploiter
(depending upon whether he works in an unproductive or in a productive enterprise) because he performs the global function of capital.
From all this it follows that:
1 the non-ownership of the means of production does not necessarily
   imply being oppressed or exploited since the non-owner can be
   also the exploiter or the oppressor (inasmuch as he performs the
   global function of capital);
2 non-ownership does not necessarily imply performing the function
   of labour because a non-owner can perform also the global function of capital;
3 non-ownership does not imply productiveness because a non-owner
   can be both productive and unproductive (of surplus value), inasmuch as he performs the function of the collective worker, and
   non-productive if he performs the global function of capital.
On the basis of these remarks it should now be clear why a definition of classes in terms of production relations should always encompass not only the ownership element (the determinant instance)

but also the expropriation and the functional elements (determined instances).

Let us now return to that section of the new middle class dealt with specifically in section IV and which, in terms of the functional element of the production relations, performs both the global function of capital and the function of the collective worker. As we have seen, section V deals with the income of this section of the new middle class. There I make the following points:

1   The income of those agents performing the function of capital (work of control and surveillance) is called *revenue,* while the income of those performing the function of labour is called *wage.*
2   Therefore, the income of all those agents who perform both the global function of capital and function of the collective worker is made up both of a revenue and of a wage component.
3   While the wage component is determined by the culturally determined subsistence minimum, the revenue component is not.
4   The determination of the revenue component is still an unsolved problem.

To solve this problem, let us recall that the typical capitalist production process is the unity in domination of the labour process and of the surplus value producing process. We have seen that unity in domination of these two aspects of the capitalist production process means that use values are produced only as a means for the production of exchange values. We have also seen that, generally speaking, to perform the function of labour means to take part in the labour process and thus in the surplus value producing process, while to perform the function of capital means to take part in the capitalist production process exclusively from the point of view of the surplus value producing process, i.e. to carry out the work of control and surveillance.(18)   Now, Marx provides an explicit and detailed analysis of how wages (the income of the labourers, both productive and unproductive) are determined, basically by referring to the value of these agents' labour power.   In other words, Marx analyses only the determination of the income of those agents who only perform the function of labour (or function of the collective worker).   Revenue, for Marx, is that part of surplus value spent unproductively by the *individual* capitalist; it is a residual category and as such presents no particular difficulties. With the advent of the global capitalist, however, i.e. with the advent of that structure which collectively and hierarchically carries out the function of capital, what used to be the function of the individual capitalist as capitalist becomes now a function carried out by a large number of agents. The income of these agents (for sake of simplicity let us now consider here only those agents who perform exclusively the global function of capital) is called in this chapter revenue, just as the income of the individual capitalist. However, if the income of the individual capitalist can be treated as a residual category, the income of the global capitalist cannot. There must be laws determining revenues just as there are laws determining wages. I think that at least one aspect of the solution to this problem should be sought in the following direction.   It is known that wages are determined by the culturally determined subsistence minimum and that skilled labour counts as multiple of simple, unskilled

labour.   Revenues are determined in the same way, provision being
made for the fact that now we can speak of simple and skilled
'labour' only by analogy.   Quite clearly, the 'skills', knowledge,
etc. required of an agent who must control those working on a conveyor belt are quite different and cost less to acquire than the
skills required of an agent who must control the work of technicians
and engineers.   There is, thus, a similarity between wage and revenue determination.   But there is also an important difference.   We
know that besides the economic determination of wages (value of
labour power) there are also political and ideological wage determinants, i.e. that in certain periods and for certain sectors of
the working class wages might not correspond to the value of those
sectors of the working class's labour power.   I discuss in section
V the example of the labour aristocracies.   However, as far as revenue is concerned, the ideological and political determinants of
revenues are much more important than for wages *because the non-
labourer*, in order to be such, i.e. in order to perform the work of
control and surveillance, *must be hierarchically higher than the
labourer he controls*.   Thus, the political and ideological components are a *constant feature* of revenues but not of wages.   It is
only on this basis, i.e. on the basis of a determination of revenues first of all in terms of value of 'labour' power, that it can
be concluded, as I do at the end of section V, that as far as revenue is concerned, 'income differentiation is functional for the
maintenance of the authoritarian and hierarchical structure of the
enterprise.'

Chapter 2 (The economic identification of the state employees)
attempts to test the relevance of the theory submitted in the first
chapter when applied to state enterprises.   We should first of all
rid ourselves of the false notion, which is dying out only with some
difficulty, that state enterprises cannot be capitalist in nature.
The following quotation by Lenin should clarify this point once and
for all.   In a speech pronounced in 1921, in which he discusses the
economic nature of concessions, Lenin had the following to say:(19)
   What are concessions from the standpoint of economic relations?
   They are state capitalism.   The Soviet government concludes an
   agreement with a capitalist.   Under it, the latter is provided
   with certain things: raw materials, mines, oilfields, minerals,
   or, as was the case in one of the last proposals, even a special
   factory (the ball-bearing project of a Swedish enterprise).   The
   socialist state gives the capitalist its means of production such
   as factories, mines and materials.   The capitalist operates as a
   contractor leasing socialist means of production, making a profit
   on his capital and delivering a part of his output to the socialist state.
What we have here is a separation, within a system in transition between capitalism and socialism, between the legal ownership of the
means of production (which belong to the socialist state) and the
real ownership of the means of production, which are now in the
hands of the capitalist.   The two cardinal points, then, in order to
find out whether a certain type of production is capitalist in
nature or not are: 1, to whom does the real ownership revert?   and,

2, are the means of production basically used to produce profits (surplus value) or to meet needs? If those two criteria are applicable to a system in transition, they are applicable, even more so, to a capitalist economy. Therefore, the fact that, legally speaking, the (capitalist) state owns certain means of production does not help us very much in finding out about the nature of a certain production process and production relations.

Having said this, we can now provide a very short summary of chapter 2. The method followed here is the same as the one followed in chapter 1. This method can be formulated very schematically as follows. We start, first of all, from an analysis of the capitalist production process both productive and unproductive. On the basis of this, we analyse the capitalist production relations. Finally, we identify the major classes in terms of these production relations. Before we proceed, however, I should warn the reader that the procedure just outlined coincides not with the method of inquiry but with the method of presentation.(20) In other words, what just said should not be taken to mean that the determinant role reverts to the capitalist production process rather than to the capitalist production relations. I start with a discussion of the capitalist production process simply because its nature is, at first, more evident than that of the corresponding production relations. However, as we will see further down in this Introduction when we will discuss, in a necessarily cursory way, the nature of the capitalist economic structure, it is the capitalist production relations which play the determinant role.

This chapter is divided into three sections. I will disregard here the third section, which is a discussion of the political implications inherent in my type of approach. Rather, I should like to spend a few words on the first two sections, which are of a more theoretical nature. In section I, I introduce the term 'state activities', since the term 'state enterprises' implies some sort of productive activity. State activities on the other hand, encompass capitalist (both productive and unproductive) as well as non-capitalist state activities. However, my discussion is limited to those activities the nature of which is basically technico-administrative (such as schools, hospitals, etc.) and does not concern itself with those institutions the basic function of which is the domination of the working class (e.g. police). In this section I search a criterion on the basis of which the capitalist state activities can be separated from the non-capitalist ones. In order to do this I reconsider the capitalist production process and I conclude that a convenient way to separate the productive (of surplus value) from the unproductive capitalist production process is to define the former as production *for* and *of* surplus value and the latter as production *only for* surplus value. In the former the formula M – M' represents a real production of surplus value. In the latter, the same formula represents no production but only appropriation of surplus value. It represents capital accumulation for the single, unproductive capitalist, but no real accumulation, i.e. as far as social capital is concerned. It follows that a state activity, whenever it conforms itself to either one of the two principles just mentioned, whenever, i.e. it is production of and for surplus value or just for surplus value, can be considered as a capitalist

activity, either productive or unproductive. It follows, then,
that - aside from political and ideological considerations - the
collocation in terms of production relations of those agents taking
part in these activities must be carried out along the same lines
provided in chapter 1.

What about the non-capitalist state activities? These are characterized as being production *neither of nor for* surplus value. They
spend money not in order to increase it but in order to meet needs.
They produce a commodity (e.g. a non-material commodity, a service)
which is not a capitalist commodity. In fact, even if this commodity is the unity of exchange value and use value, the dominant role
reverts not to the former but to the latter. Thus, in terms of production, there is a basic difference between capitalist and non-
capitalist state activities. However, we should be careful in distinguishing production process and production relations. The conclusion I reach is that the non-capitalist state activities, by
being immersed in, and thus dominated by, a capitalist economic
structure, produce non-capitalist commodities just as capitalist
commodities are produced, i.e. by extracting surplus labour. Therefore there is a similarity between the production relations upon
which an unproductive capitalist enterprise is based on the one hand
and the production relations at the basis of the non-capitalist
state activities. In conclusion, then, the collocation of these
state employees, at the level of production relations follows the
one indicated for the agents employed in the non-productive capitalist enterprises.

The reader will have realized that one of the fundamental concepts
used in the study of social classes is that of dialectical determination. In chapter 3 (On dialectical determination: an operational
definition) I attempt to define, as precisely as possible, such a
concept. Since I have already hinted at the basic elements of this
concept above in this Introduction, I will not summarize any more
the content of this chapter but will proceed to revise one important
point.

In this chapter I distinguish the method of presentation from the
method of inquiry. The latter, in turn, is subdivided into logical
and historical analysis. In discussing the nature of these two
aspects of the method of inquiry, I state that 'a logical analysis ... can be carried out at various levels of abstraction while an
historical analysis is always an analysis on the conjunctural level.
An historical analysis, then, is the logical outcome (on the most
concrete level of abstraction) of an analysis (logical) which necessarily must begin on the highest level of abstraction only to descend to more and more concrete levels.' This statement is incorrect
and should be reformulated. In order to do this, I will start from
my conclusions about the nature of the two types of analysis. As I
say in chapter 3, a logical analysis is an analysis of determination, overdetermination, correspondence, contradiction, etc. among
the various instances of a society. It should be added that a logical analysis is also an analysis, first of all, of the nature of
these instances. For example, the study of the capitalist production relations deals not only with the nature of the ownership,

productiveness, and functional aspects, but also with the relationship among these three aspects. An historical analysis, on the
other hand, deals with the factors accounting for the discrepancy,
accelerations, retardations, etc. in the rhythm of development of
the various instances.(21) We can say, thus, that the former analysis studies how this 'pure model' is modified by, adapted to, etc.
particular circumstances. It studies the particular form taken by
the pure model under particular, e.g. geographically, historically,
etc. delimited, circumstances. E.g. once the logical analysis of
capitalism has been carried out, we can inquire into the specific
form taken by capitalism in a certain country, its deviations from
the model, the reasons why it develops earlier than, or later than,
in another country, etc. It is then clear that these two types of
analysis imply each other. In fact, while an historical analysis
implies a logical one (since it can be considered as a concretiza-
tion of a theoretical model) also the latter implies the former
because it is obviously impossible to find out about the structure
of a society, its lawn of development, etc., without an historical
inquiry. As I mention in this chapter, the price one pays for failing to base a logical analysis on an historical one are the functionalist, structuralist view in sociology and the 'homo economicus'
in economics. From this, it follows that these two types of analysis are only two aspects of the method of inquiry and can be separated only as a didactical device. This is why I think that to pose
the question of the priority of one type of analysis in relation
to the other is to pose a false problem.(22)

Since the nature of both logical and historical analysis is dialectical (accelerations, delays, modifications, etc. are the way the
relative independence of the determined instances manifests itself
concretely, historically), it follows that the method of inquiry is
dialectical as well. To make this point clear, let us consider the
law of the tendential fall of the profit rate. Here we have, from
the point of view of logical analysis, a main tendency, which at
this level of analysis, is the determinant instance, and a number of
countertendencies, which are the determined instances. Since the
determined instances can be dominant vis-à-vis the determinant one,
the theoretical basis is provided for the fact that at the beginning
of the cycle the countertendencies are stronger than the general
tendency (tendential fall of the rate of profit). An historical
analysis is just the study of the particular forms taken by these
countertendencies in a certain country and at a certain period, of
how, when, and in what measure they react on the basic tendency,
etc.

The concept of dialectical determination is only one of the three
basic concepts on which the analysis of social classes, as carried
out in this book, rests. The other two basic tools of research are
the concepts of levels of abstraction and of stages of capitalist
development. These three concepts are strictly interrelated. In
fact, first of all, when classes are studied at several levels of
abstraction, we must presuppose a certain stage of development.
E.g. when we study the change in the characteristics of the working
class in shifting from the first (the pure capitalist economic
structure) to the second (the socio-economic system) level of abstraction, we must specify whether, e.g. we consider the stage of

private or of monopoly capitalism. Vice versa, when we consider the
change in the elements making up social classes in shifting from one
stage to another (e.g. from private capitalism characterized by
formal subordination of labour to capital, to private capitalism
characterized by real subordination) we must place our analysis at a
certain level of abstraction (e.g. the level of the socio-economic
system). In short, each stage of capitalist development can be studied at several levels of abstraction, and each level of abstraction
applies to several stages of development. The concept of dialectical
determination is the mechanism connecting one stage to another and
one level to another. In this book I distinguish between four
levels of abstraction (to be discussed in some detail shortly) and
three stages of development. If, for explanatory purposes, we set
these two dimensions on a system of co-ordinates, we get a scheme as
shown in Figure 1.

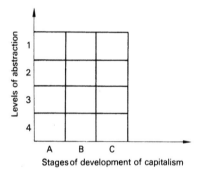

FIGURE 1

For example, when we locate our research in situation 1C, we
study the general characteristic of classes at the highest level of
abstraction and at the stage of monopoly capitalism. At this level
we consider only the working class and the capitalist class.(23)
Situation 1C can be thus compared both to situation 2C and to situation 1B. In the former case we introduce the middle classes (both
old and new), the superstructure, and the class struggle. In the
latter case we must distinguish between legal and real ownership of
the means of production, between function of capital and global
function of capital, etc. A passage from situation 1C either to 2C
or to 1B implies the concept of dialectical determination. Moreover, the analysis of situation 1C is already dialectical because
it considers the determination of the functional and the productiveness elements by the ownership element. An historical analysis of
situation 1C would consider, for example, the particular causes
which retard the development of monopoly capitalism in a certain
country (e.g. Holland) and thus of the characteristics of these two
classes as they appear under this stage of capitalist development.
Or, to give another example, an historical (comparative) analysis
of situation 2C would consider the particular ideology of the new

middle class in a certain country (e.g. Holland) versus a different
type of ideology of the same class in a different country (e.g.
Italy, where technicians and employees are much more proletarian in
their outlook). Therefore, an historical analysis can be carried
out at all levels of abstraction and not only on the conjunctural
level, contrary to what I state in chapter 3.

It should be stressed that only a clear distinction between
stages of development and levels of abstraction on one side and between logical and historical analysis on the other, can avoid
muddled and spurious categories. For example, E. Koga (24) speaks
of three dimensions of knowledge in the social sciences, i.e. the
global social system (which studies how labour becomes wage labour,
how the means of production become capital, etc.), the stages of
development of a social system (which searches the dominant forms
of existence of capital and, within each stage, the change in the
relationships among classes), and the specific and concrete situations at a certain time or in a certain country (which provides the
subject with an immediate basis for action). In fact, the first
and third 'dimensions' are only two different levels of abstraction
(the third dimension corresponding to what I call the conjunctural
level of abstraction) and only as such should be set against the
concept of stages of development.(25)

We have seen that the three basic tools of research used in this
book are the concepts of stages of development, of dialectical
determination, and of levels of abstraction. Since the former two
concepts are dealt with in some detail in chapters 1 and 3 respectively, while only a cursory treatment is given to the latter concept, a few words on the levels of abstraction are now in order.

The concept of levels of abstraction is only a theoretical tool
which allows the researcher to start from what is essential for the
study of the phenomenon under consideration (the highest level).
By considering an ever increasing number of supplementary aspects
(intermediate levels), the researcher finally comes down to the
lowest level of abstraction where, given the richness of details
considered, 'the life of the subject matter is ideally reflected
as in a mirror'.(26) In this book I distinguish between four levels
of abstraction, even though most of the analysis is carried out only
on the two highest levels. The first level is that of the *pure
capitalist economic structure*. On this level we consider only what
is determinant in a capitalist society, i.e. its economic structure.
Moreover, this structure is considered in its pure form, i.e. we disregard the modifications brought about by the determined factors.
The analysis of these modifications is carried out only at lower levels of abstraction. I have mentioned above, for example, that in
chapter 2 I analyse the modifications undergone by the capitalist
economic structure due to the introduction of what I have called the
non-capitalist state activities.

Contrary to what might be assumed, already at the highest level
the economic structure is not an undifferentiated entity. It was
Althusser's merit to have introduced the concept of structural complexity, the unity of the economic, the political, and the ideological where the former plays the determinant role. Moreover, in
'Reading Capital',(27) Althusser and Balibar face the question of
the internal structure of the economic base, i.e. disregarding the

political and ideological (determined) instances. Althusser mentions the existence, within the economic base, of two elements, the
labour process and the social relations of production 'beneath
whose determination this labour-process is executed'.(28)   However,
he does not extend this aspect of his analysis to class-divided
societies and, specifically, to the capitalist society. Moreover,
he only mentions that the two elements are 'indissociable' without
going into the question of what kind of relationship is there between the production relations and the production process. Balibar
explores another region on the pure capitalist economic structure,
i.e. the existence of two types of relations (production relations):
(29)

> Now we find that *production* itself is a complex totality, i.e.
> that nowhere is there a simple totality, and we can give a pre-
> cise meaning to this complexity: it consists of the fact that
> the elements of the totality are not linked together once but
> twice, by two distinct connections. What Marx called a *combina-
> tion* is not therefore *a simple relationship between the 'factors'
> of any production, but the relationship between these two con-
> nections and their interdependence.*

These two connections are what Balibar calls the property connection
and the real or material appropriation connection. (30)

It seems to me that Althusser's and Balibar's treatment of the
problem (31) is insufficient even in terms of their own approach.
This is not the place to evaluate and modify their contribution,
nor to proceed to an analysis of the economic structure at this
level of abstraction. However, I will provide, in a very schematic
fashion, an indication of the direction in which such an analysis
should be carried out, as well as some points of difference between
the above mentioned authors' approach and my own approach. The
scheme in Figure 2 is meant to facilitate the understanding of the
results of an analysis the details of which must be postponed to
another occasion.

The capitalist economic structure is made up of two components,
i.e. the capitalist mode of production and the capitalist production process. We know already that the latter is the unity in domination of the surplus value producing process and of the labour process. We now see that this process is linked to the capitalist mode
of production by a relation of determination. The capitalist mode
of production is also a unity of two elements, the capitalist production relations and the capitalist production forces, where the
former determine the latter.(32)   Moreover, the capitalist production relations are considered as the production relations upon which
the surplus value producing process rests (when the owner, the non-
owner, and the means of production are considered),(33) or, as the
production relations upon which the labour process rests (when only
the non-owner and the means of production are considered). Finally,
the former relations dominate the latter.

Thus, the capitalist production relations can be regarded from
two angles: the production relations linking together the elements participating in the surplus value producing process and the
production relations linking the elements participating in the
labour process. The relation between the non-owner and the means of
production is a relation of domination of the former over the latter

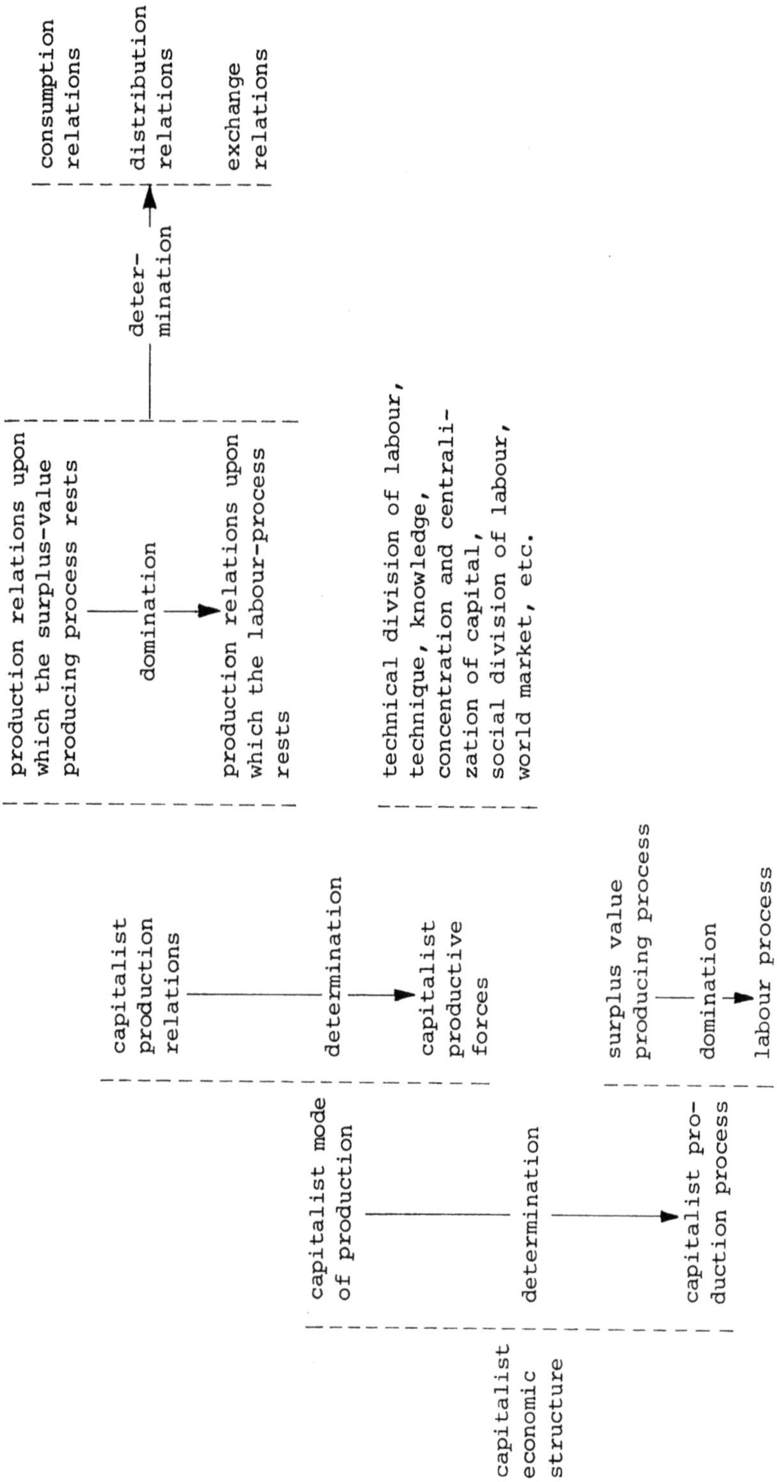

consumption relations

distribution relations

exchange relations

deter-mination

production relations upon which the surplus-value producing process rests

domination

production relations upon which the labour-process rests

technical division of labour, technique, knowledge, concentration and centralization of capital, social division of labour, world market, etc.

capitalist production relations

determination

capitalist productive forces

surplus value producing process

domination

labour process

capitalist mode of production

determination

capitalist production process

capitalist economic structure

FIGURE 2

or vice versa according to whether we consider the labour process or the surplus value producing process.(34) In other words, in the former aspect of the capitalist production process it is the worker who utilizes the means of production while in the latter aspect it is the means of production which utilize the worker. But this is not all. The capitalist production relations are not only the unity of two types of production relations, they are also a unity in dominance. This means that the non-owner/means of production relation characteristic of the surplus value producing process dominates the same relation characterizing the labour process. That is, when we add the third element of the capitalist production relations (the owner) we do not have a simple addition, but a change in the nature of the relation between the owner, the non-owner, and the means of production. It is this nature (capitalist) which becomes dominant within the production relations.

Thus, the worker utilizes the means of production as vehicle and object of his own work only because constant capital must absorb, suck, variable capital, because this is the only way materialized labour can transfer its value to the product, dead labour can live, surplus value can be produced. The owner, inasmuch as he performs the function of capital, is then the agent through which all this can happen, the vehicle through which capital can realize its self-expanding nature. The addition of the owner, then, is the way this change in the nature of the production relations takes place, i.e. the way the production relations become capitalist. If this is so, it follows that the fact that the capitalist production process is the unity in domination of the labour process and of the surplus value producing process is determined by the fact that the capitalist production relations are the unity in domination of the production relations upon which the labour process rests and of the production relations upon which the surplus value producing process rests. Determination of the capitalist production process by the capitalist production relations means that the direction of domination within the former (labour process dominated by surplus value producing process) is determined by the direction of domination within the latter. These necessarily schematic remarks should be enough, I think, to hint at the fundamental differences between this approach and that of Althusser's school.

The second level of abstraction is that of the *capitalist socio-economic system*. At this level we introduce the superstructure (both political and ideological) as well as the class struggle in all its three aspects, e.g. economic, political, and ideological. Following and modifying Harnecker, we can say that the socio-economic system presents four characteristics:(35)

(a) it is made up of three regional instances, i.e. the economic, the political, and the ideological;

(b) the economic structure is always determinant in the sense outlined above in this Introduction; of particular relevance is the fact that it is the determinant instance which determines to which instance the dominant role reverts;

(c) the dominant instance (which can be both the determinant and the determined ones) is such in the sense that it plays the fundamental role in the reproduction of the determinant instance. For example, 'in the case of the feudal mode of

production it is not the economic laws which ensure the reproduction of the system. In order for the surplus to be appropriated by the land-owner, the active and fundamental intervention of the superstructural element is necessary. Without a
relationship of dependency basically tied to ideological and
juridical-political factors, the serfs would not go and till
the land of the lord or would not surrender part of their
labour.... Therefore, it is the ideological and political-
juridical superstructure which is dominant in this mode of
production,(36) since it is through them that the reproduction
of the mode of production (37) is ensured.'(38)

(d)   finally, the socio-economic system while producing material and
non-material commodities, reproduce also the capitalist production relations. This point is further worked out in chapter 4,
to which the reader is referred.

A *concrete society,* however (and this is the third level of
abstraction) is not exclusively a capitalist one but is made up of
several, qualitatively different structures. As Lenin remarked, in
1921 the economic structure of the Soviet Union was made up of 'at
least five different economic systems, or structures', i.e.:(39)

'first, the patriarchal economy, when the peasant farms produce
only for their own needs, or are in a nomadic or semi-nomadic
state...; second, small commodity production, when goods are
sold on the market; third, capitalist production, the emergence
of capitalists, small private capital; fourth, state capitalism,
and fifth, socialism.'

An analysis of contemporary capitalist society is clearly beyond
the scope of this Introduction. At this juncture I can only provide
some indications of the methodology to be followed for such an analysis. I think Bettelheim's suggestions (40) are extremely useful.
As far as the economic structure is concerned, for example, it is
useful to start with an analysis of each component structure and of
its laws of development. Each component structure is considered,
as it were, in its purity. This, however, is only the first stage.
Its drawback consists, as Bettelheim remarks, in considering the
economic structure at this level of abstraction as a simple summation of various, independent components. Therefore, I suggest that
the second stage of research must be that of inquiring how each of
these components is dominated by the pure capitalist economic structure. I provide an example in chapter 2 of how the production
relations underlying the non-capitalist state activities are dominated by the pure capitalist production relations. We can say, therefore, that the economic structure at this level presents itself as
a unity in domination of several economic structures. Since each
of these structures is a unity in determination of a typical production process and of the production relations to it corresponding, we
can say that the economic structure at the level of the concrete
society is a unity in domination of several unities in determination. Clearly, here we are interested not in an historical analysis but in a logical one, in the nature of the system's various
component parts, in the nature of their relationship, and how this
relationship in turn modifies their initial nature. Third, as
Bettelheim rightly points out, since each national economy is only
a part of the world economy, a study of the former must always

consider its place in the latter. For example, as far as the
imperialist system is concerned, each national economy must be
placed in the hierarchical imperialist chain. Finally, each economic structure originates its own political and ideological structure.

   If we now consider not only the economic, but also the ideological and political aspects of a concrete society, we can realize how
complex the subject under consideration is. Each concrete society
is made up not only of a complex economic structure but also of a
complex ideological and political structure, where the determinant
role reverts only to the former while the dominant role can revert
to each one of the three structures. Finally, at the fourth and
last level of abstraction, the *conjunctural level,* we consider a
certain concrete society at a specific juncture of its development,
i.e. we consider the synthesis of all the contradictions of a certain society at a specific moment of its development. For political
action, this is the relevant level of abstraction.

After this long detour, we can now introduce concisely the fourth
chapter (Reproduction of social classes at the level of production
relations). Section I provides an overview of some fundamental
theoretical concepts necessary for an evaluation of N. Poulantzas'
latest book.(41) Such a discussion, even though not introducing
new theoretical elements, serves the purpose of bringing to the
fore some essential characteristics of my approach. The summary of
the analysis of the capitalist production relations serves also
another purpose, that of providing the opportunity to introduce, in
section II, the concept of positions, i.e. a fractional unit of the
capitalist production process. A position has a technical content
(the technical content of the function performed), i.e. a content
in terms of the concrete operations required by that position and
thus given by the technical division of labour. But a position has
also a social content, i.e. a content in terms of capitalist production relations. In order to understand this, we must recall that
the capitalist production process rests on the capitalist production
relations and that these relations bind together the agents and the
means of production from three different points of view. If we now
split the capitalist production process in fractional units or positions, it follows that each of these positions must rest also on
the capitalist production relations. Let us mention again that of
the three aspects of the capitalist production relations, it is the
ownership element which plays the determinant role and that, thus,
several combinations of these three aspects are possible. All these
combinations are subsumed within the capitalist production relations
as a whole. However, a fraction of the capitalist production process, a position, rests upon only *one* of the possible ways the determinant (ownership) element and the determined (functional and productiveness) elements can combine. In other words, generally speaking, a position implies that the agent filling it is either the
owner or the non-owner, either the labourer or the non-labourer, and
either the exploiter (oppressor) or the exploited (oppressed).
Thus, and given the relation of determination between the ownership
and the other two aspects of the capitalist production relations,

several combinations of the dychotomous aspects of the capitalist production relations are possible. On the other hand, when we consider a specific position we focus on which of these several possible combinations has crystallized itself in that particular position. For example, a position (the worker) can rest upon the non-owner/labourer/exploited combination, while another (the foreman) can rest on the non-owner/non-labourer/oppressed (and exploiter), combination. Thus an agent of production becomes such by simply filling a position and in so doing not only must perform certain operations but becomes also a carrier of (an aspect of) the capitalist production relations. Therefore, an agent can be placed, at this level of abstraction, in the social structure, given the social content of the position he occupies.

Against this background, I submit the thesis that the reproduction of social classes depends on the reproduction of positions and on the reproduction of agents, where the determinant role reverts to the former. The former depends, if we disregard political and ideological factors, on the changes in the capitalist production process and thus in the change in the techniques applied to this process. Since the production process under capitalism is constantly revolutionized, due to the constant introduction of new techniques, constant changes take place also within the technical content of the fraction of this process. This change in the technical content of positions can also cause a change in their social content. The reproduction of agents on the other hand, is fairly fixed since only by way of exception and under a favourable conjuncture does an agent leave a position with a certain social content (the one which collocates the agent in the social structure, i.e. the content in terms of production relations) to occupy another position with a higher social content. Thus, in order to explain changes in the social structure we must begin with the (changes in) the reproduction of positions before we can focus on the reproduction of agents.

In section III I continue the analysis of the position and I introduce the concept of value required, i.e. of the value the labour power of an agent must have in order for that agent to be able to fill that position. The moment an agent fills a position, the individual value of his labour power adapts itself to the value required by that position (and which is determined by the position's technical content). If we now consider the devaluation of an agent's labour power, we can distinguish two cases. On the one hand, the value of one or more of the commodities making up the culturally determined subsistence minimum can decrease, due to increased productivity. This is called *wage goods devaluation* and, in turn, is subdivided into general wage goods devaluation (if the commodities, the value of which has decreased, are common to the whole of the working class) and partial wage goods devaluation (if it affects only a sector of the working class). On the other hand, the value required by a certain position can decrease, due to its technical dequalification. In this case, the value of the agent's labour power is automatically decreased (devalued). I call this *devaluation through dequalification*. The distinction between these two types of devaluation of labour power is important because only the latter serves to explain the proletarianization of the new middle class. In fact, the introduction of new techniques means, for the great majority of positions, that less skills, education, etc. are required to perform the now simpler operations, i.e. it means a technical dequalification of positions, that the new value required is lower and thus that the value of the labour power of the agents filling those positions is also lower. In short, technical dequalification of positions means devaluation of labour power. But technical dequalification of positions can mean also fragmentation of tasks, less responsibility, and thus loss of (part of) the work of control and surveillance, of the global function of capital. Thus technical dequalification can mean also social dequalification, a dequalification in terms of production relations.

Both types of devaluation of labour power are ways for capital to increase relative surplus value. While the effects of wage goods devaluation on relative surplus value are a subject of detailed analysis in Marx's works, the way devaluation through dequalification increases relative surplus value has been less explored. In this section I consider the process of proletarianization of that section of the new middle class which, in terms of the function performed, performs both the global function of capital and the function of the collective worker. In terms of creation of (relative) surplus value, and keeping in mind what said above in this introduction, I summarize the effects of such a process as follows:

1   all the time previously spent in performing the function of the collective worker is paid less due to the devaluation of labour power;

2   of the time previously divided between the two functions, more time goes to the performance of the function of the collective worker and less to the performance of the global function of capital;

3   therefore, as we have seen above, more time can be devoted to either surplus value creation (productive labour) or surplus value appropriation (unproductive labour), and less time can be spent in non-productive activities;

4   the extra time spent on the performance of the function of the collective worker is also paid less than under the initial circumstances;

5   of the time previously spent performing both functions, one small fraction is now devoted only to the global function of capital. The final effect, however, is an absolute increase in surplus value.

6   inasmuch as the global function of capital disappears to make room for the function of the collective worker, disappear also the political and ideological revenue component which cause a rise of the revenue above the value of the agent's 'labour' power.

The remaining of section III is devoted to a comparison of similarities and differences between the two types of devaluation of labour power, and to a discussion of a few tentative criteria to determine under which circumstances which type of devaluation of labour power can be dominant vis-à-vis the other. Sections IV to VII use the conceptual framework worked out in the first three sections to interpret the changes undergone by the Italian middle class since its origins. In particular, these sections deal with the process of proletarianization undergone by technicians and employees.

Not everybody, of course, agrees on the existence of such a process, which has been denied in many quarters, even by authors of Marxist inspiration. For example, in a recent study of Italian technical high school graduates (THSG),(42) Corbetta, after examining a sample of 700 graduates (43) reaches the conclusion that it would be wrong to talk about the proletarianization of technicians. (44)

Before examining Corbetta's argument, let us review some of the concepts used in his study. The jobs performed by the THSG (45) are divided into 'consistent' and 'non-consistent', according to whether they require at least some of the (technical) knowledge acquired at school. In turn, the consistent jobs are subdivided into qualified jobs, i.e. 'production technicians with direct responsibility on machinery and personnel' (e.g. foreman, shop-worker, head of department, etc.),and 'production technicians without direct responsibility' (as, e.g., those engaged in maintenance, testing, assistance, etc.). The dequalified jobs are subdivided into 'execution technicians' (e.g. analysts in laboratories, time-keepers, draftsmen, etc.), and 'partially technical employees' (e.g. salesmen of technical products, employees of sales and purchases departments, etc.). The non-consistent jobs are 'non-technical employees' (e.g. salesmen of non-technical products), 'workers', 'teachers', and 'self-employed'. Moreover, the classes of origin of this type of agents are either the 'middle class' (including the small middle class) or the subordinated classes (i.e. workers and farmers).

Now, one of the results of this study is that, within the consistent jobs, the qualified ones tend to be occupied by agents coming from a middle class milieu, while the dequalified ones tend to be occupied by agents coming from the dominated classes. Moreover, within the non-consistent jobs, the position of worker tends to be filled in by the dominated classes, while the other positions, i.e. in the sphere of the 'tertiary sector', tend to be filled by the middle class. These are sufficient grounds for Corbetta to deny the proletarianization of this type of technicians since 'the proletarian classes remain in a proletarian condition'(46) and the consistent-qualified jobs still remain an apanage of the middle class.

This conclusion, however, rests both on an insufficient definition of proletarianization and some theoretical confusions. Let us start from Corbetta's (implicit) definition of proletarianization. From what was said above, it would seem that as long as the middle class keeps occupying the consistent-qualified positions and the subordinated classes the most proletarianized positions (workers), there can be no proletarianization of this type of agents. Supposedly, only if the consistent-qualified positions were filled by agents coming from a proletarian (subordinated classes) milieu, only then could we speak of the proletarianization of the THSG. As long as the mechanism of upward social mobility does not work for the subordinated classes, we cannot consider these jobs as being proletarianized. As we will see below, one of the basic weaknesses of Corbetta's argument is that he does not analyse positions, either in their technical or in their social nature. The author must thus consider a position as being proletarianized when proletarians fill it. However, if a worker would fill a capitalist position, would

that position be proletarianized, or would not rather the worker
become a capitalist? But let us not run ahead of the logical sequence of our argument. Aside from the many objections that can be
raised against this kind of approach, some of which will be examined
shortly, it should be pointed out that Corbetta's conclusion can be
accepted (in terms of his own analysis and categories) only if we
define as proletarian positions those of worker, execution technicians, and partially technical employees, and as middle-class positions those of production technicians with and without direct responsibility, non-technical employees, teachers, and self-employed.
It would be difficult, however, to see the rationale behind such
spurious categories. On the other hand, if we would not do so, we
could not accept Corbetta's contention because the consistent-
dequalified jobs tend to be filled by the dominated classes (thus,
we would have to accept the thesis of the proletarianization of the
execution technicians and of the partially technical employees) and
the 'tertiary sector' positions within the non-consistent jobs tend
to be filled by the middle class (and thus we would have to accept
the 'embourgoisification' thesis of those positions, a position
which is clearly untenable). Thus, even in terms of Corbetta's
own data, we can accept his conclusion of a lack of proletarianization of the THSG only if we focus our attention on the lowest and
highest groups of positions (the workers) and the production technicians), thus disregarding the two intermediate groups of positions.
  The problem, however, is not so much one of a consistent application of certain concepts. Rather, we must question the theoretical
validity of those concepts and of the theoretical framework they
imply. First of all, it should be said that Corbetta's categories
are spurious. In fact, in terms of production relations, given that
all those agents do not own the means of production and are expropriated of surplus labour (either directly or in the form of surplus
value), the basic distinction is between those who perform the function of the collective worker and those who perform also (or exclusively) the global function of capital. Therefore, the distinction
must be the one between those production technicians with direct
responsibility who perform the global function of capital on the one
hand and all the other positions on the other hand. The latter are
subdividable into groups requiring different levels of skills and
thus characterized by different values required. Now, as we will
see in chapter 4, the class of origin of the agents is relatively
independent of their position in the class structure, since such a
collocation depends also on political and ideological factors.
Thus, if Corbetta is right in emphasizing that the more qualified
positions tend to be taken by the middle class and the less qualified positions by the members of the dominated classes, it is also
true that the level of skill and the value required by a position do
not determine automatically the class (or section of a class) of
origin of the agents who are to fill that position. For instance
the position of a teacher, even if it requires a value of labour
power lower than that of an executive technician (which, however, is
not at all certain, given the process of dequalification undergone
by this latter position) might still tend to be occupied by members
of what Corbetta calls the middle class rather than by members coming from workers' families because the structure of values (one of

the aspects of the ideological realm) still assign a higher class collocation to a teacher than to a production technician. Therefore, not only we should rebuild Corbetta's categories: we should also introduce political and ideological determinants explaining what Corbetta does not explain, i.e. the discrepancy between the class of origin (or fractions of it) and the class collocation of the agents of production. The proletarianization thesis can thus be rejected only by 1, building spurious categories in terms of production relations; 2, focusing only on those jobs for which there is correspondence between class of origin and class collocation; and 3, using a concept of proletarianization which relies basically on the class of origin of the agents rather than on their class collocation, i.e. rather than on the positions (and changes undergone by these positions) occupied by these agents.

Implied in what just said is our second point of criticism. If it is true that, when there is a discrepancy between the supply of a certain type of agents and of a certain type of positions, only agents of a certain social origin will *tend* to fill the more dequalified positions, it is also true that *there is a proletarianization* of those technicians who have acquired a certain education, skills, training, etc., and who, because of the insufficient supply of suitable (consistent) positions, must fill (and this takes place through a complex process of social selection) 'lower', i.e. dequalified positions. A technician who, because of the discrepancies of the labour market must fill the position of worker (47) can and should be considered as having been proletarianized. But this kind of proletarianization, however, must not be confused with what I have called devaluation through dequalification because in the latter the value of the agent's labour power is devalued due to changes in the technical and perhaps social content of the position. Up to now, on the contrary, we do not yet consider changes within positions and only focus on agents having to occupy positions the value required of which is lower than the value of the agent's labour power.

We now come to the third point of criticism, i.e. to the lack in Corbetta's analysis of the study of positions. We have said that the type of proletarianization just considered is explainable in terms of an imbalance between the supply of a certain type of agents and of a certain type of positions, so that some agents have to occupy positions the value required of which is lower than the value of the agents' labour power. This type of proletarianization, however, does not constitute the essence of the process, it springs from a discrepancy between two different types of supply and thus is essentially a conjunctural phenomenon. To clarify this point, let us make a comparison with the relation between values and prices of commodities. Given the nature of capitalism, only by chance will prices coincide with the value of commodities, i.e. only when supply and demand will coincide. However, to explain the value of a commodity, one has to start from a situation of equilibrium, of coincidence between the supply and the demand of that commodity. If we now go back to our problem, we can agree with Corbetta that the discrepancy between the demand for a certain type of agents (given supply of a certain type of positions) and the supply of those agents (given e.g. the working of the school system, i.e. of the ideological which, as we know, is relatively independent of the

economic) is a permanent characteristic of capitalism. When the
supply of certain agents exceeds the demand, some of these agents
(socially selected) will have their labour power dequalified,
independently of the changes undergone by the positions. But, just
as in the example of the relation between prices and values, we must
assume - to explain values - a situation of equilibrium between
supply and demand, in the same way to explain the proletarianization
of technicians and employees, we must assume a coincidence between
the supply and demand of certain agents. Having assumed such a coincidence (which is also a correspondence between the economic and
the ideological-political) we can proceed to a study of proletarianization *in terms of production relations,* i.e. to the study of devaluation through dequalification, and thus to a study of positions.
This is the aspect which, unfortunately, is missing in Corbetta's
study. By focusing only on one of the two basic elements of the
social structure, the agents of production, and thus by losing sight
of the other element, the position, Corbetta cannot face the all-
important question whether or not the consistent-qualified positions
have undergone any changes in their technical (and perhaps social)
nature. He does talk about the positions of execution technician
and partially technical employee as 'dequalified', but this has no
impact whatsoever on his analysis. On this basis, no matter what
happens to those agents who cannot fill those positions, as long as
the middle class (never explicitly defined, even less so in terms
of production relations) keeps occupying those positions, we are
not allowed to talk of proletarianization of technicians. Yet, if
the number of some of these qualified positions would decrease
because some would become dequalified and if the remaining qualified positions would still be occupied by members of the middle
class, there would be indeed a process of proletarianization going
on.

In order to say something about this last point, we should carry
out a comparison of positions over a certain period of time. This
is not possible on the basis of the data provided by Corbetta. However, some data can be used to provide indirect evidence that a process of devaluation through dequalification of the consistent positions has indeed taken place. We can compare the percentage of THSG
occupied in qualified positions and in dequalified positions in the
1958-9 sample (one year after their first job) and in the 1968-9
sample (about three years after graduation). While in the 1958-9
sample about 40 per cent were production technicians and 25 per cent
were employed in dequalified positions, in the 1968-9 sample the
proportions are exactly reversed: 25 per cent in qualified positions and 40 per cent in dequalified positions.(48) Or, if we consider only those agents employed as technicians, thus only the production and execution technicians, we see that of the 1958-9 sample
two-thirds were production technicians and one-third execution technicians, while in the 1968-9 sample the production and execution
technicians had reached a share of 50 per cent each. It is on the
basis of this indirect evidence and of the theoretical objections
listed above that Corbetta's denial of the proletarianization thesis
does not seem to be sufficiently well founded.

In the present book I will not attempt to provide an overview of
the many theories of social classes, even though a few indications

of how the theory submitted differs from those of other Marxist and non-Marxist authors (such as Poulantzas, Braverman, Mallet, Mandel, Dahrendorf, Giddens, etc.) can be found now and then, especially in chapters 1 and 4. Rather, the major thrust of this book is that of working out an economic identification of classes at the present stage of capitalism and with particular reference to the imperialist countries. The necessarily cursory review together with the explanatory additional remarks, provided in this Introduction, were meant to bring to the fore and to complete some of the major themes of this book. In order to further sharpen the lines of demarcation of the approach emerging from the present work, let us now examine a different concept of social classes, e.g. that submitted by A. Swingewood in 'Marx and Modern Social Theory'.(49) This author's definition of class sounds as follows:(50)

> A social class is thus defined both in terms of property owner-
> ship or non-ownership and thus the degree of control over, or
> subservience to, exploitation, and the degree of personal free-
> dom its members enjoy. This latter element is crucially import-
> ant for understanding the evolution of class consciousness in a
> modern capitalist society.... Marx's theory of class, therefore,
> emphasizes the economic relation between the mode and relations
> of production, and the subjective awareness by the worker of his
> freedom, his similarities with other workers and the authority
> and power of a dominant class. It is the conjunction of these
> two components, the objective and the subjective, which creates
> class consciousness.

Even though this is not the place for a discussion of what determines class consciousness, it should be briefly mentioned that such a consciousness is not determined by the degree of personal freedom but, by the objective position agents have in the class structure and by the way the awareness of such a position is modified, distorted, crippled, etc. by the economic, political and ideological struggle. (51) But, aside from this problem, at least three orders of criticism can be moved against this definition of class. First of all, there is no distinction between legal and real ownership. This leads Swingewood to draw the wrong conclusions about the 'non-propertied' managers who cannot form part of a dominant class since they own no property in the means of production.(52) The distinction between legal and economic ownership is of fundamental importance just in order to avoid concluding that only those who are the legal owners of the means of production can be considered as capitalists. This is why, in Swingewood's opinion, both the top manager and the lowest foreman, not having the property of the means of production, 'simply command in the name of capital'(53) and thus must be classified en bloc within the new middle class.

Second, according to Swingewood, the ownership of the means of production is directly related to exploitation. Now, we have seen that between the ownership element and the productiveness (or exploitation) element there is no identity but a relationship of determination. In fact, it is possible that the owner be both the exploiter and the exploited.(54) Or, it is possible that the non-owner, while being economically oppressed, performs a function (the global function of capital) the essence of which is to help the owner to exploit. This brings us to the third point, i.e. to the

fact that there is practically no analysis of the functional element within the capitalist production relations. Swingewood hints
at such an analysis when he talks about the 'technical workers'. In
this connection he says that 'their supervisory work function is
firmly set within a formal bureaucratic hierarchy, their role en-
meshed with the administration of labour power and the extraction of
surplus value'.(55) However, not only is this the extent of Swingewood's analysis of the functional element within the production
relations, but also there is confusion between the concept of productive labour and the function of capital. 'At the same time',
says Swingewood, 'the concept of "productive labour" and productive
workers is enlarged; the division of labour ramifies throughout production so that specialized occupations and professions (engineers,
scientists) tied to capital emerge to function as the administrative
arm of exploitation.'(56) Clearly, an agent, when performing the
function of capital, i.e. when being 'the administrative arm of
exploitation', cannot be a labourer and even less a productive one.
   These insufficiencies are also at the origin of Swingewood's
inability to identify the middle class in terms of production relations.(57)

> The category of the middle class ... consists of variegated
> groups such as the small producers, the petit bourgeoisie (em-
> ployers of small fractions of labour); those engaged in the
> 'circulation of commodities' (marketing, buying, selling); the
> middle men (wholesalers, shopkeepers, speculators); those who
> 'command in the name of capital' (managers, etc.) and their
> assistants, supervisors, secretaries, book-keepers, clerks; and
> finally an 'ideological' group embracing lawyers, artists,
> journalists, clergy and state officials such as the military and
> the police.

What we have here is not a definition but simply a residual category, a list of all types of jobs the performance of which indicates
that the agents do not belong either to the working or to the capitalist class, and thus must be collocated in the middle class. While
the two basic classes had been defined (even though in an insufficient manner) in terms of production relations, the middle class is
treated only in terms of the technical content of the functions performed. Second, since the middle class is not identified in terms
of production relations but only described through a list (categories) of jobs and since - with the development of capitalism, with
the increasing socialization of labour, and thus with the creations
of new branches of industries, i.e. of new types of jobs - new jobs,
professions, etc., come constantly to the fore, it is quite evident
that Marx's correct argument that the new middle class tends to
increase (58) must be seen by Swingewood as being in contradiction
with the similarly correct argument that the capitalist society
tends towards polarization. In reality, *the growth of the new
middle class and its tendential proletarianization are only two
aspects of the same process,* process however that can be understood
only if the middle classes (just as the two fundamental classes) is
defined in terms of production relations. To deny the tendency towards class polarization means not only to make a serious theoretical mistake (which derives both from a lack of definition of the new
middle classes in terms of production relations and from a non-

dialectical approach, i.e. an approach which sets class polarization against growth of the middle classes as irreconcilable poles). It means also to provide a theoretical basis for wrong political practices the end results of which can be catastrophic for the proletariat.(59)

In the course of this Introduction I have mentioned a few qualifications the reader should bear in mind in order to give a correct evaluation of this work. For example, I have said that I focus my analysis only on the developed capitalist countries; or that this is not a review of the various previous theories of social classes but that references to other authors are made only when necessary to bring certain points into sharper relief. It is now time to introduce a further qualification: the emphasis in this work is on the typical production unit rather than on the general 'macroeconomic' aspects of capitalist production. This is so exclusively for one reason, i.e. because I have focused my analysis on relatively unexplored areas, as e.g. the functional aspect of the production relations within the production unit.(60) I do not think it is relevant to criticize my approach by pointing out, e.g. that I do not consider the realization problem (61) or any other apsects of the Marxist theory, if they are not strictly relevant to the topic discussed. After all, one can do only one thing at a time. What one should do, however, is - since the macro level is not a simple summation of what happens at the micro level - to warn against a simple generalization of concepts worked out at the level of the individual productive unit to the level of the economy as a whole. In this connection, I shall provide only one example. In this work I concentrate upon the social division of labour inside the production unit (62) and only occasionally I consider the social division of labour at the level of the economy as a whole. This means that certain concepts take on a different meaning according to whether we refer to one level of analysis or to the other. Let us see how the concept of 'producer' changes when we consider the social division of labour within the production unit or among production units (thus considering the economy in its totality).

On a social scale, by socialization of labour we understand not the concentration of people working under one roof (this is only a secondary aspect) but the two interrelated phenomena of capital concentration and specialization of social labour (or social division of labour).(63) The former phenomenon means that within each branch of production the number of capitalists decreases. The latter means that, at the same time, the number of branches increases. As Lenin remarks: (64)

> In each branch of industry, which has now become more specialized, the number of capitalists steadily decreases. This means that the social tie between the *producers* becomes increasingly stronger, the producers become welded into a single whole.... *The manufacturer who produces* fabrics depends on the cotton-yarn manufacturer; the latter depends on the capitalist planter who grows the cotton, on the owner of the engineering works, the coal mine and so on and so forth. The result is that no capitalist can get along without others.

It is clear, then, that here Lenin considers the capitalist as the producer while in the present work I consider the capitalist (as capitalist) as the typical example of non-producer. Are these two views irreconcilable? Not at all. When one considers the social divisions of labour on a societal level, among production units, the producer is the capitalist because the production unit is considered in its entirety and is *symbolized* by the capitalist. The final production is the outcome of many intermediate commodities, each of them coming from different branches. Here the focus is on the increasing number of branches, on the reduction of the production units within each branch, and thus on the increasing interdependence of the production units upon each other or, which is the same, on the fact that the final product is the outcome of one social production process. At the level of the production unit, on the other hand, i.e. within the production unit, we must distinguish between the producer (the agent performing the function of labour) and the non-producer (the agent performing the function of capital).(65) Now we focus on the social division of labour within the enterprise, on the form taken by the division between the labourer and the non-labourer (characteristic of all class societies) within the capitalist production unit, i.e. on the fact that there are those who perform the function of labour and those who perform the function of capital. Thus, producer in the former case is the name given to the capitalist as the agent symbolizing the production unit, the enterprise; in the latter case, it is the name given to the agent who, within the enterprise, *really* produces.

We shall now conclude this Introduction by discussing briefly some criticisms which have been moved to the theory submitted below in chapter 1. In a recent paper, J. Urry (66) has advanced a number of substantial critical remarks and modifications of my theory.(67)   I shall focus here on what seem to me to be the most fundamental ones. First of all, Urry implies that I identify classes under monopoly capitalism only in functional terms.(68)   In fact the ownership element is 'rendered irrelevant because of the focus on real ownership (and) it is thus reduced to a question of power and control as reflected in the social division of labour'.(69)   The fact is that I state very clearly that I am interested, as a first step in my research, in an identification of classes in terms of production relations and that I do this by starting from the highest levels of abstraction. Thus, on the level of the capitalist economic structure, we do not consider either legal relations (legal ownership of the means of production) nor social relations (e.g. political relations). These relations are considered and analyzed only at lower levels of abstraction. Real ownership is the power to dispose of the means of production and of the labour power (and thus of product).

It is clear that, with the separation between legal and economic ownership, the function of capital personified reverts to those agents who are the real owners of the means of production and of the labour power and that the legal owners fall outside the production process and thus the production relations. To focus on the real ownership does not at all render the dychotomy owner/non-owner irrelevant but, on the contrary, gives it a specific meaning under monopoly capitalism. I should add, moreover, that to do so does not

mean to conflate the concept of real ownership and that of function
of capital. From what was said above it should be clear that while
the former concept, the power to dispose of the means of production
and labour power, always implies performing the function of capital
the reverse is not true, since, under monopoly capitalism, the work
of control and surveillance is performed also by agents who do not
own the means of production, who cannot hire or dismiss labour
power, and thus who cannot dispose of the product.

The productiveness element is, again according to Urry, made also
irrelevant, since I treat unproductive labourers in the same way as
productive labourers, the only difference being that the former are
directly expropriated of surplus labour (economic oppression) rather
than in the form of surplus value (exploitation). Now, if one considers unproductive labourers as agents performing the function of
capital as Urry does, it is clear that the productiveness element
becomes irrelevant. The mistake, however, resides in giving a wrong
definition of function of capital, in not distinguishing between
unproductive labour and non-labour, between those agents who participate in the labour process, even though unproductively, and those
agents who participate only in the surplus value producing process,
who perform the work of control and surveillance. Further below I
will consider Urry's own interpretation of function of capital.
Thus, far from identifying social classes only in terms of the
social function performed, I give an identification in terms of the
ownership, productiveness, and functional aspects, where only the
former has a determinant character.

A second major criticism concerns the concept of function of
capital. According to Urry, I consider the capitalist production
process as made up of two distinct processes, the labour process and
the surplus value producing process. Therefore I am 'forced to argue
that the work of supervision and management splits into two, into
unity and coordination as part of the collective labourer function,
and control and surveillance as part of the global function of capital'.(70) Now, when I refer to the capitalist production process as
the unity in domination of two processes, I do not mean the addition
of two processes. I mean that the capitalist production process can
be regarded both as labour process and as surplus value producing
process, that the latter dominates the former, i.e. that the labour
process under capitalism becomes basically production of surplus
value and that this takes place by introducing within the production
process an agent (who performs the function of capital) who does not
labour in the precise sense that he does not take part in the labour
process, in the production of use values. As far as the distinction
between the two aspects of the work of supervision and management
goes, moreover, it seems to me that what Marx says in the third volume of 'Capital' leaves no room for doubt about the correctness of
this statement.

Thus, my concept of function of capital, far from being 'insufficient', narrows down what is specific of the capitalist as capitalist within the production process, i.e. control and surveillance
in order to produce surplus value, in order to allow capital to
realize its self-expanding nature. It is important, however, to
realize that under monopoly capitalism this function starts being
exercised also by agents who have no (real) ownership of the means

of production. Urry's concept of function of capital, on the other hand, is in my opinion heterogeneous since it encompasses 'first, the direct control and supervision of each productive enterprise; second, the reconversion of commodities into money in the sphere of circulation; third, the discovery, implementation, and monitoring of technical development in the means of production; and fourth, the reproduction of necessary labour power'.(71) Thus, not only unproductive labourers (second category) perform, according to Urry, the function of capital, but even certain productive labourers (third category, i.e. scientists, technicians, engineers, etc.). In my opinion, we have here not only an erroneous concept of function of capital and function of labour, but also of productive and unproductive labour, since the work of non-manual labourers is here considered as unproductive.

I think that one source of confusion, one factor which facilitates the conflation of unproductive labour and of the function of capital (72) is that, before the division of labour between production and sale units took place, and when the capitalist enterprise was still relatively small, the sale of commodities was carried out only by the capitalist. This is why some authors think that the sale of commodities, no matter by whom carried out, automatically implies performing the function of capital. But, does not Marx say that the commercial worker belongs to the better (then) paid sector of the working class? Let us quote once more what Marx has to say on this:(73)

> In one respect, such a commercial employee is a wage worker like any other. In the first place, his labour power is bought with the variable capital of the merchant, not with money expended as revenue, and consequently it is not bought for private service, but for the purpose of expanding the value of the capital advanced for it. In the second place, the value of his labour-power, and thus his wages, are determined as those of other wage-workers, i.e. by the cost of production and reproduction of his specific labour-power, not by the product of his labour....
> However, we must make the same distinction between him and the wage-workers directly employed by industrial capital, which exists between industrial capital and merchant's capital, and thus between the industrial capitalist and the merchant.

The commercial employee is thus clearly a worker, at least in terms of production relations. As soon as a certain part of the capitalist production process is performed not any more by one agent but by a large number of agents, the social division of labour, i.e. the division between labourers and non-labourers (those who control, even though in their turn are controlled) is introduced in that section of the production process just because surplus labour must be extracted - and the only way to extract it is by controlling the labourers - in the same way as surplus value must be extracted from the productive labourers.

It is for these reasons that I disagree with Urry's notion of the new middle class which is 'by definition responsible for one or more functions of capital. They are thus involved in organizing, arranging, implementing and devising the conditions, procedures and practices which enable commodity production to take place'(74) by consuming unproductively part of the growing surplus value. It is

clear that here the conditions of existence of the new middle class
are given in terms of realization of surplus value, while the nature
of this class is explained in terms of production of surplus value,
in terms of the useful and necessary (for capitalism) character
their labour has in order to create surplus value. We have, in
other words, a definition of the new middle class not in terms of
production relations but in terms of the capitalist production process. In fact Urry does not even distinguish between these two
levels of analysis. It is also for this reason that an analysis of
the functional aspect within the capitalist production relations becomes unnecessarily complicated. But an analysis of this aspect, as
important as it is, should not substitute a complex analysis of all
the elements of the capitalist production relations.

NOTES

1 An indication of the complexity of this structure can be found
   in chapters 1 and 2 but I am still far from having provided a
   complete treatment of the problem. More will be said about the
   complex nature of the economic structure further down in this
   Introduction.
2 For a discussion of the various levels of abstraction, see further
   down in this Introduction.
3 It should be stressed that for me the concept of dialectical
 - determination is a tool which serves to explain all forms of
   society and not only the capitalist one. Thus, I disagree with
   Colletti's argument according to which 'the fundamental principle of materialism and of science ... is the principle of non-
   contradiction' and that, however, 'capitalist oppositions are ...
   dialectical contradictions and not real oppositions ... [because]
   for Marx, capitalism is ... an *upside-down*, inverted reality
   (alienation, fetishism).' See L. Colletti, Marxism and the Dialectic, 'New Left Review', September–October 1975, pp. 28-9.
4 The term 'economic oppression' will be explained shortly.
5 The following examples are taken from chapter 6 of the first
   draft of a DPhil. thesis to be submitted by P. Fairbrother at the
   University of Oxford entitled 'Consciousness and Collective
   Action: A Study of the Social Organization of Unionized White
   Collar Factory Workers', parts of which were kindly made available to me by the author. The research was conducted in an alu-
   minium factory in South Wales between September 1973 and September 1974. The study examined the activity of the membership of
   one white collar trade union. The jobs represented by the union
   included: production foremen; production, supplies and costs
   supervisors; security officers; nurses; metallurgists; technicians; chemists; senior administrative staff; technical specialists; senior metallurgists; production superintendents; senior
   and project engineers; chief draughtsmen; maintenance superintendents.
6 Ibid. Notice that here the foremen seem to perform both the global function of capital and the function of the collective worker.
   On the agents performing both of these functions, see below.
7 Ibid.

8   Ibid.
9   Ibid.
10 Ibid.
11 Ibid.
12 Inasmuch as they perform the function of the collective worker,
    they are either exploited or economically oppressed. Inasmuch
    as they perform the global function of capital, they are exploi-
    ters or economic oppressors. However, since they do not own the
    means of production, the performance of the global function of
    capital does not imply for them the appropriation of surplus
    value (or surplus labour). They themselves must work longer
    than the time necessary for the reconstitution of their labour
    power (we will see shortly how this labour power is determined
    inasmuch as an agent performs the global function of capital)
    and are thus oppressed (they cannot be exploited since, in their
    role as agents of capital, they are non-labourers and thus can-
    not produce surplus value). Thus, the inherent contradiction
    to which they are exposed, is not only that for a part of the
    working day they are on the side of labour and for the other
    part of the working day they are on the side of capital, but
    also that, when they are the agents of capital, when they per-
    form the global function of capital, they are, unlike the
    capitalist, *both* exploiters or oppressors *and* oppressed.
13 But, as shown in section III and further elaborated later on in
    this Introduction, the unproductiveness of those performing the
    function of capital must be distinguished from that of the
    unproductive labourer.
14 See K. Marx 'Capital', vol. III, p. 300.
15 A corollary of this is that unproductive capital differentiates
    itself from industrial capital, as G. Kay rightly points out in
    discussing commercial capital, in that the former engages in un-
    equal exchange while the latter exchanges all the commodities it
    handles at prices tendentially equal to values, See G. Kay,
    'Development and Underdevelopment', MacMillan, 1975, p. 87.
16 'Capital', vol. II, p. 144.
17 In chapter 2, section III, I analyse some of the dangers inherent
    in confusing these two levels of analysis, as far as the unpro-
    ductiveness of the labourers is concerned.
18 Not to be confused with the work of supervision and management
    which encompasses both the work of control and surveillance and
    the work of co-ordination and unity of the labour process.
19 V.I. Lenin, Report on the Tax in Kind delivered at the Meeting
    of Secretaries and Responsible Representatives of R.C.B.(B)
    Cells of Moscow and Moscow Gubernia, 9 April, 1921, 'Collected
    Works', no. 32, Moscow, 1965, pp. 296-7.
20 For a discussion of the difference between these two methods,
    see chapter 3.
21 This should not be interpreted as if logical analysis admits of
    an harmonious development of capitalism. One of the basic laws
    of capitalism is its unequal development, i.e. the contradic-
    tion between the various component parts of society (which does
    not exclude the possibility of temporary states of correspon-
    dence). The task of historical analysis is to inquire how
    uneven development concretizes itself in a specific, histori-
    cally determined setting.

22 E.g. M. Godelier posits the priority of structural analysis on
    historical analysis. H. Veltmeyer agrees on this. See Towards
    an Assessment of the Structuralist Interrogation of Marx:
    Claude Levi-Strauss and Louis Althusser, 'Science and Society',
    vol. 38, no. 4, pp. 385-421.
23 Failure to recognize that Marx's works are not only at the high-
    est level of abstraction is at the basis of many misunderstand-
    ings of Marxist theory. Thus, A. Giddens writes: 'As regards
    Marx's "abstract model" of classes, this scheme presents no
    particular difficulty; the bourgeoisie are those who possess
    and deploy capital, while the proletariat are the mass of pro-
    perty less workers who sell their labour-power to the former
    grouping. However, on the empirical level, as Marx was well
    aware, this neat simplicity is not easy to reconcile with the
    complicated structure of actual forms of society'. (A. Giddens,
    'The Class Structure of the Advanced Societies', London, 1973,
    p. 97.)
24 E. Koga, Problèmes théoriques de l'organisation des classes et
    du travail productif, 'Critique de l'économie politique',
    January-March 1973, pp. 54-75.
25 Koga's article - which I read only in course of writing this
    Introduction - contains some untenable propositions (such as,
    e.g., the identification of productive labour and labour pro-
    ducing material commodities) but also some interesting points
    which, at times, come very close to some of the conclusions to
    be found in chapter 1 of this book. Koga hints, for example,
    at the two functions within the capitalist production process,
    functions which he calls function of production and function of
    oppression; at the fact that 'with the development of capit-
    alism' the work of surveillance (which encompasses both func-
    tions and which was a prerogative of the individual capital-
    ist) becomes the prerogative of certain salary-earners; at the
    fact that this category of agents forms a part of the new middle
    class; and finally at the fact that for certain of these agents
    the function of production is more important that the function
    of oppression (e.g. the contremaitre) while for other agents it
    is the latter function which is more important (e.g. the mana-
    ger). Since a comparison of Koga's and my position would take
    us too far, I shall only mention that the points of difference
    are much greater than the points of similarity and that only at
    first sight do we seem to have come to some similar conclusions.
26 Marx, 'Capital', vol. I, p. 19.
27 L. Althusser and E. Balibar, 'Reading Capital', London, 1970.
28 Ibid., p. 170.
29 Ibid., p. 215.
30 These two types of connections are radically different from what
    I call, in chapter 1, the production relations upon which the
    labour process rests and the production relations upon which the
    surplus value producing process rests. A discussion of how
    Balibar's and my approach differ would be too long a detour.
    Therefore, I will limit myself here to give only an indication
    of the nature of my criticism of Balibar. First of all, Bali-
    bar's concept of real appropriation connection seems to be based
    on a misunderstanding of the capitalist's double role in the

production process. Second, according to Balibar, the relation
between the property connection and the real appropriation connection is a relation of homology (or not) while in reality it
is a relationship of subordination.
31 Approach followed also by other authors as e.g., Poulantzas,
Harnecker, etc.
32 This excludes, of course, the thesis of the neutrality of the
forces of production. Such a thesis will be criticized in
chapter 3, in discussing the transition between capitalism and
socialism. Concerning a capitalist society, A. Gorz has the
following to say: 'Most orthodox communist parties clung to
the view that capitalist relations of production were stifling
the development of the productive forces and that socialism, by
tearing down the so-called superstructure of the capitalist
state and of capitalist social relations, could set free at one
blow a potential for socio-economic development and growth.

This view still pervades the political attitude of the Western European communist parties. They usually consider all
available productive capacity, all available manual, technical,
professional and intellectual skills as forces that will be
valuable and useful during the transition period.... [But] we
can no longer assume that it is the productive forces which
shape the relations of production.' (A. Gorz, Technical Intelligence and the Capitalist Division of Labor, 'Telos', 12,
Summer 1972, p. 27.) While it is true that the capitalist productive forces are not neutral, it is also true, as shown in
chapter 3, that they, due to their relative independence, at a
certain stage of their development, enter into contradiction
with the capitalist production relations. This is only one of
the fundamental differences between Gorz's theory and the theory
expounded in this book. I will mention only one more point of
radical divergence. According to Gorz, technicians in the
manufacturing industries have a double function: 1, they keep
'production to a certain pre-determined technical standard' and
2, they maintain 'the hierarchical structure of the labor force
and [perpetuate] capitalist social relations'. (Ibid., p. 31.)
Gorz adds: 'There is ample documentary evidence for the fact
that this second aspect of this role takes precedence over the
first.' (Ibid.) Thus, 'they are the workers' most immediate
enemy.' (Ibid., p. 34.) Therefore, in Gorz's view, the technicians basically perform the function of capital, where to
perform this function does not mean to carry out the work of
control and surveillance, but to be carriers of capitalist technology. However, the technicians 'are themselves frustrated,
estranged and oppressed from above.' (Ibid., p. 35.) Consequently, 'All we can do in times of uneasy and restless "peace"
is to impress upon technical personnel that they have more to
win that to lose by the abolition of hierarchical regimentation
and privilege.' (Ibid.) The voluntarism implicit in this
approach is evident. To impress certain ideas on the technicians and on the new middle class in general will become possible only when the process of proletarianization (i.e. the
double process of tendential devaluation of skilled labour
power and of tendential disappearance of the global function of

capital) will have sufficiently eroded these agents' positions of privilege.

33   Since we know that the ownership element is the determinant one vis-à-vis the productiveness and the functional elements, for sake of brevity I refer to the agent of production as the owner or non-owner.

34   K. Marx, 'Resultate....', p. 18.

35   What I call socio-economic system is called by Harnecker the global structure or mode of production and is considered as the first level of abstraction. Thus what is missing in Harnecker's scheme, as in all those writers who adhere to Althusser's and Balibar's approach, is a study of the structure of the economy as indicated above. It is for this reason that in the writings of these authors as well as of all the writers who adhere to this school of thought, there is no trace of an analysis of what I call the unproductive capitalist economic process and of the production relations corresponding to it. An indication of this analysis can be found in chapters 1 and 2. Thus, the capitalist economic structure at this level of abstraction is made up of both the pure (productive) and of the unproductive capitalist economic processes and relations. Only one of these processes and relations are, however, dominant, namely the productive ones. Thus we have here a unity in domination, a structure made up of a dominant and a dominated set of production processes and relations. See M. Harnecker, 'Los Conceptos elementales del materialismo historico', Siglo XXI, Editores, 1971, chapter VIII.

36   Socio-economic system, according to my terminology.

37   See note 36.

38   Harnecker, op. cit., pp. 141-2.

39   Lenin, op. cit., pp. 295-6.

40   See C. Bettelheim, 'La Transition vers l'économie socialiste', Italian translation, 'La transizione all' economia socialista', Milan, Jaca Books, 1969, pp. 8-9.

41   My criticism of this work is quite different from that of Jean-Marie Vincent (État et classes sociales, 'Critiques de l'économie politique', no. 19, pp. 4-26) and of C. Colliot-Thélène (Contribution à une analyse des classes sociales, 'Critiques de l'économie politique', no. 19, pp. 27-47 and no. 21, pp. 93-126). An appreciation of these two articles is beyond the scope of this Introduction.

42   They are the 'periti industriali' i.e. those who take a diploma from the 'istituti tecnici industriali'.

43   The years of graduation were 1968-9 while the interviews, through questionnaires, were carried out in 1972. The sample was taken in Northern Italy. For reasons of comparison, Corbetta took also another sample of 245 THSG who got their diploma in the years 1958-9.

44   See P. Corbetta, 'Tecnici, disoccupazione e coscienza di classe', Bologna, 1975. Corbetta's argument rests on two points but I will disregard the one dealing with the lack of 'left-wing consciousness' of those agents filling dequalified positions. To tackle this point would presuppose a discussion of Corbetta's 'left-wing consciousness' indicators and would not, in any case,

bring us very far since, as we will see, the author focuses
only on the agents of production thus paying no attention to
changes in the technical and social nature of the positions
occupied by those agents.

45   The sample is statistically representative.
46   Corbetta, op. cit., p. 57.
47   Notice that it is not infrequent in today's Italy for a THSG to
     hide the fact that he has a diploma in order to find employment
     as a worker.
48   Notice, however, that the decrease in agents employed in consis-
     tent-dequalified positions derives almost exclusively from a
     decrease in production technicians without direct responsibility.
49   A. Swingewood, 'Marx and Modern Social Theory', Macmillan, 1975.
50   Ibid., p. 114.
51   R. Miliband discusses how the school system, the mass media,
     etc. affect class consciousness. See 'The State in Capitalist
     Society', London, 1969. At least three remarks should be made.
     First, class consciousness is acquired differently by indivi-
     duals than by the masses, which can acquire it only through
     action (see E. Mandel, 'Lenin en het probleem van het prolet-
     aries klassebewustzijn', Sun, Nijmegen, 1970). Second, there
     are various levels of class consciousness, and the working
     class should be subdivided in separate parts according to the
     degree of their class consciousness (ibid.). This point, of
     fundamental importance is disregarded also by some Marxist
     authors as e.g. Z. Bauman, 'Lineamenti di una sociologia
     marxista', Editori Riuniti, Rome, 1971, p. 58. Third, it is
     impossible for the working class to achieve a developed class
     consciousness without an organization which wages an economic,
     political, and ideological fight against the class enemy under
     the leadership of a vanguard. (See I Quaderni di Avanguardia
     Operaia, 'La Concezione del Partito in Lenin', vol. I, Milan,
     1970.)
52   Swingewood, op. cit., p. 164.
53   Ibid., p. 116.
54   For the case of the artisan, see Marx, 'Resultate...', p. 64;
     'The German Ideology', pp. 70-4; and 'Theories of Surplus
     Value', vol. 1, pp. 407-9.
55   Swingewood, op. cit., p. 126.
56   Ibid., p. 128.
57   Ibid., p. 116
58   As Swingewood says: 'Marx even suggests that with the growth
     of corporations and the gradual diffusion of the division of
     labour to all sectors of industry and commerce, managers and
     the supervisors increase in number.' (Ibid., p. 116.)
59   See chapter 4, section VII, of this book. Also C.H. Anderson
     seems to be unable to choose between a dichotomous and a tri-
     chotomous class model. 'We are able to decipher two major
     trends in the shape of the class structure through the applica-
     tion of the Marxist economic theory of capitalist development.
     First, the class structure tends toward polarization between an
     increasingly concentrated capitalist class and an expanding
     proletariat.... A second trend in class structure which accom-
     panies the first...is the rise of a "surplus" class or new

middle class. This introduces a third major grouping and suggests that, depending upon one's purposes, a trichotomous class
model may be utilized as well as a dichotomous one. For example,
descriptively speaking, the trichotomous model may at times
prove to be more useful whereas in terms of revolutionary
theory the dichotomy of class structure may be more powerful.'
('The Political Economy of Social Class', Prentice Hall, 1974,
p. 51.) This view is unsatisfactory since it seems to imply a
schism between the theoretical and the revolutionary aspects of
Marxism, which is untenable for anyone who has understood that
Marxism is the science of proletarian revolution.

60   This aspect of my theory has been applied by T. Johnson in an
interesting paper on the professions. See T. Johnson, The
Professions in the Class Structure, forthcoming in the 'Proceedings of the British Sociological Association, Annual Conference, 1975.

61   As J. Urry does in his New Theories of the New Middle Class,
forthcoming in 'Amsterdams Sociologisch Tijdschrift'.

62   As Harnecker rightly points out, one should not conflate a production unit - which encompasses a whole production process -
and an enterprise. The former can of course encompass several
of the latter. See Harnecker, op. cit., p. 28.

63   See V.I. Lenin, 'What the "Friends of the People" are ...,'
pp. 175-7.

64   Ibid., p. 176, emphasis added.

65   For sake of simplicity, we consider here only the pure capitalist economic structure, so that we can talk interchangeably
of producer and of labourer and vice versa of non-producer and
of non-labourer.

66   See Urry, op. cit.

67   Related also to a previous article by the same author, Towards
a Structural Theory of the Middle Class, 'Acta Sociologica',
16, pp. 75-87.

68   New Theories..., p. 13.

69   Ibid.

70   Ibid., p. 17.

71   Ibid., p. 18.

72   Thus, Giddens criticizes the concept of unproductive labour
without being able to grasp the essence of this concept.
'Since workers in administrative occupations are "non-
productive" and depend for their existence on appropriating a
portion of the surplus product of manual (?) labour, it would
appear that they effectively form part of the dominant class.
But, on the other hand, since they are, with manual workers,
separated from control of their means of production, they must
sell their labour on the market in order to secure the means of
their livelihood.' Giddens, op. cit., p. 96.) After what has
been said in this Introduction, the primitiveness of such an
interpretation of Marx should be evident.

73   'Capital', vol. III, pp. 292-3.

74   Urry, New Theories ..., p. 24.

Chapter 1

ON THE ECONOMIC IDENTIFICATION OF THE NEW MIDDLE CLASS

INTRODUCTION

In this essay (1) I will restrict my field of analysis to classes in
their relation to the economic structure. This limit should not be
interpreted as an attempt to define classes in purely economic terms
(only possible on the highest level of abstraction) but on the contrary — given that a complete definition of classes must be worked
out in terms of the economic, the political, and the ideological —
as an attempt to find out what is the limited yet fundamental (determining) role of the economic in the definition of classes. Since
there is an economic, political and ideological structure as well as
the corresponding levels of social relations (class struggle), it is
more accurate to assign the determining role to the economic structure and, (as we will see in section I below) within this structure,
to the production relations, rather than to the economic. Social
relations and the superstructure (i.e. the political and ideological
structure) are thus determined. This calls for a discussion of the
nature of the economic structure and of its relation to the superstructure and class struggle, a relation which can be defined as one
of determination and overdetermination. As used here, these concepts are a modified version of those developed by Althusser. As we
will see, they are particularly useful not only in understanding the
relation between economic structure and superstructure (and class
struggle) but also the relation between the various elements within
the economic structure i.e. between the mode of production and the
production process and, within the mode of production, between production relations and distribution relations.
   We will focus our attention on the capitalist system (and in particular on its monopolistic stage) which we will analyse only on the
two highest levels of abstraction. Even within these limits the
problem is a complex one and requires a discussion — albeit cursory
— of some basic theoretical concepts including what I will call direct and indirect overdetermination. The focus is on the new middle
class as identified in relation to the economic structure (and
especially the production relations). The 'old' middle class, (i.e.
the small entrepreneurs) and strata of the petty bourgeoisie which
are only indirectly tied to the economic structure of the capitalist

43

system and whose analysis can be more properly undertaken at lower levels of abstraction, will not be analysed here for lack of space. The fact that only toward the end of this essay will we be able to come up with a scientifically accurate and precise concept of the new middle class reflects the difficulties met in clarifying some of the basic concepts used (such as the function of the collective worker and what I will call the global function of capital as it operates in both the productive and unproductive phases of the capitalist production process), upon which the concept of new middle class must be built. This extensive preparatory work is necessary, however, if one wants to avoid falling into mistaken interpretations associated with Marxist analysis which always resolve themselves into one of the following positions (a) the concept of middle classes as unproductive labourers (2) or (b) the concept of middle classes as non wage labourers.(3) Lack of space does not allow me to enter into a detailed criticism of these two erroneous interpretations. I will only point out the following: as far as the former interpretation goes, why should a nurse in a state hospital, for example, not belong to the working class and a nurse in a private hospital belong to it? Even abstracting from political and ideological considerations, from the purely economic point of view, is not the nurse working in a public hospital like the productive worker expropriated of surplus labour, the only difference being that the latter is expropriated of surplus labour *in the form of* surplus value? Why should the form of expropriation determine the objective collocation in the class structure? As far as the second interpretation goes, the formal identification of wage earners as the proletariat (and of non wage earners as the middle classes) rests on methodological deficiencies and leads to the absurd conclusion that the manager (i.e. the production agent which under monopoly capitalism is capital personified) is objectively speaking part of the working class. It could be objected that the manager does not receive a wage. But, if wages are defined as the income of the working class, the reasoning is circular. If wages, on the other hand, are tendentially related to the value of labour power (and in this case the manager would not belong to the working class), then we would restrict the definition of the working class to those wage earners whose wage is determined, tendentially, by the value of their labour power. We would then provide a definition in terms of distribution and not in terms of production relations (the manager would then, in terms of production relations, be part of the working class). The same methodological deficiency would therefore vitiate the concept of middle classes. In other words, why should the new middle class (that part of the middle class which owes its birth and development to the advent of monopoly capitalism) receive an income higher than the value of its labour power?

One (but only one) essential element of the answer (an answer to be focused to begin with at the level of *production* relations) is that this class performs both the function of the collective worker and the global function of capital (a precise definition of these terms will be provided in section III). They do not own (either legally or economically) the means of production and yet part of their time is devoted to performing the function of capital. Therefore, their income (as we will see in section V) is made up of two components: the wage component (connected with performing the function of the collective worker) and the revenue component (connected with performing the global function of capital). In other words, their income is only partly determined by the value of their labour power, the other parts being connected with a position of privilege vis-à-vis the working class and thus explaining the variance with the wages of the working class. Moreover, as we will see in section VI, these two functions are combined in a varying balance in the sense that 1, different positions combine these two functions in different ratios, and 2, over the time, the balance within a position can change. This change, e.g. the decrease in the time devoted to performing the global function of capital and the corresponding increase in the time going to performing the function of the collective worker (a change which must be connected with the devaluation of labour power; a constant tendency under capitalism) in turn explains the process of proletarianization of the new middle class (basically employees (4) and technicians) again in terms of production and not only distribution relations). To talk about proletarianization (always leaving aside political and ideological considerations) as decreasing wages (i.e. to stay on the level of distribution relations) is to go no further than describing (and not explaining) this phenomenon.

The last two sections (on the income of the new middle class and on its proletarianization) are an attempt to prove the analytical usefulness of the concept of new middle class I am submitting, when applied concretely. This concept brings in proper perspective the function (i.e. the two functions) performed by this class in the capitalist production process. This element, in combination with the other three elements defining a class at the economic structure level (see section II) provides a rigorous definition of this class. It should be kept in mind, however, throughout the reading of this essay, that the analysis given here is limited to the economic aspects of the new middle class (and, moreover, only at the two highest levels of abstraction) and that very little attention is paid to the ideological and political instances. Yet no class, when analysing a concrete society, can ever be defined only on the economic level: its economic identification (the difference between economic definition and economic identification has to do with the levels of abstraction we use in our analysis and will be explained in section III) is, however, a necessary although not a sufficient step. Only when the limits of our research are clearly defined in such a way, can we examine the relevance of the economic structure for the concept of class.

If the following analysis is correct, then the political implications should be obvious. The policy of those left wing forces which aim at an alliance with the new middle class by trying to win back to this class a lost position of privilege is doomed to failure. Only a correct theoretical understanding of the nature of, and processes being undergone by, this class will provide a basis for winning this class away from the forces of reaction. The role of the revolutionary vanguard, then, must be that of making clear to those strata in the process of proletarianization that, *objectively* speaking, it is the proletariat and not the bourgeoisie which must be looked upon as their natural ally.

1   AN OUTLINE OF THE THEORETICAL BACKGROUND (5)

If we examine the capitalist production process, we see that it is
made up of three elements:
(a) the labourer (producer)
(b) the means of production (6)
(c) the non-labourer (non-producer), who appropriates to himself
    the surplus labour in the form of surplus value.
These three elements, in order to participate in the production process must enter into relation with each other (Marx, 'Capital' II,
34: 'Grundrisse' 489), i.e. they must enter into *production relations*. Or, to introduce a terminology which we will use later, the
production relations are relations between the agents of the production process and the means of production.(7)   Under capitalism, the
producer does not own the means of production (which belong to the
non-producer, the non-labourer) and must, thus, sell his labour
power in order to obtain the culturally determined necessities of
life. Since the non-labourer owns both the means of production and
the labour power, he owns also the product and thus can appropriate
the surplus labour incorporated in it. The transformation of the
product into money (sale) allows the capitalist to realize the surplus labour incorporated in the commodity in the form of surplus
value. The capitalist's income derives from surplus value while the
labourer's income is tendentially given by the value of his labour
power. Thus, production relations determine *distribution relations*.
(8) Let us call, as a first approximation, the system of production
and distribution relations the *mode of production*. To each mode of
production there correspond a production process simply because production relations are the relations into which the agents enter when
participating in the production process. We can thus define the
economic structure as the unity (actually a unity in determination)
(9) of the mode of production and the production process corresponding to it.
That the capitalist production process is made up of these three
elements does not tell us anything about the specific nature of this
process. Marx provides, especially in 'Capital', Vol. I, and in
'Resultate des Unmittelbaren Produktionsprozesses'(10) an analysis
of this process the outcome of which was to identify the process as
the unity in domination of two aspects of it: the labour process
(which is the 'process which, by using useful labour, creates with
given use values new use values' (Marx, 'Resultate': 10 [462]) and
the elements and general nature of which never change) and the surplus value producing process, (the process producing value and thus
surplus value).(11) Unity in domination refers to the subordination
of the former to the latter, or that use values are produced only as
a means for (and thus are subject to the laws of) the production of
exchange values. (12) An implication of this analysis is that,
under capitalism, only that labour which produces surplus value is
productive labour. The double aspect of the capitalist production
process is summarized in Table 1.

TABLE 1   The capitalist production process

	constant capital	variable capital				
quali-tative aspect	necessary additions to labour-power (means of production)	concrete labour (labour-power in action)	= labour-process		use value	
			domination =	capitalist =production process	domin-ation =	capitalist commodity
quanti-tative aspect	depositories of material-ized labour (constant capital)	abstract labour +(variable capital in action	=producing surplus value		ex-change value	

Limits of space force us to assume a knowledge of the analysis summarized in Table 1. A few words, however, must be spent on the fact
that, if the mode of production determines the production process,
and if, under capitalism, the latter has a double aspect (as labour
process and as surplus value producing process), then it follows
that there must be two types of production relations or that production relations too can be regarded from two different perspectives.
Let us call these two sets of relations the production relations
upon which the labour process rests and the production relations
upon which the surplus value producing process rests.(13) Without
elaborating the argument, we will simply state that the former set
of relations invests only the producer and the means of production,
while the latter set of relations invests also the non-producer, the
non-labourer.(14)   Moreover, not only do we have two sets of relations, (not only can we consider the capitalist mode of production
from two perspectives) but the relations underlying the surplus
value producing process dominate the relations upon which the labour
process rests.(15)   Therefore, the capitalist mode of production
when we focus only on the production relations can be defined as the
unity in domination of two aspects of it, the mode of production
upon which the surplus value producing process rests and the mode of
production upon which the labour process rests.(16)   Thus, it is the
unity in domination of the capitalist mode of production which is
the origin of the nature of the capitalist production process, as
the unity in domination of the labour process and the surplus value
producing process.
    But in what sense is the mode of production the origin of the
production process? What is the content of the relation between
these two elements of the economic structure?(17)   The answer is: a
relation of determination. This concept, first introduced by
Althusser ('For Marx': 101) is used here in the following modified
sense: First of all, the determinant instance (e.g. the economic
structure vis-à-vis the superstructure, or within the economic
structure, the mode of production vis-à-vis the production process

or within the mode of production, the production relations vis-à-vis the distribution relations, etc.) determines the determined instance (superstructure, production process, distribution relations, etc.) in the sense that the former calls into existence the latter as a condition of its own existence. For example, the capitalist economic structure, being based as it is on antagonistic production relations (exploitation), generates class struggle. This conflict could jeopardize the reproduction of the economic structure itself. Thus, the political and ideological structures, by limiting class stuggle, make possible such a reproduction. Secondly, the determined instance modifies, reacts upon, the determinant instance, i.e. the determinant instance is overdetermined by the determined one. for example, class struggle and thus superstructure make necessary the introduction of production processes (e.g. provision of services by the state) different from the capitalist one and thus modify the economic structure (in the sense that this structure is not a purely capitalistic one). Overdetermination thus implies relative autonomy of the determined vis-à-vis the determinant instance. Thirdly, the determinant instance sets the limits to its overdetermination by the determined instances.(18)   For example, the non-capitalist sector must always be subordinated to the capitalist one, or the capitalist system will cease to be such.

The concept of overdetermination as used here, is useful for the purpose of our discussion for two reasons. First of all, it allows us to interpret the relation between production and distribution relations. The former determine the latter, which in turn, being endowed of a certain autonomy, modify the former up to a certain extent. The following quotations are necessary to prove the point.

The relations and modes of distribution thus appear merely as the obverse of the agents of production. An individual who participates in production in the form of wage labour shares in the products, in the results of production, in the form of wages. The structure of distribution is completely determined by the structure of production. Distribution is itself a product of production, not only in its object, in that only the results of production can be distributed, but also in its form, in that the specific kind of participation in production determines the specific forms of distribution, i.e. the pattern of participation in distribution ... In the shallowest conception, distribution appears as the distribution of products, and hence as further removed from and quasi-independent of production. But before distribution can be the distribution of products, it is: 1, the distribution of the instruments of production, and 2, which is a further specification of the same relation, the distribution of the members of the society among the different kinds of production ... If it is said that, since production must begin with a certain distribution of the instruments of production, it follows that distribution at least in this sense precedes and forms the presupposition of production, then the reply must be that production does indeed have its determinants and preconditions, which form its moments. (Marx: 1973: 95 and 97).

Therefore the economic structure is not a simple but a structured unity in which only one element, the production relations, play the determinant role in the sense explained above:

The conclusion we reach is not that production, distribution, exchange and consumption are identical, but that they all form the members of a totality, distinctions within a unity. Production predominates not only over itself, in the antithetical definition of production, but over the other moments as well ... A definite production thus determines a definite consumption, distribution and exchange as well as *definite relations between these different moments*. Admittedly, however, *in its one-sided form*, production is itself determined by the other moments. For example, if the market, i.e. the sphere of exchange, expands, then production grows in quantity and the division between its different branches becomes deeper. A change in distribution changes production, e.g. concentration of capital, different distribution of the population between town and country, etc. Finally, the needs of consumption determine production.(19)

These remarks are important because, if it is true that distribution relations can play an important part in the final shaping of the economic structure and thus of the social classes, it is also true that they always react upon a basic structure in which the ultimate explanation must be sought. But they are also important — and this brings us to the second point — because they serve to introduce what I call the direct and the indirect overdetermination of the concept of classes. The overdetermination of the economic structure is a reflection of the intervention of the superstructure and class struggle on the former. I call this type of overdetermination, when applied to the economic identification of classes, *indirect overdetermination* of the concept of class because it is only a reflection of the intervention of the superstructure and class struggle on this identification. But the peculiarity of the definition of classes is that this overdetermined identification of classes is only a *basis* for the definition of classes, a basis which is directly changed by the outcome of the dialectical relation economic structure/superstructure/class struggle. Therefore, we have also a *direct overdetermination* of the identification of class, the change the definition of class undergoes due to the class struggle and super structure, the change which writes off an automatic identity between the economic identification of a class and its definition, since this definition must be given in economic, political, and ideological terms.(20)

We can now close this section with a few remarks on the levels of abstraction to be used in this paper. Basically, we will stay on the two highest levels of abstraction, the level of the *pure capitalist structure* (21) and the level of the capitalist socio-economic system. On the former level we isolate only what is essential in a capitalist system. That is, we concentrate on the production relations typical of capitalism. But, to each economic structure there corresponds a political and ideological structure (super-structure) and also the corresponding levels of class struggle. Therefore, we define the next to the highest level of abstraction, *i.e. the socio-economic system, as the totality of social relations and structures corresponding to a certain economic structure*. We will not use more concrete levels of abstraction, e.g. what I call *the level of the concrete society*. On this level we examine the coexistence in domination of several socio-economic systems and thus of several

economic structures. Within a concrete society, however, only one
socio-economic system, and thus only one mode of production, is
dominant. Within the capitalist concrete society, it is the capitalist economic structure which is dominant, a dominance which is
reflected both in the dominance of the capitalist mode of production
over the other modes of production and in the dominance of the capitalist production process over the other production processes.
Given the determinant role of the capitalist mode of production, we
can say that this is the key element within a capitalist concrete
society. Poulantzas in his 'Political Power and Social Classes'(22)
carries out a magistral analysis of the capitalist state (i.e. the
political structure corresponding to the capitalist mode of production) and shows how it is not a 'pure' capitalist state but the
result of the influence and modifications brought about by other
socio-economic systems.

II   THE DEFINITION OF CLASSES ON THE PURE CAPITALIST ECONOMIC STRUCTURE LEVEL

What has been said in the previous section was necessary for a definition of the two fundamental classes on the highest level of
abstraction (the pure capitalist economic structure level) because
on this level classes are definable purely in terms of the economic
structure. An analysis, even though a necessarily concise one, of
the elements making up this structure and of the relations binding
these elements together was thus necessary. We now need a definition of classes to be applied not only on this level but also on
more concrete levels of abstraction.(23) Among the several definitions of classes, I have chosen the very well known one given by
Lenin in his pamphlet 'A Great Beginning'.(24) Lenin defines
classes as 'large groups of people (25) differing from each other
1 by the place they occupy in a historically determined system of
   social production,
2 by their relation (in most cases fixed and formulated in law) to
   the means of production,
3 by their role in the social organization of labour, and
4 consequently, by the dimensions of the share of social wealth
   of which they dispose and the mode of acquiring it'.
Let us consider briefly how these four elements should be interpreted when defining the two fundamental classes on the highest level
of abstraction.(26) The first element focuses on the fact that,
under capitalism, within the production process, there is a class
which produces and another class which does not produce. This can
be expressed concisely by saying that the first element focuses on
the producer/non-producer dichotomy. But since the capitalist production process is essentially production of surplus value, the
producer is regarded, at least on this level of abstraction, as producer of surplus value, as productive labourer. Therefore, the non-
producer is considered as appropriator of surplus value. Thus, the
first element also implies another dichotomy: the exploited/
exploiter. The second element focuses on the ownership of the means
of production or on the owner/non owner dichotomy. In this connection, we can conveniently introduce the distinction between legal and

economic ownership. Strictly speaking, the difference between juridical and real ownership is irrelevant on the pure capitalist mode
of production level and will only be used in the next section, i.e.
on the socio-economic system level. We have seen that

> it is the owners who have real control of the means of production
> and thus exploit the direct workers by extorting surplus-value
> from them in various forms. But this ownership is to be under-
> stood as real economic ownership, control of the means of pro-
> duction, to be distinguished from juridical ownership which is
> sanctioned by the law and belongs to the (juridical) superstruc-
> ture. Certainly, the law generally ratifies economic ownership,
> but it is possible for the forms of juridical ownership not to
> coincide with real economic ownership.(27)

This distinction will become particularly useful when we come to
consider which changes in the production process, and thus in the
economic identification of classes, accompany the emergence of the
joint-stock company.

The third element focuses on the separation between the labourer
and the non-labourer; the labourer/non-labourer dichotomy typical
not only of capitalism but also of all class divided societies.
Since the first element of the definition focuses on the producer
and the third element on the labourer, and since, when the essence
of capitalism is considered, there is a coincidence between the producer and the labourer, it would seem that one of the two elements,
or criteria, is redundant. But this is not so. The first element
focuses on the surplus value producing process. It thus focuses, if
we consider the pure capitalist mode of production level, on the
fact that the capitalist production process is essentially production of surplus value. Therefore, the producer, in a capitalist mode
of production, is the producer of surplus-value. His antagonist is
the non-producer, he who appropriates to himself the surplus value
created by the producer. In other words, what is essential in this
relationship between producer and non-producer is the element of
exploitation. We can express all this in a synthetic form by saying
that the first element focuses on the *producer as exploited* (and thus
on the non-producer as exploiter). The third element focuses on the
social division of labour within the production process, the most
macroscopic and important element of which is the separation between
the labourer and the non-labourer. We can express all this by saying
that the third element focuses on the *producer as labourer*.

By focusing on the third element alone, we would stress the fact
that this production process is divided, basically, between labourers
and non-labourers so missing the fact that the specific and characterizing object of the production process is surplus value. On the
other hand, by focusing only on the first element, we would indeed
catch the essence of the capitalist production process but we would
also exclude the possibility of considering changes which have been
brought about by the social division of labour affecting the prota-
gonists of the capitalist production process, something which we will
do in the next section. There, we will see that, once we leave the
highest level of abstraction, there is no necessary identity between
the producer and the labourer.(28) Finally, as far as the fourth
element is concerned (the distribution relations) they are, as Lenin
says, a consequence of the first three elements (or production

relations). Moreover, we may also attach a precise meaning to the
term 'consequence': i.e. a relation of determination, as discussed
in the previous section. It might be useful to add that, for a concise depiction of the (tendential) correspondence between production
and distribution, reproduction schemes might be a useful device.(29)
This is what Lenin himself seems to have had in mind as the following quotation, written twenty years earlier than the above-given
definition, would suggest:

> ...one cannot even discuss 'consumption' unless one understands
> the process of the reproduction of the total social capital and
> of the replacement of the various component parts of the social
> product. This example once again proved how absurd it is to
> single out 'distribution' and 'consumption' as though they were
> independent branches of science corresponding to certain indepen-
> dent processes and phenomena of economic life. It is not with
> 'production' that political economy deals, but with the social
> relations of men in production, with the social system of pro-
> duction. Once these social relations have been ascertained and
> thoroughly analysed, the place in production of every class, and,
> consequently, the share they get of the national consumption, are
> thereby defined (emphasis added, G.C.). (Lenin: 1967: 63)

It is perhaps useful to slightly modify the fourth element of
Lenin's definition by adding one more qualification. It would add
clarity to the definition of classes to add also the origin of a
class' income.(30) I suggest, therefore, that the fourth element
be made to encompass: (a) the share of social wealth going to a
class, (b) the mode of acquiring it, and (c) the origin of it. We
have now all the elements necessary for a definition of the two
basic classes (the working class and the capitalist class) on the
level of abstraction of the pure capitalist economic structure.
The *working class* thus is defined: 1, in terms of the first element of Lenin's definition, as the producers (in the sense of producers of surplus value), and thus as the exploited; 2, in terms of
the second element, as the non-owners of the means of production;
3, in terms of the third element, as the labourers; 4, and in terms
of the fourth element (distribution relations, a consequence of production relations) as those agents whose income (a) is determined by
the value of their labour power, (b) is produced by themselves, and
(c) is thus paid back to them by the capitalists. The *capitalist
class* is exactly the opposite of the working class and is thus
defined as: 1, the non-producers (and thus the exploiters), 2, the
owners of the means of production , 3, the non-labourers, and 4,
those whose income (a) is derived from surplus value, (b) is limited
by the extent of that surplus-value (and by the needs of capital
accumulation), and (c) is not produced by them, yet is produced in
their own enterprise, by 'their own' workers.

We have introduced, then, four fundamental dichotomies, i.e. the
producer/non-producer, the exploited/exploiter, the labourer/non-
labourer and the owner/non-owner. Let us group the terms of these
dichotomies in the following two equivalences: 1, labourer = non-
owner = exploited = producer; 2, owner = non-labourer = non-
producer = exploiter. Then, the first equivalence becomes a concise
way of defining the working class on the level of the pure capitalist structure (and considering only the production relations upon

which the surplus value producing process rests) while the second
equivalence depicts the capitalist class, given the same pre-
suppositions.

III   THE ECONOMIC IDENTIFICATION OF THE PROLETARIAT AND THE
      BOURGEOISIE ON THE SOCIO-ECONOMIC SYSTEM LEVEL

The definition of class on the highest level of abstraction as a
prelude to its application to more concrete levels is a necessary
but clearly insufficient step. If we stopped here, not only would
we commit the sin of economicism but we would also, even within the
frame of a purely economic definition of classes, disregard important changes undergone by the capitalist economic structure during
its various stages of development. It is to the analysis of these
changes that we must now turn, in order to arrive at a precise definition of what it means to perform the function of the collective
worker and the global function of capital. Only when these concepts
have been worked out in detail, we will be able to provide a precise
economic definition of the new middle class. Thus, this section far
from being a lengthy detour is a necessary condition of our analysis.

(a)   Formal and real subordination of labour to capital

In section I above we introduced the concept of the capitalist mode
of production (at the highest level of abstraction) as the unity in
domination of the mode of production upon which the labour process
rests and the mode of production upon which the surplus value producing process rests. There we gave a restricted definition of
these two modes of production, i.e. we considered only their social
conditions, the relations between labourer and means of production
on the one side and the relations between labourer, means of production, and non-labourer on the other. Both modes of production, or
better, both aspects of the capitalist mode of production have also
economic and technical conditions (see note 16, section I). In other
words the former mode of production is given by all the economic,
technical, and social conditions upon which the labour process rests
and the latter mode of production is similarly defined as the economic, technical and social conditions supporting the surplus value
producing process. Thus, the capitalist mode of production is the
unity in subordination of the mode of production upon which the
labour process rests and of the mode of production upon which the
surplus value producing process rests, as defined above. This is,
then, our extended and final definition of the capitalist mode of
productions. (31)
     Having said this, we can start with the analysis of changes which
characterize the mode of production upon which the labour process
rests during the transition from the feudal to the capitalist mode
of production. We have already mentioned that the elements and the
general character of the labour process are valid for all human
societies. The elements (the producer and the means of production)
and the general character (the production of use values) are 'the
absolute determinations of human labour in general as soon as it has

cast away its purely animal character . . . (and) are valid also
for the men who work independently one from the other and who produce in a relation of exchange not with society but with nature:
Robinson, etc.' (Marx. 'Resultate': 58) The elements and general
nature of the labour process, then, do not change, but the conditions of the labour-process, the mode of production upon which the
labour-process rests, do change.   The interesting thing is that,
as Marx has shown, these three orders of conditions do not have to
change at the same time, i.e. that there might be, as in the transition from feudalism to capitalism, lags among them.   In this case,
only the social and economic conditions (and more precisely within
the social conditions, only the production relations) change, while
the technical conditions lag behind, at least in this stage.   Let
us take these latter conditions first.   At first, the capitalist
enterprise is but an assemblage of former artisans under one roof,
each one of them producing the whole commodity.   'At first capital
subordinates labour on the basis of the technical conditions in
which it historically finds it' (Marx, 'Capital' I: 310).   A shoe-
factory, for example, is simply a collection of so many shoemakers,
each one of them making so many pairs of shoes a week with raw
materials, tools, etc. provided by the capitalist and under the
latter's supervision.   Thus, the technical conditions of the labour-
process do not change, or at least they do not change drastically.
Only the intensity and length of the labour process are modified
(increased) due to its subordination to the surplus value producing
process.   But from the point of view of technology, the capitalist
production process takes place on the basis of the old, precapital-
ist labour process.   In other words the technique of both the
labour-process and of the surplus value producing process does not
undergo any significant changes.   Things are different with regard
to the economic conditions of the capitalist production process.
True, the economic conditions of the labour process do not change
due to the lack of change in the technical process: e.g. the amount
of capital needed to start a certain labour process does not change.
But now the labour process is subordinated to the surplus value producing process;   that is the capitalist starts a labour process only
as a means to start a surplus value producing process.   Therefore,
the amount of capital needed to start a business is now determined
by the surplus value producing process, i.e. by competition, because
the capitalist wants to start a viable (competitive) business.
Therefore, within the capitalist mode of production, the economic
conditions of the surplus value producing process subordinate to
themselves the corresponding conditions of the labour process.   As a
result, the economic conditions of the capitalist mode of production
are different from the same conditions of the feudal mode of production.(32)   A similar analysis follows as far as the social conditions (and here we restrict ourselves to that part of the social conditions which is given by the production relations) are concerned.
The production relations upon which the labour process rests are the
relations between the producer and the means of production, they are
the dominance of the producer over the means of production.   But the
producer is now engaged by the capitalist in a labour process only
because, at the same time, he is engaged in a surplus value producing process.   The production relations upon which the surplus·value

producing process rests are then the relation producer/means of
production/non-producer. As we have seen, the fact that the producer is engaged in a production process in which the surplus value
producing process is dominant, is a reflection of the subordination
of the production relations upon which the labour process rests to
the production relations upon which surplus value producing process
rests. This means that now it is the means of production which
dominate the producer, that it is dead labour which reigns over
living labour. Therefore the social conditions of the production
process are changed not only as a results of the 'introduction' of
the non-labourer but also due to the subordination of the production
relations upon which the labour process rests to the production
relations underlying the surplus value producing process. These
latter relations introduce the element of subordination (of the producer to the non-producer and to the means of production) within the
production process. But this subordination extends itself only to
part of the mode of production upon which the labour process rests
and does not encompass the technical conditions of the labour process. This stage, the first stage of the capitalist mode of production, is called by Marx the stage of *formal subordination* of the
labour process to the surplus value producing process, or of labour
to capital.(33) But the logic of capitalist development implies
also a revolution in the technical conditions of the labour process,
the subordination of the technical aspect of this process to the
surplus value producing process. Now, 'co-operation, technical
division of labour, employment of machines and, in general, the
turning of the production process into the conscious application of
the natural sciences, of mechanics, chemistry, etc. and of technology . . .' (Marx, 'Resultate': 57 [472]) are all new elements of
the technical conditions of the labour process. This process is
turned from a simple one to a scientifically organized one; to a
process split into a great number of different sections (tasks,
functions),(34) according to the technical division of labour; a
division of labour which is characteristic only of the capitalist
mode of production. That is, we witness here the coming to life of
that constant revolution in the technical conditions of labour, and
thus of the capitalist production process, which is one of the
characterizing features of capitalism. This is what Marx calls
real subordination of labour to capital,(35) the adaption of the
labour process pure and simple to the surplus value producing process, its becoming a technically divided and scientifically organized process along the lines dictated by the need to create an ever-
increasing mass of surplus value.(36)

(b)   Productive labour: extension and restriction of the concept

The change in the nature of the labour process, its real subordination to capital, also brings about a change in the notion of who is
a productive labourer. The final product is not the product of the
individual labourer any more (i.e. the individual shoemaker working
in the capitalist enterprise) but becomes the outcome of a complex
labour process in which several workers take part on a co-operative
basis.

The product ceases to be the direct product of the individual, and becomes a social product, produced in common by a collective labourer, i.e. by a certain combination of workmen, each of whom takes only a part, greater or less, in the manipulation of the subject of their labour. As the co-operative character of the labour-process becomes more and more marked, so, as a necessary consequence, does our notion of productive labour, and of its agent the productive labourer, become extended. In order to labour productively, it is no longer necessary for you to do manual work yourself; enough, if you are an organ of the collective labourer, and perform one of its subordinate functions' (Marx, 'Capital' I: 508-9).

Therefore, the notion of productive labourer is here extended to all those who take part in the labour process, even though they do not do manual work, even though they are not directly engaged in the production of use values. The technician engaged in quality control work, for example, takes part in the labour process just as much as the worker who directly produces the commodities whose quality must be controlled. The relation producer/product within the labour process is not an individual relation any more but becomes a collective relation. The production of a commodity involves a large number of labourers, due to the introduction of the technical division of labour within the labour process. The producer has become the collective labourer, the collective labour-power. Remembering what we said in section I, we see that the concept of productive labour undergoes, under capitalism, a double qualification. When we focus our attention on the surplus value creating process we *restrict* our definition of productive labour only to that labour producing surplus value; when we focus our attention on the labour process and on its real subordination to the former process, then we *extend* the definition to include the collective labourer, all those who participate to the labour-process. As Marx says:

Since, with the development of real subordination of labour to capital and thus of the specifically capitalist mode of production, the true agent of the total labour-process is not the individual labourer but a labour-power more and more socially combined, and the various labour-powers which co-operate and which make up the total productive machine, participate in various ways in the immediate production process of the commodities, or, better said, here, of the products — some working more with the hand and some more with the brain, some as director, engineer, technician, etc., some as controller, some as hand-labourer or simply as helper — an increasing number of functions of labour-power is grouped into the concept of productive labour and an increasing number of people who can carry out this labour as productive labourers, directly exploited by capital and subordinated to its process of production and surplus value creation. If we consider that collective worker which is the factory, its combined activity realizes itself materially and directly in a total product which is at the same time a total mass of commodities — where it does not matter at all whether what the individual worker does, as a pure and simple member of the collective worker, is farther or closer to the actual manual work' (Marx, 'Resultate': 74 [481])

There is thus a double movement in the determination of productive

labour under capitalism. As Balibar rightly points out, there is no
contradiction in this extension/restriction of the concept of productive labour. This double movement is made possible by the fact
that the capitalist production process, as the unity of two processes, rests on a mode of production which is the unity of two
modes of production and thus of two sets of social relations of production. Thus the possibility of imposing two contradictory qualifications on to the same concept, rests on the existence of the production relations upon which the labour-process rests and of the
production relations upon which the surplus value producing process
rests within the capitalist mode of production. The extension to
the collective labourer rests on the former production relations,
while the restriction to only that collective labourer which produces surplus value rests on the latter production relations.(37)

(c) Economic exploitation and economic oppression

Before concluding the treatment of productive labour, let us dwell
briefly on a possible source of confusion. We have seen that the
capitalist production process is based on the production and appropriation of unpaid labour in the form of value, i.e. of surplus
value. This appropriation, and this is the concept of exploitation,
does not rest on paying the worker less than the value of his
labour-power. On the contrary, the concept of exploitation can be
understood only once it has been understood that the labourer gets
the full value of his labour-power (fluctuations and other considerations aside) and yet he is exploited because of the difference between the value of his labour-power and the value this labour-power
creates. But what about the non-productive workers? Can they not
be exploited? It would be held that, since they do not produce
value and thus surplus value, they cannot be expropriated of it and
thus cannot be exploited. This is true, at least as far as terminology is concerned, but one should not draw the conclusion that the
unproductive workers are paid goods and services (wage) which in
terms of labour are the equivalent of the labour provided by them.
Even though, strictly speaking, we cannot talk of exploitation of
unproductive workers because these workers do not produce, and thus
cannot be expropriated of, surplus-value, we can talk of economic
oppression (38) of these workers. The value of their labour-power
is determined in the same way as the value of the labour-power of
the productive workers, i.e. by the value of the goods and services
going into the culturally determined subsistence minimum. The
application of this labour-power, even if it does not create value
and thus surplus value, is, just as in the case of the productive
worker, by no means limited by the value of the labour-power itself.
Take the example of the commercial worker, the typical unproductive
worker. Suppose the value of this labour-power is the equivalent of
five out of a seven-hour working day. For the remaining two hours
of the working day he does not produce value but provides the capitalist with unpaid labour. That is, while the productive worker is
expropriated of his labour in the form of value, the unproductive
worker is subjected to a direct expropriation of labour. No surplus
value is created in the commercial sphere. The commercial

capitalist only participates in the sharing of the surplus value produced in the industrial and other productive spheres. The commercial worker 'creates no direct surplus-value, but adds to the capitalist's income by helping him to reduce the cost of realizing surplus value, inasmuch as he performs partly unpaid labour' (Marx, 'Capital' III: 300). The more he performs unpaid labour, the more he is the agent through whom the commercial capitalist realizes the surplus value produced in other, productive enterprises. From the point of view of the individual capitalist it does not make any difference whether his activity is productive of surplus value or not. But from an aggregate point of view, the larger the number of productive labourers, the higher the general rate of profit, other things being equal.(39)

(d)   Technical and social contents of functions

We have introduced above the term 'function of the collective worker', a term related to the changes which take place as a result of the transition from a system of private capitalism characterized by formal subordination of labour to capital to a system of private capitalism characterized by real subordination of labour to capital.
   What does it actually mean to perform the function of the collective worker? Before we can tackle this and other related questions, an understanding of what we mean by the term 'function' is necessary. With the introduction of the technical division of labour within the labour process, this process becomes increasingly complex; from a process in which the individual labourer produces the whole commodity, to one in which the final outcome, the commodity, is produced by an ensemble of people organized as a collective labourer; as collective labour-power. The labour-process is subdivided in a number of fractional operations, i.e. fractional units logically determined by a certain technical division of labour. As a first approximation, we can say that each one of these operations is performed by different agents of production. This implies that the function performed by an agent taking part in the labour process always has a specific content which is determined by the technical division of labour, i.e. it is always an operation (in the sense defined above). But no matter what the nature of these operations is; what the specific, technical content of a function is, all functions share one common feature: that of being functions to be performed within the complex labour process. Therefore, all those agents performing one of these operations (functions) perform one of the functions of the collective labourer, of the collective labourpower. In short, they perform the function of the collective worker. We will see below that, with the advent of monopoly capitalism, a similar revolution takes place within the surplus value producing process. Of course, when the worker produces a use value (i.e. takes part in the labour process) he produces also an exchange value and thus participates in the production of surplus value. But if we consider the capitalist production process in its quantitative aspect, then we have to introduce the non-labourer also, the capitalist. He is the agent without whom no surplus value would be produced even though he does not directly produce surplus value.

Therefore, he is just as essential for the production of surplus
value as is the direct producer. Now, if under private capitalism
characterized by real subordination of labour to capital the surplus
value producing process is revolutionzed only as far as the worker
is concerned, only as far as the labour process is concerned, under
monopoly capitalism the whole of the surplus value producing process undergoes a revolutionary change. Just as under private capitalism characterized by real subordination of labour to capital the
figure of the worker changes from an individual to a collective
worker, the figure of the capitalist changes in a similar way under
monopoly capitalism. What used to be the function of one agent, of
one capitalist, under private capitalism, is subdivided now in a
number of fractional operations which, no matter what their technical content, all share the common characteristic of being functions
performed outside the labour process and yet inside the capitalist
production process, i.e. of being functions performed not any more
by an individual, but by a global capitalist. Thus, all those
agents who perform one of these operations, no matter what their
technical content, perform at the same time the global function of
capital. *Therefore, a function has always a double content.* As a
fractional operation of either the labour process or of that part of
the capitalist production process which does not correspond to the
labour-process, a function has a specific, technical content which
is determined by the technical division of labour not only within
the labour process but also within the surplus value producing process as a whole (i.e. within the complex of functions performed by
the global capitalist as capitalist). The general, social content
of a function under monopoly capitalism is determined by either
performing the function of the collective worker or the global function of capital. Thus, the specific content of a function is determined by the technical division of labour, while its general content is determined by the social division of labour to be found within an enterprise, within a capitalist production process: the division between the labourer/producer on the one side and the non-
labourer/non-producer on the other. Where does this double content
of a function come from? Simply from the fact that the capitalist
production process is never just a technical process because it is
based on production relations (the production relations upon which
the surplus-value producing process rests) which are antagonistic in
nature, because it is based on the division between producer and
non-producer, because, in other words, by simply taking part in this
process, an agent automatically falls into either one of these two
categories and thus performs either the function of the (collective)
worker or the (global) function of capital.
One should be careful not to confuse the double nature of labour
with the double nature of a function. The former is the result of
the fact that the expenditure of human labour-power is always both
concrete and abstract labour. Similarly, the latter is the result
of the fact that the division of labour within the capitalist production process is always both technical and social.(40) But the
difference to be firmly grasped is that while labour is always both
concrete and abstract (and similarly, but for different reasons, a
function has always both a technical and a social aspect), a function can never be both a function of the (collective) worker and a

(global) function of capital: an agent *either* performs one function
or another. Let us be clear on this point. Of course an agent can
perform both functions, as for example, the capitalist of the private capitalist mode of production who (as we will see soon) performs both the function of the collective worker and the function of
capital. But he does not perform both functions at the same time.
He performs two functions which exclude each other: when he performs one function he does not perform the other and vice versa.
He does not perform the same function which is both a function of
the collective worker and a function of capital. On the other hand,
when an agent takes part in the labour-process and thus the surplus
value producing process he expends both concrete and abstract labour,
at the same time. The importance of this point, the realization
that whatever time is spent in performing one social function is de-
tracted from the performance of the opposite social function (just
as whatever time is spent in performing productive labour cannot be
spent on unproductive labour) is fundamental for an understanding of
the process of proletarianization, i.e. the process which, through
the devaluation of labour-power, constantly tends to reduce the time
devoted to performing the global function of capital and thus to
increase the time devoted to performing the function of the collective worker.

Thus, the real subordination of labour to capital means, as far
as the technical conditions are concerned, the subordination of the
technical aspect of the labour process to the same aspect of the
surplus value producing process. As we know, the general nature
(production of use values) and the elements (producer and means of
production) of the labour process never change. The conditions, on
the other hand, upon which this process rests, do change. As far
as the technical conditions are concerned, these changes can be summarized as in Schemes 1 and 2. In these three schemes, the producer/
labourer always takes part in the labour process, whether this process is considered in terms of its general nature or in one of the
two forms under which it appears in the capitalist mode of production. The production of bread, for example, always presupposes the
baker and his means of production. It is relevant to talk about the
social content of the baker's function within the production process
only in schemes 1 and 2, i.e. only within a capitalist production
process. The technical content of his function changes too with the
advent of the capitalist mode of production characterized by real
subordination of labour to capital. That is why in scheme 1 we
refer to the producer as the individual labourer while in scheme 2
we refer to the collective labourer. Similarly, as Marx has shown,
the revolution in the technical conditions of the labour process
implies also the substitution of the machine for the tool. The
baker, considered as taking part in the specific production process
which produces the use value bread, is only considered as applying
his concrete labour by means of the means of production (we do not
consider his labour as an abstract labour because we now only consider the labour process). When this specific production process
(production of bread) is considered within the frame of a specific
mode of production, e.g. the capitalist mode of production, then we
have to qualify our description of the elements of this specific
labour process by referring to the individual (or collective) baker

Scheme 1:   *private capitalism characterized by formal subordination*
            of labour to capital (simple labour-process)

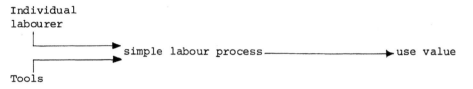

Individual
labourer

simple labour process —————————— use value

Tools

Scheme 2:   *private capitalism characterized by real subordination of*
            labour to capital (complex labour-process)

Collective
labourer
(technical
division
of labour)

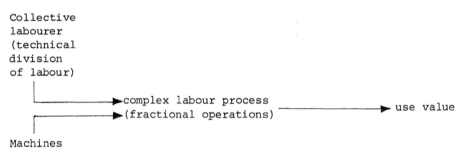

complex labour process
(fractional operations) ——————— use value

Machines

These two schemes can be usefully compared to the following one:

Scheme 3:   *labour process in general*

Producer

labour-process ———————————— use value

Means of
production

and the tools (or machines) he uses. Now we consider *how* he produces bread, not only technically but also socially (i.e. by being
either the individual or the collective labourer).
    We have called the technical, specific nature of a function an
operation, i.e. a fractional unit logically determined by a certain
technical division of labour. We have also called the general,
social nature of a function its being part either of the function of
the (collective) worker or of the (global) function of capital. We
have also said that, with the introduction of the technical division
of labour, one agent performs only one function. But this was a
first approximation introduced in order to stress the fact that the
capitalist production process is internally subdivided in a number
of functions, in a number of operations with a specific social significance. But an agent can, and usually does, carry out more than
one function. We can thus introduce the term *position* to refer to

one or more functions (considered both from the technical and from
the social point of view) which, in a certain enterprise, are carried out by one agent. Thus, the same technical division of labour
applied to a certain specific production process — e.g. the production of bread given a certain technology — originates the same
structure of functions in several enterprises engaged in the production of bread but not necessarily the same structure of positions:
a certain position in enterprise A can be fragmented in a number of
functions in enterprise B. In other words, a function (as an operation) depends only on the technical division of labour, while a position (as an ensemble of operations) depends on how this technical
division of labour is organized in a certain enterprise. The term
position is preferred to the term *job* because the latter, as used in
bourgeois social sciences, refers only to the technical aspects of
the position. The *job content* is thus purely a technical description, a description in terms of operations. By using the term position we want to emphasize that an agent, in performing one or more
functions, is never only doing a technical job: at the same time
his activity has also a social significance, a social function, i.e.
he either performs the function of the (collective) worker or the
(global) function of capital.(41)

*(e)   The function of capital and the double nature of the work of
supervision and management*

The remarks made above should make clear why, from now on, when we
talk about a function we will always specify not only its technical
but also its social content. The same remarks should also have made
clear what is the function of the producer within the labour-process
subordinated to the capitalist production process: he only performs
the function of labour, either of the individual or of the collective labourer. Let us now consider the function of the agent of production who does not take part in the labour process, and yet is
indispensable for the capitalist production process, for the production of surplus value: the capitalist. While radical changes
take place as far as the producer is concerned in shifting from the
first to the second stage of private capitalism, the figure of the
non-labourer, the capitalist does not undergo radical alterations.
Let us then see what these functions are, i.e. what the nature of
the capitalist's work is under private capitalism, what does it
mean to perform the function of capital. Under conditions of private capitalism, the capitalist performs a *work of supervision and
management* which has a *double nature*. On the one hand this work is
necessary due to the co-operative nature of the labour process (and
thus of the production process) and would thus be necessary also in
the a-historical hypothesis of the same technical process based on
non-antagonistic relations of production.(42) On the other hand,
this labour is necessary due to the fact that, under capitalism, the
relations of production are antagonistic, i.e. that there is an
antithesis between the labourer as producer of surplus value (or
surplus labour, in the case of unproductive labourers) and the non-
labourer as the appropriator of surplus value. From this point of
view, then, this second aspect of the work of supervision and

management is necessary not only under capitalism but also in any antagonistic mode of production in which the expropriation of surplus labour in whatever form takes place within the production process. What changes, from one mode of production to another, is the form this second aspect of the work of supervision and management takes. For example, the manager under the slave system is the person (a slave himself) who takes instruction from the master; who replaces the master when he is absent; who thus has more freedom of action and a more privileged position than the other slaves, and who has the possibility of gaining freedom. Basically, then, the capitalist can perform not only his function as a capitalist, a function which corresponds to the maintenance of economic exploitation and oppression, a function which is one aspect of his work of supervision and management and which we call *work of control and surveillance,* but also a function as the producer, as the co-ordinator of the labour process, a function which corresponds to the other aspect of the work of supervision and management and which we call *work of co-ordination and unity* of the labour process. Therefore, *to perform the function of capital basically means to carry out the work of control and surveillance.*(43)   The capitalist as capitalist performs the function of capital while as producer; as a member of the labour-power, he performs one of the functions of the collective worker, i.e. carries out a work of co-ordination and unity of the labour-process. The capitalist as such performs the work of control and surveillance because he must impose discipline on the worker. Labour must be performed regularly, properly and continuously. The worker must not ill-use or damage the machines; must not waste raw materials; must not only re-produce his own labour-power but must also produce surplus value, by working for a time longer than that contained in his wage, etc. Of particular importance is that since the quantity produced is a function of both the length of the working day and of the intensity of labour, it is necessary that the labourer works with an average degree of intensity. The capitalist, through his work of control and surveillance, will see to it that this happens or, if possible, will force the labourer to work at a higher-than-average degree of intensity because this extra-intensity will bring him extra surplus value. Of course he will also try to increase his absolute surplus value at the same time. (Marx, 'Resultate': 15 : 17 [464-5])

[It should be pointed out that while control and surveillance is always the content of the function of capital, the forms this function takes can change from the most brutal to the most subtle. In his discussion of Taylorism, H. Braverman is rightly emphatic on this point:

> Control has been the essential feature of management throughout its history, but with Taylor it assumed unprecedented dimensions. The stages of management control over labor before Taylor had included, progressively: the gathering together of the workers in a workship and the dictation of the length of the working day; the supervision of workers to ensure diligent, intense or uninterrupted application; the enforcement of rules against distractions (talking, smoking, leaving the workshop etc.) that were thought to interfere with application; the setting of production minimums; etc. A worker is under management control when

subjected to these rules, or to any of their extensions or variations. But Taylor raised the concept of control to an entirely new
plane when he asserted as an *absolute necessity for adequate management the dictation to the worker of the precise manner in which work
is to be performed.*(44)]

Thus, if we use the following abbreviations:

w.s.m. = work of supervision and management
w.c.u. = work of co-ordination and unity of the labour-process
w.c.s. = work of control and surveillance
sPP   = surplus value producing process
LP   = labour process
FCW   = function of the collective worker
FC   = function of capital
CPP   = capitalist production process
p.l.   = productive labour

we can summarize what has been said above concerning the double
nature of the capitalist's work of supervision and management and
thus the double function he carries out, both as a capitalist and as
a producer, as in Scheme 4.

Scheme 4

```
  ┌──► w.c.s.      = FC  = sPP ──────────┐
w.s.m.                      +            │  CPP proper
  └──►w.c.u. (p.l.) = FCW = LP (sPP)─────┘
```

Thus, the capitalist as capitalist, i.e. as capital personified,
must always carry out the function of capital, the work of control
and surveillance. Moreover he can also carry out one of the functions of the collective worker, the work of co-ordination and unity
of the labour process. Inasmuch as he performs the function of the
collective worker, he carries out productive labour.(45) But attention should be paid to the fact that we are here dealing with the
capitalist production process proper, i.e. with the production of
surplus value. If the capitalist operates in an unproductive (of
surplus value) sphere, such as the commercial sphere, then even
this part of his work of supervision and management cannot be considered as productive labour. Take, for example, a capitalist operating in a productive activity and performing both the function of
the collective worker and the function of capital. Inasmuch as he
performs the function of the collective worker he is productive,
i.e. his labour is incorporated in the collective labour-power, in
the collective labour process and thus in the production-process.
In this case, and to this extent, he *carries out productive labour.*
This must not be confused with the fact that he operates in the productive sphere, i.e. that he has advanced money in order to produce
surplus value and that he carries out his work of supervision and
management in that sphere. Since he carries out this work of supervision and management in the productive sphere, he *performs a productive function,* disregarding whether his labour is productive (function of the collective worker) or not (function of capital) (Marx,
'Resultate': 84 [486]). To be precise, when the capitalist performs
the function of capital he performs neither productive labour nor

unproductive labour because these two categories can be applied only to the labourer, and the capitalist as such is the non-labourer. Thus, to perform a productive function has nothing to do with performing productive or unproductive labour.

The capitalist performs a productive function only if he is the agent through which capital, by being invested in the productive sector, can realize its self-expanding tendency. Only then can the capitalist perform productive labour (if he carries out the work of co-ordination and unity of the labour-process).

[It is interesting to note that in the transitional forms preceding a fully developed capitalist production process, we can already find agents performing both the function of capital and the function of labour. I think here of the sub-contracting and of the 'putting out' systems. The following description, by H. Braverman, provides a couple of examples:

In cotton mills, skilled spinners were put in charge of machinery and engaged their own help, usually child assistants from among their families and acquaintances. Foremen sometimes added to their direct supervisory function the practice of taking a few machines on their own account and hiring labor to operate them.... In the United States ... the contract system, in which puddlers and other skilled iron and steel craftsmen were paid by the ton on a sliding scale pegged to market prices, and hired their own help, was characteristic of this industry until almost the end of the nineteenth century. (46)

The basic difference between these agents and the individual capitalist is of course that the former did not own the means of production (either legally or really) while the latter does. Already at this stage we witness a tendency for the function of capital to make room for the function of labour whenever these two functions are performed by the same agents. We will discuss this tendency further down in connection with the proletarianization of the new middle class. Without going into a detailed discussion, I will only mention that the two processes — i.e. the tendential disappearance for certain agents of the function of capital in these transitional systems and of the global function of capital under monopoly capitalism (the latter term will be explained further down and is essential for the understanding of the nature of the new middle class) — cannot be superficially equated. The former reflects the transitional stage towards capitalism, the latter presupposes not only a fully developed capitalist system but even monopoly capitalism.]

(f)   The function of the collective worker: first approximation

The capitalist, then, performs the function of capital which has been defined as the work of control and surveillance. He can also, in his capacity as co-ordinator of the labour process, perform one of the functions of the collective worker, the work of co-ordination and unity of the labour process. While only the capitalist performs the function of capital, the function of the collective worker is obviously performed also by the labourers. Thus, what does it mean to perform the function of the collective worker? In the case of the capitalist (as co-ordinator, not as capitalist) it means as we know, to perform the work of co-ordination and unity of the labour-process. But what does it mean to perform the function of the collective worker in general, i.e. including also the work of co-ordination and unity performed by the capitalist? Let us start, first of all, from the individual labourer of private capitalism characterized by formal subordination of labour to capital. His function is to carry out the whole labour process individually, i.e. to produce individually the use value, and thus to produce surplus value. Thus, *to perform the function of labour (of the individual worker) means to take part individually in the labour-process, to produce individually use values, in order to produce surplus value.* It means to carry out the whole labour-process and thus to be the individual agent through which the capitalist can produce and appropriate surplus value. It means to be the individual labour-power which allows capital to perform its function by being expropriated of surplus labour in the form of surplus value. On this basis, we can define what it means to perform the function of the collective worker. *To perform the function of the collective worker means to take part in the complex, scientifically organized labour process as a part of the collective labour-power, to produce collectively use values in order to produce surplus value.* It means to be part of the collective agent of production whose exploitation allows capital to perform its function, the production (and thus the appropriation) of surplus value. Therefore, given that the capitalist production process is the unity in subordination of the labour process and the surplus value producing process, to be a *labourer* means to take part in the labour-process and thus to perform the function of labour (either the function of the individual worker or of the collective worker). *To be a non-labourer means to take part in the capitalist production process exclusively from the point of view of the work of control and surveillance,* to perform exclusively the function of capital, to take part in the capitalist production process exclusively from the viewpoint of the surplus value producing process (extraction of surplus value). In short *it means to take part in the capitalist production process while not participating in the labour process.*(47)

(g) The unproductive capitalist production process and the second approximation to the concept of the function of the collective worker

It will have been noticed that the definitions given above concern exclusively the pure capitalist mode of production level, the mode of production corresponding to the production process whose essential feature is the production of surplus value. Therefore, these definitions can be considered correct only on this level of abstraction, only as a first step in the direction of a more comprehensive set of definitions. As a second step in this direction we must now consider the extension the concept of 'function of the collective worker' undergoes at the socio-economic system level of abstraction. To do this, we must introduce a new concept, the *unproductive capitalist production process.* We will introduce this concept by examining the nature of the production process taking place within the

typical unproductive capitalist enterprise, the commercial enterprise.

Productive labour has often been equated with performing the
function of the collective worker because in 'Capital' the discussion of the collective worker takes place within the framework of
the discussion of productive labour. In volume one of 'Capital',
Marx implicitly compares the function of a productive worker when
the production process is the unity of 1, the simple labour process
and the value producing process and 2, the complex labour process
and the surplus value producing process. While in case 1 the determination of whether a worker is productive or not is made on an
individual basis, in case 2 it is made on a collective basis due to
the complex organization of labour. This is why Marx stresses the
fact that the collective, and not the individual worker is productive. This, however, does not imply that the collective worker is
always a productive worker. Let us take a non-productive (of surplus value) branch such as commerce. Since there is no production
of surplus value in this branch, can we also say that there is no
collective worker in it? This would amount to denying that there is
technical division of labour within this branch, which is obviously
nonsensical. If there is division of labour, there must also be a
collective worker, whether productive or not. A commerical enterprise — as with an industrial one — is organized in such a way that
there are those who perform the functions of capital (control and
surveillance) on the one side, those who perform the function of the
collective worker on the other, and those whose function has a
double nature (for the moment we will ignore those who perform both
functions). Confusion might arise here as to the meaning of performing the functions of the collective worker in an unproductive
enterprise. Before the social division of labour separated one from
the other the commercial and the industrial spheres were combined in
the figure of the entrepreneur. The commercial activity was the
exclusive prerogative of the entrepreneur, it was (and still is)
purely unproductive (the time spent in selling had to be subtracted
from the time spent on production). Thus, one might be tempted to
think that all those who work in the commercial enterprise are not
only unproductive but, having taken over what used to be the tasks
of the capitalist, perform also the function of capital, i.e. that
there is no collective worker in the unproductive sphere.(48) (This
could be the reasoning behind the identification of productive
labour with the working class, or proletariat and of the unproductive
labourer with the capitalist class).

But we have already seen that there must be a collective worker
in the unproductive sphere, i.e. that there are agents in the unproductive sphere who perform the function of the collective worker.
What do we mean by this? To get this point clear, we must go back
to the production process. The production process in the unproductive enterprise is the unity of the labour process and the process
connected with the appropriation of (share in) the surplus value
produced elsewhere. Here the workers are economically oppressed
(direct appropriation of labour) rather than exploited (appropriation of labour in the form of value) and are the agents through
which the capitalist appropriates surplus value. Thus, there are
those the expropriation of whose labour is the mechanism through

which the capitalist appropriates (rather than producing) surplus value (those who are subjected to the mechanism of economic oppression), and those who help to maintain that system of economic oppression by performing the function of capital. Take a bank, for example. A bank sells services, non-material capitalist commodities, non-material unities in domination of use values and exchange values. The labour process in a bank consists in providing these services to the customers (safe deposits, loans, etc.). It is those who carry out this labour process, who provide these services — either individually (as in very small branches) or collectively — who are the labourers. Normally, this labour-process is carried out by a collective worker. On the other hand, there are those whose function is to oversee the labour process in its despotic organization, who ensure that labour is provided continuously and at the required speed, with the needed degree of efficiency and skill, etc. These are the agents who perform the function of capital (or, as we will see soon, the global function of capital). Thus, if we consider the *unproductive capitalist production process (i.e. the unity in domination of the labour process and the surplus-labour producing process)*, we submit the following definition: to perform the function of the collective worker in an unproductive capitalist enterprise (production process) means to take part in the complex, scientifically organized labour process as a part of the collective labour-power, to produce collectively use values in order to allow the capitalist to share in the distribution of surplus value produced elsewhere. If we combine the two definitions concerning the function of the collective worker, both in the productive sphere (productive, or pure, capitalist production process) and in the unproductive sphere (unproductive capitalist production process), we can submit the following *general definition: to perform the function of the collective worker means to take part in the complex, scientifically organized labour process* (i.e. in the production of use values, either material or not) *as a part of the collective labourer, as agents through which capital in the productive sphere produces and appropriates directly surplus value (economic exploitation) or through which capital in the unproductive sphere participates in the sharing of the surplus value produced in the productive sphere of the economy (economic oppression)*. It means to be part of the collective labour-power which allows capital to perform its function by being expropriated of surplus labour either directly (economic oppression) or indirectly in the form of surplus value (economic exploitation). This is why, in terms of the third element of Lenin's definition the unproductive labourer is a member of the proletariat as much as the productive labourer.

If we now assume no changes in the figure of the capitalist, i.e., if we assume that the work of control and surveillance (both in the productive and in the unproductive sphere) is still carried out on an individual bases, we can complement scheme 4 above as in Scheme 5.

Scheme 5

$$
\begin{array}{l}
\text{w.c.s.} \qquad = \qquad\qquad\qquad \text{FC}\\[4pt]
\text{w.s.m.}\\[4pt]
\qquad \text{w.c.u.} = \text{FCW} =
\end{array}
$$

w.c.s. = FC

w.s.m.

w.c.u. = FCW =

LP(p.l.) + sPP   = CPP (proper)

LP(u.l.) +   slPP = CPP (unproductive)

where the following two abbreviations should be added to those
preceding scheme 4 above:
slPP = surplus labour producing process
u.l. = unproductive labour

*(h)   The non-labourer under monopoly capitalism and the global func-
tion of capital*

Our discussion has so far focused on the changes which take place in
the figure of the producer/labourer due to the changes in the mode
of production which characterize the transition from a feudal to a
capitalist mode of production and, within the capitalist mode of production, from the capitalist mode of production characterized by
formal subordination of labour to capital to the capitalist mode of
production characterized by real subordination of labour to capital.
The figure of the non-labourer, the capitalist, has been examined
only to allow a complete discussion of the labourer. It is now time
to analyse this other protagonist in the capitalist production process, the other supporter of the capitalist mode of production, the
capitalist. This analysis has already been carried out as far as
the two above-mentioned stages of private capitalism are concerned.
We will not repeat it, then, but will pass on to an analysis of the
transformations undergone by the capitalist in the stage of monopoly
capitalism. First of all, therefore, we must consider what changes
in the capitalist mode of production and production process have
been brough about by the emergence of the joint-stock company.
    First of all as Marx noticed in his analysis of the joint-stock
company; as Hilferding subsequently examined in detail in his
'Finance Capital' and as the bourgeois social scientists redisco-
vered with great fanfare in the 1930s (49) the development of the
joint-stock company resulted in the separation between its legal,
juridical ownership and its real economic ownership. Now it is the
stock-holders who have the legal ownership of the means of production while the economic ownership, the control of the means of production (i.e. the capacity to determine their use, to hire and dismiss labourers, to decide what, and how much to produce, etc.)
belongs to the top managers.(50) *Secondly,* this separation implies
also that the legal owners of the means of production (in this case
the stock-holders) fall outside the capitalist production process:
they have no function to perform within this process. As we know,
the individual capitalist's task used to be two-fold. He performed
both the function of capital and the function of the collective
worker. As a capitalist, however, he was considered as only

performing the function of capital, the work of control and surveillance. Now the function of capital is no longer performed by the
legal owners, by the stock-holders, but by those who control the
means of production, the joint-stock company. It is the managers
now who have become the non-labourers within the capitalist production process: *the work of control and surveillance is connected to
real and not to legal ownership.* But this is true only as a first
approximation. In reality, and this is the *third* point to be made,
the function of capital is not performed only by those few top managers who control the company. Now this function has become the task
of a complex, hierarchically organized ensemble of people who collectively perform what used to be the function of an individual
capitalist. That is, the work of supervision and management, in its
double sense, is not only separated from the legal ownership of the
means of production but is carried out collectively by a hierarchically organized bureaucratic structure. This implies that both the
work of co-ordination and unity of the labour process and the work
of control and surveillance are no longer an individual but a collective task. This means in turn that, 1, a further technical division of labour is introduced in the labour process because the work
of co-ordination and unity has also become a collective task (and
thus subdivided in several operations) and 2, the equivalent of the
labour process's technical division of labour is introduced in the
work of control and surveillance which is now split into several
operations, i.e. organized in a structure of functions (operations).
Therefore, the work of supervision and management becomes a global
work of supervision and management in which the function of the collective worker is still, as before, a collective function (even more
so, given that the work of co-ordination and unity is now also a
collective task), and in which what used to be an individual function of the capitalist has now become also a collective task, carried out not only by the few who control the corporation but also by
a great number of people who perform parts of the work of control
and surveillance without having either the real or the legal ownership of the means of production. Therefore, 1, the technical division of labour is carried to its logical conclusion and reaches all
aspects of the labour process (including also the work of co-
ordination and unity) and 2, the function of capital becomes the task
of a structure, not of an individual; that is, transformed into the
global function of capital.(51) Next, we have to examine this
structure. The *fourth* point is, then, that at the top of this
structure we find all those who only perform the global function of
capital, the social nature of whose functions is exclusively connected with the antithetic nature of the capitalist mode of production.
Those performing this function are contributing to the 'overseeing
(of) the labour process in its despotic organization'. They carry
out collectively that function which earlier was characteristic of
the capitalist as capitalist and not as the co-ordinator of a co-
operative labour process. Therefore, while under private capitalism
it was possible to defend the thesis that the capitalist was performing a 'useful' activity (i.e. was participating to the labour
process) now this argument can no longer be defended vis-à-vis those
who only perform the global function of capital. *Fifthly,* among
those who only perform the global function of capital we should

distinguish those (the top managers) who have the real ownership of
the corporation and those who do not. This category, then, combines
together the top manager and the foreman who only supervises, without taking part in the labour process. *Sixthly,* aside from the
positions in which only the global function of capital is performed,
there is a whole gradation of positions where both aspects of the
work of supervision and management are performed. That is, those
who fill in these positions on the one hand carry out the function
of the collective worker, and on the other hand carry out the function of exploitation and oppression, and thus perform the global
function of capital. Thus, within the framework of a joint-stock
company, the global function of capital is carried out by a structure in which we can find not only agents performing the global
function of capital alone but also agents performing both the global
function of capital and the function of the collective worker. An
engineer in a steelworks, for example, who is head of an office and
who, therefore, is responsible for the technicians working under
him (i.e. for their productivity) performs both the global function
of capital, because he oversees the despotic organization of the
labour-process, and the function of the collective worker, because
as an engineer, he takes part in that labour process. The same can
be said for a chemist who, besides carrying out tests himself as a
part of the production process, must also carry out some managerial
functions. From this point of view, there is no difference between
the double nature of the work of supervision and management of a
capitalist under the individual capitalist mode of production and
the work of all those who, under the monopoly capitalist mode of
production, have taken over this work from the capitalist. Differences do, however, exist. I am referring not only to the fact that
under private capitalism the work of co-ordination and unity and the
work of control and surveillance were individual activities, while
now they are collective tasks. I am referring also, and this is the
seventh point, to the fact that while in the private capitalist the
function of capital is always dominant vis-à-vis the function of the
collective worker, the complex structure performing the work of
supervision and management under the monopoly capitalist mode of
production is made up of a hierarchy of positions at the top of
which the function of the collective worker is either non-existent
or is of minimal importance, and at the bottom of which the function
of the collective worker is predominant and the global function of
capital is almost non-existent; through a gradation of positions
which are the outcome of different combinations of the two functions. Let us call *private bureaucracy* all those who perform the
global function of capital either exclusively or, if in combination
with the function of the collective worker, only in so far as they
perform the global function of capital. We can now summarize the
changes mentioned above concerning the figure of the capitalist in
the following two statements:
(a)   the global function of capital is separated from the legal
      ownership of capital;
(b)   the global function of capital is performed by a structure a
      first part of which only performs this function and has the
      real ownership of capital, a second part of which performs
      this function without having the real ownership of capital,

and a third part of which does not economically own capital
and performs both the function of the collective worker and
the global function of capital (in a variable balance).(52)
With the advent of the complex structure performing the global function of capital, we witness also the birth of a series of disciplines the aim of which is (a) to help the manager to carry out a
rational (i.e. rational from the capitalist point of view) economic
policy such as, for example, operational research, marketing, and
industrial relations, and (b) to organize in an efficient way not
only all those agents who perform the function of the collective
worker but also all those who perform the global function of capital
(e.g. scientific organization of labour). In the last analysis,
however, all these new disciplines, which rest on the application of
economics, mathematics, statistics, sociology, psychology, etc.,
have one fundamental purpose in common, namely the maximization of
the profit rate of the enterprise either by reducing the costs of
production or by helping to set the highest possible prices compatible with a monopolistic situation.(53)

*(i)   The work of co-ordination and unity in the capitalist produc-
tion process as a whole*

In volume II of 'Capital' (1967: Ch. I) Marx summarizes the process
of circulation of money — capital as shown in Scheme 6.

Scheme 6

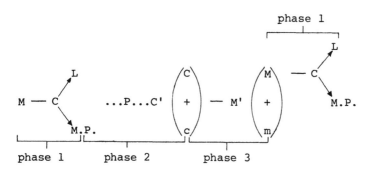

The scheme can be subdivided, for reason of convenience, into
three phases. In the first phase the capitalist advances a certain
sum of money (M) with which he buys commodities (C) in the form of
labour power (L) and means of production (M.P.). In this phase, the
capitalist converts his money into elements of production. The production process has not yet started, all the capitalist has done has
been an act of exchange, a formal transformation of money into commodities. This phase will be examined in some detail after the analysis of phase 2. Let us move now on to phase 2. With the two elements of production (L and M.P.) the capitalist starts a production
process (...P...) at the end of which he obtains a commodity (C'),
a product, which in terms of value is greater than the commodities

(C) which originally entered the production process by an amount c, a surplus product. Here phase 2 ends and phase 3 begins. The product (C') must now be sold on the market, since the capitalist does not produce for himself but produces in order to sell. The product (C') is now transformed back into money (M') and the sum of money which accrues to the capitalist is bigger than the initial amount (M) by the difference m, the surplus-value. In this third phase, then, just as in the first one, there is no production proper, but only exchange, no real transformation of the elements of production into a product but only a formal transformation. Now the capitalist has at his disposal enough money (M) to start a new production process, i.e. enough money to buy again labour-power and means of production.

If we assume money employed in the productive sphere (i.e. if we assume the capitalist production process proper), then only phase 2 is the real production process; the other 2 phases are formal transformations of money into means of production and labour-power or of the product back into money. The implicit assumption here is the lack of a social division of labour in the sense, for example, that both the production proper and the commercial activity are performed by the same enterprise. Therefore, the labour process is here technically subdividable at least into 3 sub-processes: the purchase of the means of production and labour-power, their transformation into the product and the sale of the commodity produced. Take the third or commercial phase, for example: When the capitalist sells the commodity C' which has been produced in his own enterprise, *he takes part in the labour process not in the sense pointed out, i.e. not as the co-ordinator of that part of the labour process corresponding to phase 2. He takes part, now, in a different phase of the labour process, in that phase the outcome of which is the sale of C', its transformation in M'.* Assume, to begin with, that this is the task of the individual capitalist. In selling C' the capitalist provides at the same time both concrete labour (the labour needed for the sale of commodity A differs from the labour necessary to sell commodity B) and abstract labour, i.e. the quantity of labour needed to sell that particular commodity. From this point of view, his activity does not differ from that of the labourer in phase 2 who produces a use value (through concrete labour) and an exchange value (through abstract labour). Just as the labourer takes part in the labour process in phase 2 through his concrete labour and in the surplus value producing process through his abstract labour, so the capitalist participates in the labour-process in phase 3 through his concrete labour and in the surplus value realizing process (a part of the surplus value producing process) through his abstract labour. Similarly, when the individual capitalist performs phase 1, he both provides concrete labour — because to buy the means of production and labour-power needed for his, technically specific, production process he needs a certain type of means of production and labour-power, with certain concrete, useful qualities — and abstract labour, because to buy those means of production and labour power he needs a certain period of time.(54) In phase 1 just as in phase 3, then, the capitalist performs the whole of this phase's labour process by providing concrete labour. To understand what happens in phases 1 and 3 when we shift from the two sub-labour-processes

performed only by the individual capitalist to the same sub-labour-
processes performed co-operatively by a number of agents, we just have
to recall what happens in shifting from the production process carried out by the feudal artisan to the capitalist production process.
The artisan is the only agent who performs both the labour process
and the value producing process: there is no non-labourer within
the production process as yet. With the advent of capitalism, the
same labour process is now performed by a number of agents: now
there are those who perform the labour process and thus the surplus
value producing process, and those who only control and oversee (the
non-labourers). With the growth in the size of the enterprise, with
the advent of the joint-stock company, and with the growing complexity of the labour-process and of the work of control and surveillance, phases 1 and 3 are now also characterized by a process in
which we find, 1, those who take part in the labour process (participation in the production of use values as a whole by the purchase of
the means of production and labour-power on the one hand, sale of
the product on the other) and thus in the surplus value producing
process as a whole (even though they are unproductive), 2, those who
only control and oversee and thus who only take part in the surplus
value producing process, only perform the global function of capital
and, 3, those who perform both functions. This becomes even clearer
if we introduce the separation of the commercial from the productive
enterprise. In a bank, for example, there are those who sell C' (in
this case services) and those who make sure that this C' is exchanged
for a certain value, who make sure that the value exchanged for C'
covers not only constant capital and 'variable' capital but also the
average rate of profit, i.e. who make sure that the labourer is sufficiently oppressed. This means that now the work of co-ordination
and unity of this labour process is carried out by a complex, hierarchical and bureaucratic organization, just as in the productive
enterprise. If we now go back to the joint-stock company carrying
out all these 3 phases, we see that the work of co-ordination and
unity is carried out in all 3 phases of the labour process and that
in all these 3 phases there will be those agents who, by performing
collectively one part of the total labour process, take part in the
labour-process and thus perform the function of the collective
worker, and those agents who by performing the work of control and
surveillance in all the 3 phases, perform the global function of
capital.

*Thus, the work of co-ordination and unity can be carried out by
the capitalist in all the three phases and not only in phase 2.*
This is so because the three phases are, just as in the above-
mentioned operations, technically determined parts, segments of the
labour-process but which unlike those operations, are not performed
by an individual but collectively. This is how the capitalist performs the function of the collective worker. But since he performs
this function not only in phase 2 but also in the other two phases,
we can draw the conclusion that, even when we assume a pure capitalist production process, *to perform the function of the collective
worker the technical content of which is the work of co-ordination
and unity of the labour process, is to perform productive labour
only in phase 2 of the labour process.* This is why it is mistaken
to assume a necessary identity between the work of co-ordination and

unity (function of the collective worker) and productive labour.
This conclusion obviously does not change whether this work is performed by the individual capitalist or by the collective capitalist,
whether phase 3 is detached, due to the social division of labour,
from the other two phases or not.

(j)   The capitalist production process quantitatively considered

Let us consider further phases 1 and 3. When the individual capitalist purchases the elements of the labour-process, i.e. those elements which have .the necessary qualities (technically determined)
for his labour process, he expends concrete labour, he participates
in the labour process in its totality. But when he buys *those* means
of production and labour-power (expenditure of concrete labour) he
buys also exchange-values, i.e. a certain amount of abstract labour
which was necessary, under average conditions of productivity, to
produce them. For example, as we have seen, not only does he buy
a machine (use value) but a machine with a certain value. We have
also seen that the purchase of the use value is subordinated to the
purchase of the exchange value. For example, to preserve the value
of the constant capital advanced, it is necessary that the value of
the means of production entering the production process be not
higher than the socially necessary value, i.e. since the value of
the means of production is the same as the value of the commodities
which make up the means of production before entering the production process, it is necessary that the value of those commodities
corresponds to the labour-time socially necessary to produce them
and no more. Otherwise the capitalist would not be able to recover
all the anticipated constant capital. The question now is: does
the capitalist participate in the surplus value producing process
in its totality because he buys exchange values (just as he participates in the labour process in its totality by buying use values) or
because he expends abstract labour (i.e. because he expends so many
hours in the purchase of that machine)? The same problem applies
also to phase 3. The answer is: both. This question can be tackled
if we recall what Marx says about the amortization of constant capital.
    Let us consider phase 2, the productive phase. Given the means
of production and the labourer, when the latter applies his labour-
power to the former he applies, as we know, both concrete and abstract labour. Marx shows that the application of concrete labour is
the transformation of the use value means of production into the use
value product (i.e. the labour process) and thus the transfer of the
means of production's value to the product's value. Therefore, each
moment of work is both the transfer of old value (through concrete
labour) and the creation of new value (through abstract labour)
(Marx, 'Capital' 1: 200 and ff). This new value 'is the surplus, of
the total value of the product, over the portion of its value that
is due to the means of production' (Marx, 'Capital' 1: 208). It is
'an actual and not, as in the case of the value of the means of production, only an apparent reproduction. The substitution of one
value for another is here effected by the creation of new value'
Marx, 'Capital' 1: 208), while in the case of the means of

production this substitution is effected by the transfer of old value. The creation of surplus value is nothing other than the creation of new value pushed beyond the point at which the worker has created (through his abstract labour) value equal to the value of his labour-power. *Thus, the capitalist production process* which has been so far characterized as the unity (in subordination) of the labour process and the surplus value producing process *can also, if only the quantitative aspect is considered, be defined as the unity of what can be called the value transferring process (which quali-tatively speaking is the labour-process) and the value (and thus surplus value) creating process proper.* If the following abbrevia-tions are used,

CPP = capitalist production process
LP = labour process
sPP = surplus value producing process
vTP = value transferring process
then summarizes the point just made:

Scheme 7

CPP = LP + sPP = vTP + sPP

where, of course, the sign '+' should not be understood as indicat-ing addition but unity. Thus, the value transferring process, even though taking place during the labour process, through concrete labour, is part of the process which results in the creation of the commodity's exchange-value. The value transferring process only takes place during the labour process but is not the same as the labour process. This is the result of the *double effect of concrete labour:* the creation of use values and the transfer of the means of production's value to the product. The two processes are of a com-pletely different nature. The value transferring process refers to the quantitative aspect of the production process while the labour process refers to its qualitative aspect. Thus, the former process takes place during, but is not the same as, the latter process. In section I we considered the capitalist production process as the unity in domination of the labour process and the surplus value pro-ducing process, i.e. we considered it as the unity of two qualitat-ively different processes (and this is the basis for the contradic-tory nature of this process). Thus the commodity was also consid-ered as the unity in domination of two qualitatively different aspects of it: the use value and the exchange value. Here we con-sider only the quantitative aspect of the capitalist production pro-cess, i.e. the transfer of the constant capital's value (transfer which takes place through concrete labour, i.e. during the labour process; yet it is not the same as the labour process), and the creation of new value. This one-dimensional (i.e. only quantita-tive) analysis of the capitalist production process is necessary in order to explain why the commodity's exchange value is not only equal to the new value created by labour but also to the value transferred from the used up constant capital.

Let us now go back to phase 1. *If the capitalist production*

process as a whole can be divided into three phases, then the same
operation can be carried out also both as far as the labour process
and as far as the surplus value producing process are concerned
(even though, only the application of abstract labour in phase 2 is,
strictly speaking, generating surplus value). The individual capitalist takes part in the labour process in its totality during phase
1 by ·purchasing those use-values (labour-power and means of production) which are to be the elements of the labour-process. He thus
expends concrete labour because, as we have seen, the purchase of
the elements of the labour process varies with the technical nature
of this process. But, and here we link up with the analysis of
amortization, to purchase use values means also, as we have seen,
above, to purchase exchange value (we leave aside the elements of
subordination as irrelevant for the present discussion). In terms
of the abbreviations in scheme 6 above, the use value of M is transformed into the use values of C while the exchange-value of the
former can be said, by analogy, to have been transferred to the
latter (exchange of equivalents). Thus, the capitalist's concrete
labour in phase 1 both transfers the exchange value and transforms
the use value of M into C: concrete labour is the means for the
exchange of equivalents. Conversely, in phase 3, when the capitalist applies his concrete labour in order to sell 'his' commodities
(the labour necessary to sell the commodities varying according to
the use value) he also transfers the value of C' into that of M'.
This means that the individual capitalist, by expending his concrete
labour in phases 1 and 3, both carries out these two sub-phases'
labour process thus participating in the labour process in its
totality, and takes part in the surplus-value producing process,
broadly understood, not as the actual production of surplus value
but as the process resulting in the creation of the commodity's
exchange value, as the quantitative aspect of the capitalist production process, because, through his concrete labour, he buys (or
sells) exchange-value, the constant capital and variable capital
necessary for the surplus value producing process (in its strict
sense).

But, at the same time, the capitalist expends abstract labour
(i.e. so many hours for the purchase (or for the sale) of commodities). Here the similarities with the worker in phase 2 end. In
fact now there is no addition of new value because we are now in
phase 1 and 3, both unproductive. The position of the individual
capitalist is here essentially similar to that of the artisan who
buys his means of production and sells his product on the market.
If the labour process is understood not in the strict sense, as
the actual transformation of means of production and labour-power
into the product as a use value, but broadly, as the process which,
qualitatively speaking, encompasses all three phases, then the capitalist, by the application of his labour-power, participates in
phase 1 and 3 not as capitalist but as labourer. There is, quite
obviously, no function of capital to be performed because there is
no work of control and surveillance to be performed. This had to
be said in order to avoid confusing the expenditure of abstract
labour with the performance of the function of capital. Just as
the worker in phase 2 expends both concrete and abstract labour, so
does the individual capitalist in phases 1 and 3, because he is

actually carrying out these two phases not as capitalist but as
labourer. We have seen the double effect of the capitalist's concrete labour; how he performs both the labour process and the value
transferring process. But he expends also, and at the same time,
abstract labour. The fact that this abstract labour does not add
any value to the commodities bought (or sold) does not imply that
the expenditure of abstract labour in the unproductive phases is of
no importance. Marx devotes a considerable part of the second
volume of 'Capital' to the analysis of the turnover period. One
conclusion that can be drawn from that analysis is that, *just as
there is an average time necessary to produce a commodity so there
is an average time necessary to sell it*.(55) If a capitalist manages to reduce the length of phase 3 vis-à-vis the average length,
he manages also to increase correspondingly his annual rate of
profit. The same holds for the purchase of the elements of the
labour process. Once phase 3 has been completed, any delay in
starting phase 1 anew will be reflected negatively in the annual
rate of profit. Thus, even though only phase 2 is important as far
as the production of surplus value is concerned, phases 1 and 3 are
important when it comes to the yearly rate of profit. It is because
of this; because of the importance the rate of profit has for the
capitalist; because of his need to reduce and even eliminate from
his production process phase 3, that the commercial enterprise branches out from the industrial enterprise. But we are still abstracting from such a development, we still assume that the individual
capitalist alone is carrying out phases 1 and 3. Then, what is said
above, should show that the capitalist, by providing abstract labour
in the unproductive phases, participates in the capitalist production process as a whole from its quantitative point of view. His
labour, which is unproductive labour, does not participate directly
in the creation of the commodity's exchange value, yet it is necessary for that creation. He does not take part in the surplus value
producing process strictly speaking but takes part in that process
if considered as a whole, as the ensemble of all 3 phases. This
means that, while the capitalist production process proper (phase 2)
can be depicted as in scheme 7 above, the part of the capitalist
production process corresponding to phases 1 and 3 can be depicted
as in Scheme 8.

Scheme 8

CPP = LP + lPP = vTP + lPP

lPP stands for labour producing process; the expenditure of abstract
labour by the individual capitalist during the purchase or sale of
commodities. This is why the answer to the question we posed above
'does the capitalist in phases 1 and 3 participate in the surplus
value producing process in its totality because he buys exchange
values or because he provides abstract labour?' was: both. When he
buys exchange values (exchange of equivalents) he, through his concrete labour, carries out the value transferring process. When he
sells the product he performs the same operation. But at the same

time, through his abstract labour he provides (unproductive)
labour; takes part in the quantitative aspect of the capitalist
production process as a whole not by adding value but by adding
labour, socially necessary labour in the double sense that 1, it is
necessary for the capitalist production process as a whole and, 2,
its duration is socially determined. *Therefore, the individual
capitalist takes part in the labour process as a whole, 1, by performing the work of co-ordination and unity of the labour process in
phase 2 and, 2, by carrying out, through his concrete labour, phases
1 and 3.* Consequently, he takes part in the capitalist production
process as a whole, quantitatively considered, 1, in phase 2 where
he actually produces surplus value, i.e. is a productive labourer,
and, 2, in phase 1 and 3 where he is an unproductive labourer.

We have seen that the individual capitalist is only a labourer
and not a capitalist in the two unproductive phases. In other words,
while in phase 2 he performs both the function of the collective
worker and the function of capital, in phases 1 and 3 he only performs the function of labour. In these two unproductive phases he
is not a capitalist in the sense that he does not perform the function of capital. The fact that the purchase (and sale) of use
values is subordinated to that of exchange values should not be
interpreted as the performing of the function of capital. The capitalist as labourer takes part here in a process in which the labour
process is subordinated to the surplus value producing process, as
does the worker in phase 2. The fact that his participation in the
labour process is subordinated to the surplus value producing process
does not mean that he performs the function of capital because the
worker's participation in the former process is also subordinated to
his participation to the latter process. The worker also expends
concrete labour (through which he both carries out the labour process and the value transferring process) and abstract labour
(through which he adds new value, i.e. performs the surplus value
producing process). But this does not mean that he performs the
function of capital.

Having said this the role of the capitalist, both as capitalist
and as labourer, within the capitalist production process as a whole,
where phases 1 and 3 are also split into a number of operations and
positions performed by a number of people, is more easily understood. With the growth in the size of the enterprise, with the
growing complexity of its production process, phases 1 and 3 become
separate branches of collective activity; either separate branches
within the large-scale enterprise (joint-stock company) or separate
branches of capital. In the commercial enterprise for example (and
the same applies to the commercial branch of the industrial enterprise) the capitalist as capitalist (i.e. as non-labourer) enters
the production process and therefore assumes the functions typical
of him as capital personified. *First,* we have all those whose task
is to perform collectively the section of the labour process (e.g.,
the purchase and sale of the commodity) corresponding to phases 1
and 3. They take over collectively what used to be the tasks of the
individual capitalist as labourer. That is, by expending both concrete and abstract labour they do not only take part in the labour
process but also in the surplus labour producing process. The difference is that this part of the labour process (and thus of the

surplus value producing process as a whole) is now performed not individually but collectively. *Second,* we have either the individual capitalist or the global capitalist who carries out the work of control and surveillance. *Third,* in the case where this work of control and surveillance is performed by the global capitalist, we have also a number of agents whose function is two-fold: both the function of the collective worker and the global function of capital. Therefore, the capitalist as labourer now takes part in the labour process only by performing the work of co-ordination and unity of the labour process in all three phases. What used to be his function as labourer in phases 1 and 3 has been taken over by the collective labourer. *The capitalist as capitalist takes part in the capitalist production process also in all 3 phases,* because now the work of control and surveillance has become necessary in all these phases. We can thus justify the claim made above that the production process in phase 3 (and also in phase 1) is the unity in subordination of the labour process and the surplus labour producing process. In fact, Scheme 8 above applies to the case in which the capitalist as labourer carries out all the operations connected with phases 1 and 3. There is, therefore, no extraction of surplus labour and the production process in these phases is thus the unity in subordination of the labour process and the labour producing process. But when phases 1 and 3 are taken over by the collective labourer, the capitalist gives up his participation in the labour process (with the exception of the work of co-ordination and unity) and starts performing the function which is more proper to him: the work of control and surveillance. Now, the unproductive worker of phases 1 and 3 must provide surplus labour and it is the capitalist's (as capitalist) function to see to it that this actually happens. Therefore, the production process in phases 1 and 3 is characterized as in Scheme 9.

Scheme 9

$$CPP = LP + slPP = vTP + slPP$$

(k)   The global function of capital and the function of the collective worker: final definitions

The capitalist as capitalist performs the function connected with the exploitation or oppression of the labourers. These are the agents who, by participating in the labour process, participate also in the surplus value producing process. The capitalist, on the contrary, participates *only* in the surplus value producing process: without him the labour process would still take place but the surplus value producing process would not. Therefore, the general definition of 'function of the collective worker' given above can be reformulated in a more concise form as part of the following definition: *to perform the function of the collective worker means to take part in the capitalist production process as a whole (i.e. in all its 3 phases) from the point of view of the labour process and thus of the surplus labour producing process.* Conversely, to

perform the global function of capital means to take part in the
capitalist production process as a whole exclusively from the point
of view of the surplus labour producing process.(56)

The three phases in which the capitalist production process has
been subdivided are not the only ways in which this process can be
technically subdivided. Each of these phases can, in its turn, be
further split into smaller sub-phases. For example, phase 2 can be
subdivided into (A) product design, (B) production proper, and (C)
control and maintenance. Moreover, there are phases of the global
production process which, strictly speaking, do not belong to either
of the three above-mentioned phases: e.g. book-keeping. In common
with phases 1 and 3, book-keeping is a necessary but unproductive
expenditure of labour-power. The employee of private capitalism
who keeps the books performs the function of the collective worker
because, even though he does not actually produce the commodity
(not in the sense of performing manual labour but in the sense of
taking part in phase 2), he participates in the labour process in a
wider sense. The moment book-keeping, due to the introduction of
the technical division of labour within it, becomes a complex process (not only one or a few employees taking care of all aspects of
so many dossiers each, but one employee only working on a part of
the dossier, another employee on another part, etc.), then within
this sub-phase of the total production process (and even without
assuming a separate office outside the enterprise, i.e. without
assuming a social division of labour), there will be those who will
collectively perform the labour process and those who will supervise, i.e. those who perform the function of the collective worker
and those who perform (either only or in combination with the function of the collective worker) the global function of capital.

(1) Economic definition and economic identification of classes

The earlier lengthy discussion of the concepts of 'function of the
collective worker' and 'global function of capital' was necessary
because these two concepts play an important role in the definition
of classes. We can now draw on the analysis provided so far in
order to arrive at such a definition. Before doing this, however,
we have to hint briefly at the need to give different definitions of
classes on different levels of abstraction (57) and consequently to
distinguish between the economic definition and economic identification of a class. In the last section we have defined the working
class and the capitalist class on the pure capitalist mode of production level by using Lenin's definition. Since the economic definition of a class is nothing more than the class collocation of the
production agents due to the production relations, and since these
production relations (and thus the mode of production and the economic structure) can and should be analysed at several levels of
abstraction (i.e. not only at the level which analyses the pure
capitalist economic structure but also the economic structure made
up of the unity in dominance of several modes of production and production processes), it follows that the economic definition of
classes can and should vary according to the level of abstraction on
which we operate. This is what we called the indirect

overdetermination of the concept of class. If we now descend from
the pure capitalist economic structure level to the socio-economic
system level, there are at least two points which should be made.

First of all, we consider now not only the economic instance but
also the political and ideological ones. Therefore, as we said in
section I above, we introduce the superstructure and the class
struggle on all three levels and the complex relationship between
the economic structure on the one hand and the superstructure and
class struggle on the other. This means that we introduce also the
changes that the superstructure and class struggle bring about in
the economic structure and thus in the economic definition of a
class. Therefore, the economic definition of the working class on
the pure capitalist mode of production level is not the same as the
economic definition of the corresponding class on the socio-economic
system level. *To emphasize the fact that we are operating on a
different level of abstraction on which an economic definition of
classes, even though necessary, is no longer sufficient to define a
class (since, now, a definition must encompass also the political
and ideological instances) we now refer to the two primary classes
not as the working class and the capitalist class but as the proletariat and the bourgeoisie. To emphasize that the economic definition of the capitalist class and of the bourgeoisie (i.e. on different levels of abstraction), and also of the working class and of
the proletariat, is not the same because we now consider the changes
undergone by the economic structure and thus by the two primary
classes on the socio-economic system level, we introduce the term
economic identification.* Thus, we should talk about the economic
identification of the proletariat and of the bourgeoisie and about
the economic definition of the working class and of the capitalist
class. In other words, not only do economic definition and economic
identification not coincide (as we will see in a moment) due to the
indirect overdetermination of the concept of class but also the
economic identifications of the proletariat and bourgeoisie do not
coincide with the definition (which encompasses all three levels of
instances) due to the direct overdetermination of the concept of
class.

The *second point* to be made has to do with the fact that, at this
level of abstraction, we introduce also a *third primary class*, the
petty bourgeoisie which is economically identified as the middle
class. In this section we will only discuss the economic identification of the proletariat and the bourgeoisie. We will tackle the
economic identification of the petty bourgeoisie in the next section.

It is at this point that we can appreciate our previous analysis
of who is labourer and who is non-labourer (i.e. who performs the
function of the (collective) worker and who performs the (global)
function of capital), as well as the distinction made, when we dealt
with the four elements of Lenin's definition, between the first and
the third element, i.e. between the labourer and the producer. In
fact, on this level there is no necessary correspondence between the
labourer and the producer (of surplus value). While it is always
true that a producer is always a labourer, at this level of abstraction we consider agents who, even though labourers, are not producers, i.e. the unproductive labourers. This is only a reflection of
the changes, or better said, of the broadening, the first three

elements of Lenin's definition undergo when we shift from the pure
capitalist economic structure level to the socio-economic system
level.   In terms of the first element it is no longer just the producer who is exploited but we include also the non-producer as
oppressed.   This is the agent who, even though taking part in the
labour process as a whole, does not produce surplus value; this
agent should not be confused with the non-producer who does *not* take
part in the labour process, who thus performs the (global) function
of capital and thus who cannot be oppressed.(58)   In terms of the
second element we have a distinction between legal and real ownership of the means of production.   In terms of the third element we
introduce, within the labourer/non-labourer dichotomy, the distinction between the individual and collective labourer and between the
individual and global capitalist.

   The broadening of these concepts has obviously to do with the
development of capitalism, with its different stages of development.
Therefore, the economic identification of the proletariat and of the
bourgeoisie can no longer be undertaken (as was the case at the pure
capitalist mode of production level) independently of these stages
but depends on them.   Let us provide the following periodization of
capitalist development: private capitalism (59) characterized by
formal subordination of labour to capital, private capitalism characterized by real subordination of labour to capital, and monopoly
capitalism.(60)   We can now procede to identify economically the
proletariat and the bourgeoisie.

*(m)   The economic identification of the proletariat and the
bourgeoisie*

During the *first stage,* the *proletariat* is identified as follows.
In terms of the first element of the definition (the place classes
occupy in the production system) the proletariat is given by all
those agents who are economically either exploited or oppressed.
In terms of the second element of the definition (the relation to
the means of production), the proletariat is given by all those who
do not own their means of production.   In terms of the third element
of the definition (their place in the social division of labour) the
proletariat is made up of individual labourers, that is of labourers
who work in units of production in which the technical division of
labour has not yet been applied.   In terms of the fourth element
(the share of the social product, the way of acquiring it and its
origin) the proletariat is given by those (a) whose income (i.e.
wages) is determined by the value of labour-power, (b) who are paid
this income by the capitalist (since they do not own the means of
production and thus are hired by the capitalist) and (c) who are
either paid back a part of the value they themselves have produced
(if we consider the productive sector of the proletariat) or are
paid a part of the value produced elsewhere and in the distribution
of which the capitalist participates thanks to the expropriation of
their surplus labour (if we consider the unproductive sector of the
proletariat).   Therefore, the proletariat under conditions of the
private capitalist mode of production characterized by formal subordination of labour to capital is made up of all those individual

labourers who do not own the means of production, who are either
exploited or oppressed and who, consequently, are paid by the capitalist a wage (either produced by them or not), which is determined
by the value of their labour-power.

The *bourgeoisie* is under the same conditions exactly the opposite
of the proletariat. It is economically identified as all those who,
1, either economically exploit or oppress, 2, own the means of production (the distinction between the legal and real ownership is not
yet relevant), 3, are individual non-labourers, i.e. perform the
function of capital. In terms of the fourth element, they are all
those whose income (a) is derived from surplus value, (b) the extent
of which is delimited by the extent of this surplus value, and (c)
is either produced in their own enterprise or acquired through participation in the sharing of surplus value produced elsewhere.

When we shift to the *second stage,* i.e. the private capitalist
mode of production characterized by real subordination of labour to
capital, then we observe no changes as far as the bourgeoisie is
concerned. Changes, however, do take place within the *proletariat.*
The first, second and fourth elements (the element of exploitation,
ownership and distribution of social product) do not change. The
third element (the place in the social division of labour) does.
Now, the proletariat is no longer given by an aggregation of individually considered producers but by the collective labour-power,
that is, by all those who perform the function of the collective
worker. Therefore, the definition of the proletariat now becomes:
all those who do not own the means of production, who perform the
function of the collective worker, who are either exploited or
oppressed and who consequently, (a) are paid a wage which is determined by the value of their labour-power, (b) are paid this income
by the capitalist, and (c) are paid back either part of the value
they themselves produced or are paid out of surplus value produced
elsewhere.

Let us now consider the *third stage,* i.e. the monopoly capitalist
mode of production. Now it is the turn of the *bourgeoisie* to undergo changes. The first and fourth elements (the exploitation and
distribution elements) do not change while the second and third (the
ownership and social division of labour elements) do change. That
is, the bourgeoisie is still the class of the exploiters (or opres-
sors) and the class which draws its income from surplus value. But
now, it is not necessary to be the legal owners of the means of production: real, economic ownership suffices. The function of capital
is carried out, now, by those who have real ownership and not legal
ownership. Therefore there is a separation between capital as function and capital as legal ownership. Moreover, the function of capital is carried out now not by an individual capitalist any more but
globally, by a hierarchically and bureaucratically organized structure, that is, it has become the global function of capital. Therefore, the bourgeoisie under the monopoly capitalist mode of production is defined as all those who, 1, exploit, or economically oppress, 2, have the real, economic ownership of the means of production, 3, are the non-labourers in the sense that they perform the
global function of capital, and 4, derive their income from surplus
value, whose income is limited by the extent of surplus value and
either produce or appropriate that surplus value. The economic

identification of the *proletariat*, we repeat, does not change in shifting from the stage of the private capitalist mode of production dominated by real subordination of labour to capital to the stage of monopoly capitalist mode of production and remains: all those, 1, who do not own the means of production, 2, who perform the function of the collective worker, 3, who are exploited (or oppressed), and 4, who, consequently, (a) are paid a wage the extent of which is determined by the value of their labour-power, (b) are paid their income by the capitalist, and (c) either are paid back part of the value they themselves produced or are paid out of the surplus value produced in the productive spheres. Table 2 summarizes and compares the characteristics of both classes, as far as their economic identification goes, considered in the various stages of development of capitalism.

(n) A few comments on the managers

It might have been noticed that the identification of the bourgeoisie under conditions of monopoly capitalism fits the managers rather than the capitalist rentiers. This is so because, on the socioeconomic system level, the former, rather than the latter, are the real capital personified. This should not be taken as if the managers have now become completely independent of those who have legal ownership of the means of production. If it is true that the small stock-holders are practically powerless, the same does not apply to those who are at the top of the social structure for whom the separation between legal and economic ownership (they retain real ownership through a partial legal ownership) and the separation between capital as ownership and capital as function (they still perform managerial functions) is only partial.(61) The point is that when we consider the social structure as it appears at the level of the concrete society (something we cannot do in this paper), then we must consider also the legal owners and how legal ownership and economic ownership are combined. But from the point of view of the production process and production relations, the legal owners are not an essential element of the picture. If we want to understand their real place in the social structure we must start by examining how the production process has changed in shifting from private capitalist to monopoly capitalism. On this level, the manager, rather than the capitalist rentier, is the central figure, he, rather than the capitalist rentier, is the non-labourer, the non-producer, the exploiter. He, rather than the capitalist rentier, is capital personified. This does not imply that he has replaced the capitalist as a class. The managers are only a part of the capitalist class, the most representative part from the point of view of the production relations typical of monopoly capitalism. Thus, if one follows Lenin's definition, one can collocate the managers in the class structure unequivocally already at the level of production relations. That is, without considering the ideological and political practices and already at the level of production relations, it is possible, and indeed necessary, to classify the managers as members of the bourgeoisie.(62)

TABLE 2   Economic identification of the proletariat and of the bourgeoisie on the basis of production relations

	Bourgeoisie			Proletariat		
	private capitalist mode of production characterized by formal subordination of labour to capital	private capitalist mode of production characterized by real subordination of labour to capital	monopoly capitalist mode of production	private capitalist mode of production characterized by formal subordination of labour to capital	private capitalist mode of production characterized by real subordination of labour to capital	monopoly capitalist mode of production
No ownership of the means of production				×	×	×
Ownership (legal, formal)	×	×				
Ownership (real, economic)	×	×	×			
Individual labourer				×		
Collective labourer (function of the collective worker)					×	×
Individual capitalist (function of capital)	×					
Global capitalist (global function of capital)		×	×			
Exploited				×	×	×
Exploiter	×	×	×			
Producer				×	×	×
Non-producer	×	×	×			

IV   THE NATURE OF THE NEW MIDDLE CLASS

Table 2 in the previous section shows that, whether we talk about
the economic definition of the working class and of the capitalist
class or we talk about the economic identification of the bourgeoisie and proletariat, we always have classes in their 'pure' state.
That is, the broadening in the interpretation of the four elements
of the adopted definition, broadening which was made necessary when
we shifted from the pure capitalist mode of production level to the
socio-economic system level, does not modify the fact that the proletariat is definable, in terms of production relations, as the
exploited (or oppressed), the non-owner, the labourer. The opposite
terms identify the bourgeoisie. Thus, these two primary classes, no
matter at which of the two levels of abstraction we operate, coincide with the two basic equivalences, the only difference being that
the two equivalences on the pure capitalist mode of production level
are qualified when we shift to the socio-economic system level. But
the fact remains that no elements of one equivalence can be found in
the other or, in other words, that no elements of one class can be
found in the other class. The table shows clearly that, no matter
which stage we consider, under capitalism the bourgeoisie always
owns the means of production (either legally or really), is the non-
labourer (it performs the function of capital either individually or
globally) and is the non-producer, and thus is the exploiter. The
opposite is true for the proletariat. Classes appear here in a
'pure' state because no element of one contaminates the other.
      But we have seen in the previous section that, at the socio-
economic system level, the capitalist of private capitalism is analysed as performing both the function of capital and the function of
the collective worker (i.e. the work of co-ordination and unity of
the labour process). Thus, at the level of the production relations
(63) this capitalist presents aspects of both classes in the sense
of: 1, owning (both legally and economically) the means of production, 2, performing both the function of capital and the function of
the collective worker, 3, being therefore both the labourer (productive or unproductive, depending upon its sphere of activity) and the
non-labourer, and 4, having elements of both exploiter (or oppressor)
and exploited (or oppressed),(64) even though, as we will see, the
capitalist is only the exploiter or the oppressor. Thus, this class,
which in terms of production relations, we will call the *old middle
class*, to distinguish it from the new middle class which emerges
only with the advent of monopoly capitalism, belongs exclusively to
the capitalist class only in terms of the first above-given element,
that is, only in terms of ownership. In terms of the other three
elements this class is spurious because it is a mixture of the elements characterizing the two primary classes in their pure state:
the working class and the capitalist class.(65) Does this mean that
each aspect of this double nature has equal weight? Certainly not.
The elements of performing the function of capital and thus of being
the non-labourer and the oppressor (or exploiter) are dominant
vis-à-vis the opposite elements. And this is so because this capitalist has not only the legal ownership of the means of production
(which entitles him to the ownership of all the surplus-value produced in his factory) but also the real, economic ownership, which

confers to him the role of capital personified. *It is this role which makes it so that the function of capital (and thus the non-labourer exploiter (or oppressor) elements) outweigh the opposite elements.* This is why I said above, that this capitalist 'has elements' of both the exploiter and the exploited. True, he performs both the function of capital and the function of the collective worker, but the fundamental role within the production relations reverts to the ownership element and not to the functional element. The relation connecting the three elements of the production relations cannot be discussed here but it was necessary to stress that the fundamental role reverts to the ownership element in order not to be accused of functionalism.

These remarks are essential for an understanding of the nature of the *new middle class,* i.e. of that part of the middle classes which, in terms of production relations, owes its existence to the advent of monopoly capitalism. It will be recalled from the foregoing analysis (III*h*) that with the advent of the joint-stock company, with the separation of the legal from the economic ownership of the means of production, we witness the following phenomenon: the function of capital only pertains to those who have the real ownership of the means of production; capital takes on a global function which is no longer concentrated in the capitalist class but is diffused among those who are neither the legal nor the real owners of the means of production. That is, the function of capital (now a global function) is performed not only by the capitalist class (at this level of abstraction, the managers) but also by another class the characteristics of which are: 1, it does not own either legally or economically the means of production, 2, it performs both the global function of capital and the function of the collective worker, 3, is therefore both the labourer (productive or unproductive) and the non-labourer, and 4, is both exploiter (or oppressor) and exploited (or oppressed). It is this class which I call the *new middle class.* (66)

The essential features which distinguish the old from the new middle class are three. First of all, in terms of the first of the four above-mentioned elements, the old middle class belongs to the capitalist class (since it is the real and the legal owner) while the new middle class does not. Secondly, the old middle class performs the function of capital individually. It is the individual capitalist, at most helped by a few employees, who is the agent through which capital can realize its self-expanding nature. The new middle class, on the other hand, performs this function collectively in the double sense that this function 1, is performed both by the capitalist and by the new middle class and that, 2, within the latter, is performed by a great number of agents. Thirdly, and this is of fundamental importance, while in the old middle class the function of capital/exploiter (or oppressor)/non-labourer elements are always dominant, in the new middle class this is no longer so, as they are not the real owners of the means of production. One of the characteristics of this class is that the global function of capital and the function of the collective worker (which is no longer restricted to performing the work of co-ordination and unity of the labour process) are now combined in a varying balance. Actually, there are sections of the new middle class in which the

latter function dominates the former. This is possible because
this class, unlike the old middle class, does not comprise the real
ownership of the means of production and yet performs part of the
function of capital. *This fact, that the new middle class performs
the global function of capital even without owning the means of production, and that it performs this function in conjunction with the
function of the collective worker, is the basic point for an understanding of the nature of this class.* The lack of this understanding has not only caused much confusion concerning the nature of this
class, but also has been one of the major stumbling blocks in understanding its process of proletarianization.

[On the basis of what said both above and in the Introduction, we
can now summarize the differences between the old and the new middle
class in the following way.

Old middle class:	*New middle class:*
1 They have both the legal and the real ownership of the means of production.	1 They have neither the legal nor the real ownership of the means of production.
2 They perform both the function of capital (not the *global* function of capital) and the function of the collective worker.	2 They perform both the global function of capital and the function of the collective worker.
3 Since they have the real ownership of the means of production, the function of capital is always dominant.	3 Since they do not have the real ownership of the means of production, the global function of capital is not necessarily the dominant one. This role can also revert to the function of the collective worker.
4 When they perform the function of the collective worker they are either exploited or economically oppressed; when they perform the function of capital they are either the exploiters or the economic oppressors.	4 When they perform the function of the collective worker, they are either the exploited or the economically oppressed; when they perform the global function of capital, they are either the exploiters or the oppressors. However, since they do not have the real ownership of the means of production, when they perform the latter function, they are also economically oppressed.
5 Since they are the real owners of the means of production and since the dominant function is that of capital, they are typically the exploiters or the economic oppressors.	5 Since they are not the real owners, and since therefore the global function of capital is not necessarily dominant, their fundamental role is not necessarily that of exploiters or oppressors.
6 On the basis of point 5 above, they are always on the side of capital.	6 On the basis of points mentioned above, they are partly on the side of capital and partly on the side of labour. This is the contradiction inherent in their

position. Moreover, even when
they are on the side of capital,
they are both exploiters (or
oppressors) and oppressed. This
is an element of further contradiction inherent in their position.]

The above analysis has shown that one of the essential characteristics of the new middle class is that of performing both the function of the collective worker and the global function of capital in
different degrees and combinations. Scheme 10 and related remarks
will help us to analyse the relation between the function of the
collective worker and the global function of capital. Just as the
function of capital is performed by a hierarchically organized complex at many levels of which agents perform both the global function
of capital and the function of the collective worker, in the same
way the function of the collective worker is performed by a collective ensemble hierarchically organized at many levels of which agents
perform both functions. Therefore, the total labour-time during the
working day of a hypothetical corporation is subdivided as in Scheme
10.

Scheme 10:   Functions performed by the agents of production.

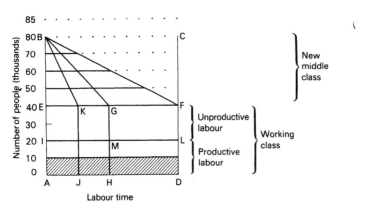

——— Time devoted to performing the function of the collective worker

· · · Time devoted to performing the global function of capital

This diagram depicts the hypothetical case of a corporation in
which 40,000 people perform only the function of the collective
worker, 40,000 people perform both functions, and 5,000 people perform only the global function of capital. Only a small number of
these 5,000 people has the real ownership of the means of production
and thus belongs to the capitalist class. Thus, this scheme implies
also the existence of agents who, while not owning the means of production, perform exclusively the global function of capital (e.g.
the foreman).(67)   Thus, in terms of labour-time it is as if
40,000 + 20,000 people perform only the function of the collective

worker and 20,000 + 5,000 = 25,000 people perform only the global
function of capital. (Those who also have the legal ownership are
not shown in this diagram.) The total labour-time during one working day going to the function of the collective worker is thus
represented by the area ABFD. If we assume that of those performing the function of the collective worker one-half are productive
labourers and one-half unproductive labourers, then the area ABGH
represents the total labour-time going to productive labour.
Marx' analysis was carried out basically on the level of the capitalist economic structure and at the stage of private capitalism.
Only in the third volume of 'Capital' does Marx analyse the double
nature of the entrepreneur's work of supervision and management. He
focuses mainly on the essential feature of the capitalist economic
structure, the production of surplus value, that is in our scheme,
on the 20,000 labourers who only carry out productive labour, i.e.
on the area AILD. Marx considers only incidentally monopoly capitalism and thus does not consider the area EBF. He mainly focuses
on how the working day of those 20,000 labourers is divided. If we
assume a rate of surplus value of 100 per cent, then the production
of surplus value is represented by the shaded area (20,000 people
working half time to produce surplus value = 10,000 people working
full time for the same purpose). But in terms of our scheme (i.e.
thus shifting to monopoly capitalism), the time going to the production of surplus value is represented by the area ABKJ.(68)

Having defined both the old and the new middle class in terms of
production relations, we can now combine the definitions of these
two classes in order to arrive at a general definition of middle
classes on the level of production relations. From this general
definition we will then be able to extract the element characterizing the middle classes. A combination of the definition of old and
new middle classes gives us the following general definition: *middle
classes*, on the level of production relations, are all those agents
of production who, disregarding whether they own the means of production or not, carry out both the function of the collective worker
and the function of capital (either individually or globally), are
both labourers and non-labourers, and can be either only the exploiters (oppressors) or also the exploited (oppressed).

Which is, then, the element characterizing the middle classes?
Let us proceed by exclusion. Not the ownership element because the
old middle class is the owner of the means of production while the
new middle class is not. Not the exploitation (or economic oppression) element either because the new middle class is both the
exploiter and the exploited. The old middle class, on the contrary,
while having elements of both the exploiter and the exploited (but
only on a level of formal logic) in reality, given its real ownership of the means of production, is only the exploiter (or oppressor).

The functional element, on the other hand, has characteristics
common to both classes because both the new and the old middle
class perform the function of capital together with the function of
labour. (However, we should keep in mind that (a) the old middle
class performs the function of capital while the new middle class
performs the global function of capital and (b) in the old middle
class the function of capital is always dominant while in the new

middle class this is not necessarily so.) Thus, we can single out
the social function performed within the capitalist production process, *the functional element, as the element characterizing the
middle classes,* both old and new. In other words, the term middle
class as used here does not refer to the position this class has in
the system of social stratification (in the sociological, empirical
meaning as determined by income, status etc.) but to its position
within the capitalist production process as determined by the social
division of labour. This is not a vertical notion with the capitalist above, the worker below, and this class in between.(69) Our
notion has rather to do with the position of the middle class between
the proletariat and the bourgeoisie, considered only from the point
of view of their economic identification. To put it concisely, this
notion has to do with the position of this class in between the
global function of capital and the function of the collective worker,
sharing both functions.(70)

What has been said should only be considered a convenient abbreviation for the definition, on the level of production relations, of
the middle classes. It would be utterly mistaken to interpret the
characterizing aspect — the functional element — as if the middle
classes could be defined only in functional terms, i.e. as if they
could be defined only as those classes performing both functions.
The identification of a class depends on all the three elements of
the production relations and not only on one of them, which in the case
of the functional element would not be even the fundamental one.

V   THE INCOME OF THE NEW MIDDLE CLASS (71)

We have seen that distribution relations are determined by production relations, or in terms of Lenin's definition of classes, that
the first three elements determine the fourth one. If our understanding of that section of the petty bourgeoisie which is economically identifiable as the new middle class is correct, then this
identification, as carried out in the previous section, i.e. this
definition exclusively in terms of production relations, should
allow us to grasp the nature of the income of the new middle class.

As we have seen, a constant feature of the proletariat's economic
identification is that it is the labourer (either individual or collective) and that, consequently, it gets an income (wage) which is
tendentially determined by the value of its labour-power. Thus, as
long as the worker performs only the function of the collective
worker and if he does not belong to the labour aristocracy; various
wage levels reflect only the various degrees of skill and thus the
various levels of the value of labour power.(72) Under the private
capitalist mode of production, the worker gets a wage (or salary)
equivalent to the value of his labour power. The capitalist, on the
other hand, lives on surplus-value. The capitalist's income depends
thus on that part of the realized surplus value which he does not
re-invest (or consume productively) in the production process. We
will call the income of those performing the (global) function of
capital *revenue* in the sense that, whether it is surplus value
directly produced in those branches, or in other branches and subsequently redistributed, it is always the income of those who maintain

(or help to maintain) the system of economic exploitation and oppression, that is, who are the channels through which capital can
perform its function, the production of surplus value. *Revenue is
the income of those performing the function of control and surveillance.*

Marx ('Capital', I: 591) employs the term *revenue* to indicate
that part of surplus value which is consumed unproductively by the
capitalist. Wages are that part of the social product which goes
to the productive labourer, that part which reconstitutes the
labour-power of the productive labourer. This is of course correct
as long as we consider the production and reproduction of capital
(as Marx does): in this case we focus our attention only on the productive labourers. But productive labour is not the same as working
class. Therefore, *wages* are the part of social product which is
used for the reconstitution of the working class (i.e. the income of
the working class). That is to say, it is used for the reconstitution of labour-power, both productively employed and not, or in
other words, for the reconstitution of those who must perform the
function of the collective labourer. Thus the unproductive part of
the working class is also paid from surplus-value.(73) Moreover,
the origin of the income of the working class (wages), i.e. whether
it is value or surplus-value, is not relevant for the definition of
wages. Just as for Marx the origin of revenue and capital is irrelevant (they both are surplus-value) for their definition, but *only
their use is relevant* (the former being spent productively, the
latter unproductively) so the origin of wages (whether from value
or surplus value) is irrelevant, the only relevant criterion being
their use: whether they are used for the reproduction of the working
class, of the collective labourer, or not. This means that whenever
the work of supervision and management of the capitalist under the
private capitalist mode of production is made up of both the function of the collective worker and the function of capital, his
income is not only made up of revenue (connected with the function
of control and surveillance) but also of wages (connected with the
work of co-ordination and unity). Therefore, the wages of supervision and management are equal to revenue plus wage.

Under monopoly capitalism, as we have seen, there is a complex of
agents performing both the function of the collective worker and the
global function of capital. Thus, the agent performing both functions has his wage determined by the value of his labour-power only
in so far as he performs the function of the collective worker. The
more this function outweighs the global function of capital, the
higher in his income will be the wage component vis-à-vis the revenue component. Conversely, the more he performs the global function of capital, the more he participates in the redistribution of
surplus value (not as a labourer but as a non-labourer) the higher
will be the revenue component in his income and thus the weaker the
relation between this income and the culturally determined subsistence minimum.

In other words, the level of wages might be due not only to the
various levels of the labour-power values, not only to the strength
of the unions and to the conditions of the labour-market (Mandel,
1968: 145), not only to political and ideological reasons (as we
shall see), but also, as in the case of the retribution of the new

middle class, to the fact that these 'wages' might actually be a
mixture of both wages and revenues *and thus might owe differences
and fluctuations also to the revenue component.*(74)   The difference
between the wage component and the revenue component is that the
former tends to level around the subsistence minimum while the
latter is not related to that minimum. *Thus, when a 'wage' is
actually made up of both wage and revenue, its relationship to the
subsistence minimum will become the weaker the heavier is the
weight of the global function of capital relative to the function
of the collective worker. The fact that many 'wages' seem to be
unrelated to the subsistence minimum is a result of this fact.*(75)

I have mentioned above that both political and ideological reasons might affect wage determination. I am not referring to the
wide-spread practice of paying different wages to people performing
the same functions, practice determined by the need to break the
unity of the working class, to create competition within it, to tie
some workers to the interests of capital by paying higher than average wages. This practice explains wage differentials on a micro-
economic level. I am referring, rather, to the *labour aristocracies.* Even though this is not the place to undertake a discussion
of these strata of the working class,(76) a few comments on their
nature are in order if we want to avoid confusing their position of
privilege (and thus, in terms of distribution relations, the discrepancy between their incomes and the value of their labour-power)
and the new middle class's position of privilege.

The labour aristocracies are those strata of the working class
which, like the new middle class, owe their privileged position to
the development of monopoly capital, i.e. of imperialism. The new
middle class is made up of those who perform both the global function of capital and the function of the collective worker. It
owes its position of privilege to the fact that it performs the
global function of capital, i.e. to its place in the production process, to its importance in relation to the surplus value producing
process. Thus, both privileged categories owe the possibility of
their existence to monopoly capitalism and, more precisely, *to the
social division of labour under monopoly capitalism.* Theoretically
speaking, the privileged position of the new middle class can be
explained simply by referring to the division of labour within the
production process, i.e. without having to resort to an international economy. On the other hand, the labour aristocracies can be
explained only by resorting to the international division of labour
brought about by imperialism (i.e. monopoly superprofits)(77) and to
the possibility of corrupting strata of the working class even
though they do not perform at all the global function of capital.
(78) The labour aristocracies are those strata of the working class
which, for a variety of reasons varying with the changes in the conjuncture, are the best suited to introduce within the working class
the ideology and the political practices of the bourgeoisie. Thus,
the labour aristocracies are only a part of that section of the proletariat which has been won over to the petty bourgeoisie. Once the
original contamination of the proletariat has been carried out,
other sections of the proletariat will develop petty bourgeois ideologies and political practices even though no positions of privilege
correspond to these ideologies and practices. In the long run,

however, a position of economic privilege is necessary to sustain
these petty bourgeois ideologies and practices.

This should not be taken to mean that the creation of labour
aristocracies is exclusively the result of a conscious design on the
part of the bourgeoisie. The working of the capitalist system
itself generates the need for strata of the working class to be won
over to the ideology and political practices of the petty bourgeoisie.(79)

Thus, we can speak of labour aristocracies only with reference to
the working class and not to the new middle class. The concept of
the labour aristocracy refers only to those who, in spite of being
part of the working class, in spite of not owing the means of production, being exploited (or oppressed), and performing the function of the collective worker, develop a vested interest in the
maintenance of this mode of production. Those performing the
global function of capital have already an interest in the maintenance of the capitalist mode of production. It would be nonsensical
to talk about labour aristocracies in their case, not only because
they, inasmuch as they perform the global function of capital, are
not part of the working class, are not labourers, but also because,
not being part of the working class, they have already, as part of
their objective nature, an interest in maintaining this mode of production. They are already 'aristocracies' vis-à-vis the working
class.(80)

The labour aristocracies are strata which, despite belonging to
the working class, develop an interest in the maintenance of the
capitalist mode of production and thus do not belong to the proletariat. This means: 1, *on the economic level,* that they are paid
levels of wages higher than the ones corresponding to the value of
their labour-power. Since, as we have just seen, these strata are
chosen for political and ideological reasons, we must draw the conclusion that, under the monopoly capitalist mode of production,
wages are determined also on account of political and ideological
considerations; 2, *on the political level,* that their political
class practices are not those of the proletariat (not joining the
revolutionary party, etc.); 3, *on the ideological level,* that they
do not develop a proletarian class consciousness.

The above remarks were necessary in order to emphasize the difference, concerning the discrepancy between wages and value of
labour-power, between the labour aristocracies and the new middle
class and in order to avoid confusing the former with the latter.
When this is clear, the question that naturally arises is then the
following: given that the income of the new middle class is made up
both of a wage and of a revenue component, how is the latter determined? This is still an open question. One point, however, seems
clear. We should avoid a functionalist explanation of the type 'the
more important functions (technically speaking, of course, since we
are now dealing only with functions whose social content is the
global function of capital), that is, the functions that are more
important from the point of view of capital, get the higher incomes'.
Perhaps the most important lesson to be drawn from the discussion
around the so-called 'Davis-Moore theory' is that this kind of
explanation does not stand a close scrutiny.(81) From a purely economic point of view, not only is there no way to prove that the

function performed by the foreman (who only carries out the work of
control and surveillance) is less important than the function performed by the managers, but also there is no logical ground on
which to base such an opinion: both agents are equally important as
far as the global capital is concerned. Yet the foreman's income
is much lower than the manager's. Of course, we are still concerned
about the determination of the revenue part from an economic standpoint: there are also political and ideological determinants. For
example, monopoly super-profits create the possibility of introducing a fictitious differentiation of functions within the global
function of capital for ideological and political reasons.(82) We
can either hold that these latter reasons are paramount, or we can
try to tie the subdivision of the surplus value, among all those
agents who globally carry out the function of capital, to the particular nature of the capitalist production process. If the latter
route is chosen, then we could establish a direct relation between
a position's high income (revenue) and its vicinity, in the hierarchical structure of positions, to those positions carrying within
themselves the real ownership of the means of production, and in
inverse relation to this position proximity, in the production process, to those who perform the function of the collective worker.
The top manager has real, economic ownership and thus has economic
power. He must delegate a part of his work of control and surveillance to lower managerial strata and to the new middle class. The
lower strata, since they are farther from the centre of economic
power, also get lower incomes. In other words, income differentiation is functional for the maintenance of the authoritarian and
hierarchical structure of the enterprise. The farther we move from
the top, the farther we move from the centre of economic power, the
lower will the incomes be until when we reach the foreman. This
agent is in constant touch with the labourers and makes sure that
they provide daily the proper amount of surplus value. If the gap
between his and the worker's income were very large, the ideological
repercussions would be extremely unfavourable to the enterprise.
The top manager, on the other hand, is safely isolated from direct
contact with the shop-floor. This, however, is nothing more than
an hypothesis and the question, as said above, is still largely
unexplored.

VI   ELEMENTS OF A THEORY OF THE PROLETARIANIZATION OF THE NEW
     MIDDLE CLASS

In the previous sections we have stressed several times that there
is no automatic correspondence between the economic identification
of classes and their definition. This is so because classes must be
defined in economic, political and ideological terms. As an example
of a non-correspondence between the economic identification and the
definition of the proletariat, we considered briefly the labour
aristocracy. We saw briefly that this stratum, as far as the economic is concerned, belongs to the proletariat on the level of production relations while it belongs to the petty bourgeoisie when
distribution, political, and ideological relations as well are considered.(83) This means that the transition of a certain part of

the proletariat to the petty bourgeoisie (labour aristocracy) does
not involve changes at the level of production relations.(84)
Things are different when we examine the reverse process, i.e. the
shift of a certain stratum of the petty bourgeoisie in to the proletariat, i.e. the proletarianization of the petty bourgeoisie.

While proletarianization as a process is the reverse of the
formation of labour aristocracies it is not its mirror image. To
anticipate our conclusions, we are now dealing with a process which
has its origins in the changing position of the middle classes in
the capitalist production process and in the production relations on
which this process rests. Here too distribution relations play an
important part since, for example, the level of income (value of
labour power) of those strata which have been proletarianized has
undergone a reduction, if not in absolute certainly in relative
terms, compared to the average value of the labour power. But
here, the fundamental, the determining change takes place at the
level of the production process and production relations. It is
this fact which has not been understood and that consequently
must be heavily stressed. A typical example of this incorrect
approach which remains only on the level of the distribution relations is provided by the definition of proletarianization given by
Simonetta Piccone-Stella (1972) who defines proletarianization as
'that process of all-round lowering of the conditions of life of a
social stratum, a process which starts basically from its conditions of work. Proletarianization is not simply a change from
ownership (and control) of the means of production to non-onwership,
but from independence to dependence in the work activity, from self-
sufficiency to subordination, from qualified and high in prestige to
unqualified roles, from a level of economic well-being to one of
simple subsistence or privation. As far as the external conditions
of the labour market go, proletarianization usually goes hand in
hand with unemployment, disguised unemployment (i.e. activities in
roles below one's level of training) and low salaries. Similarly,
as far as the internal conditions of work are concerned, proletarianization means losing control of the ultimate end of the work process, a liability to be substituted (as a consequence of dequalification) and a variable degree of exploitation. Moreover, proletarianization almost always marks a shift from forms of individual
labour to forms of collective labour'.(85)

The first noticeable thing about this definition, which is representative of the way many authors conceive proletarianization, is
its insufficiency. In fact, even if it does provide a good description of some of the major economic phenomena characterizing proletarianization, it only stays on the level of description without
providing an explanation of the process itself. It is not enough to
say that proletarianization can be explained, essentially, in terms
of a deterioration of the conditions of work: what causes this deterioration? Secondly, only the economic aspects of a complex process are here considered. Since a class is not only definable in
economic terms, a process which determines the shift of one class
or section to a different place in the social structure must be
explained also in political and ideological terms. But even if we
add the political and ideological dimensions to this economic 'definition' we still remain on the level of description rather than

analysis because we still do not examine the production relations but remain on the level of the distribution relations. Thirdly, this definition does not make a distinction between the proletarianization of the old middle class (i.e. the expropriation of the producers from their own means of production and their becoming proletarians) and that of the new middle class which is a more complex phenomenon. Consequently, this definition is more likely to introduce confusion than clarity. The proletarianization of the old middle class presents no conceptual difficulties. What we must do, is to explain the proletarianization of the new middle class because it is around the nature and dynamics of this new middle class that many of the most heated debates have revolved (and still revolve) and contradictory theories have been built: from the 'embourgeoisification' of the working class to the proletarianization of the middle class. What is, then, the essence of the process of proletarianization of the new middle class? As a first approximation, we can say that it is a process of devaluation of labour-power, from skilled to average labour-power. To understand this point it is essential to realize that the nature of a socio-economic process is never a simple mechanical, sort of cause-effect relationship but the result of an interaction between a basic tendency and a number of countertendencies which arise and develop contemporaneously with the basic tendency itself and as a part of the same process. Thus, the basic tendency and the counteracting influences are not to be understood as chronologically separated but as parts of a unity, of a whole, the development of which is contradictory because it is a development of both a basic trend and of counteracting factors. If this is understood we have the basis for an understanding of what proletarianization is and of the contradictory development which is at its origin: the development of capitalism itself, that is the constant tendency to devalue skilled to average labour while at the same time originating an ever increasing complexity in the social division of labour which constantly creates new functions, new strata of skilled labourers.

Let's make two examples. First of all, the commercial worker. As capitalism develops, commercial capital develops into a specific branch of activity. 'Specific capitals, and therefore specific groups of capitalists, are exclusively devoted to these (commercial, G.C.) functions' (Marx, 'Capital' III: 301). As a result a stratum of commercial workers is also called into being. At first the commercial worker is a skilled worker whose labour-power stands above the average because of the necessary knowledge of commercial practices, languages, etc. (Marx, 'Capital' III: 300). Therefore 'in the strict sense of the term', considering purely his place in the economic structure, without considering political and ideological factors, he 'belongs to the better-paid class of the wage-workers' (Marx, 'Capital' III: 300). However, because of the place he occupies in the social division of labour, that is given his higher qualifications and thus his higher than average income, he is more prone than the average industrial worker to middle class ideological and political influence. Therefore as a stratum, the commercial worker cannot be automatically classified among the proletariat. Yet, this situation is not static, his 'wage tends to fall, even in relation to the average labour, with the advance of the capitalist mode of production' (Marx, 'Capital' III: 300). There are at least four reasons explaining this phenomenon.

First of all, 'the division of labour within the office (implies) a one-sided development of the labour capacity' (Marx, 'Capital' III: 300), a fragmentation of tasks, devaluing the labour-power of the commercial worker (employee), who needs less knowledge and training to perform these simplified functions. At the same time 'the labourer's skill develops by itself through the exercise of his function, and all the more rapidly as division of labour makes it more one-sided' (Marx, 'Capital' III: 300). 'Secondly, because the necessary training, knowledge of commercial practices, languages, etc., is more and more rapidly, easily, universally and cheaply re-produced with the progress of science and public education the more the capitalist mode of production directs teaching methods, etc., towards practical purposes' (Marx, 'Capital' III: 300). That is, inasmuch as practical knowledge becomes generally necessary for the carrying out of the new functions, the weight of providing that knowledge is shifted from the capitalist to public education which performs the task more cheaply than the capitalist themselves would. Thus, while the general level of knowledge (at least in the developed capitalist countries) rises, thus raising the value of the average labour-power, this rise is achieved more cheaply by the introduction and expansion of practical, technical public education. Thus, the value of the commercial worker's labour power falls, *in relation to the average labour-power*, because it becomes, through this process, more and more similar in labour content to the average.

This is something which escapes the bourgeois economist. For him, the rise in the culturally determined subsistence minimum can only mean that 'we are all middle class'. He cannot understand that de-valuation of labour-power — and, at the limit, proletarianization — on the one hand and a rise in the subsistence minimum on the other can not only co-exist but are actually part of one and the same development process.(86) As the productivity of labour increases, the part of the labour day devoted to the production of the means of subsistence decreases (i.e. the rate of exploitation increases), i.e. the value of the labour-power decreases. At the same time the quantity of goods and services produced in this decreased length of time can be, due to the great technological improvements, greater than previously, i.e. the subsistence minimum can increase in abso-lute terms. In short, there is a tendency for wages to level out around an average which is increasing in absolute terms (in terms of the commodities making up the subsistence minimum) but decreasing in relative terms.(87) Thus, the development of the productive forces, the ever-increasing mass of social product make possible the rise of the subsistence minimum. But this development involves the growing complexity of the technical and social division of labour, and thus the creation of new, highly skilled strata. These strata, irrespec-tive of whether they are productive or not, because of their posi-tion determined by the division of labour, are only 'in the strict sense of the term' part of the working class. In effect, they usu-ally belong to the middle class on ideological and political grounds. On the other hand, the constant increase in the mass and rate of surplus value and the constant tendential fall in the rate of profit are only two sides of the same coin. This tendential fall forces the capitalist to constantly lower his costs; in the case of labour-power to devalue, and at the limit proletarianize, this originally highly skilled labour-power.(88)   The constant creation of new skilled functions and at the same time their down-grading to average labour-power together with a constant (irrespective of fluctuations) rise in the culturally determined minimum, which is also tendentially a smaller and smaller part of the total value produced, are all phenomena which can be explained only if their interconnections have been understood.

Thirdly, and this is a further factor pushing down the value of the labour-power of the commercial worker — value which is given by the culturally determined minimum subsistence level — 'the universality of public education enables capitalists to recruit such labourers from classes that formerly had no access to such trades and were accustomed to a lower standard of living' (Marx, 'Capital' III: 300). The same is true for other types of workers such as draftsmen most of whom are recruited from the working class. Finally, 'this increases supply, and hence competition' (Marx, 'Capital' III: 300), and thus can determine, when this competition is very keen, a drop in wages below the value of the commercial worker's labour-power. The essence of this all is that 'with few exceptions, the labour-power of these people is ... devaluated with the progress of capitalist production' (Marx, 'Capital' III: 300). This process of devaluation of labour-power, from skilled to average labour-power, we call *as a first approximation,* proletarianization. Its origin and essence goes back to the social division of labour, to the constant creation of new skilled functions and, at the same time, to the constant need of capital to devalue, to down-grade those functions to simpler and simpler ones. Only if the contradictory nature of this process is grasped, can proletarianization be properly understood.

So far we have considered a part of the petty bourgeoisie which is actually identifiable, on the level of production relations, as proletariat and which is petty bourgeoisie on political and ideological grounds and on the level of distribution relations. The proletarianization of this section of the petty bourgeoisie actually means its returning to what it already is on the level of production relations. But what we are really interested in, is a different section of the social structure: the new middle class, those who perform both the function of the collective worker and the global function of capital; those who are identifiable as middle class rather than proletariat on the level of production relations. It is the proletarianization of this middle class which needs now to be explained. The issue has often been obfuscated not only by the misunderstanding of this class' nature but also by the relatively recent introduction of the computer in the joint-stock company and by the effects this introduction has had on the internal dynamics of the new middle class. It is clear that the introduction of the computer into the enterprise is basically just another way in which capitalist enterprises (mainly the corporation) rationalize their activity; cut down costs; get a competitive edge.(89)   Rather than repeating what was said above about the commercial worker, we will simply underline the basic points again. First of all, the advent of the computer, in itself a change in the technical division of labour, brings about deep changes in the social division of labour.

New strata or workers, new functions, arise initially requiring
high levels of skill (e.g. professional technicians).(90)   At the
same time other functions are down-graded and the new functions as
well, with a few exceptions, undergo a process of de-qualification.
(91)   What follows is the stratification of the employees and technicians into two strata, the higher stratum being much smaller.
There is also a tendency for the functions (steps) in between
(those performing both the function of the collective worker and
the global function of capital) to disappear. Moreover, within
each of the two main strata, stratification takes place.(92)
    The process of devaluation of labour-power concerns these agents
as well, but now takes on a new dimension. The accumulation needs
of capital tend to degrade these functions so lowering the value of
the labour-power of those who must perform them. This means that
the same job can now be done by someone with lower skills, education, etc. But there is now another aspect to the process of labour
power's devaluation. We know that the new middle class performs
both the function of the collective worker and the global function
of capital. The accumulation needs of capital also mean that there
is a constant tendency for capital to decrease the area devoted to
the performance of the global function of capital and to increase
the area devoted to the function of the collective worker. In fact,
only through the latter function can capital appropriate to itself
surplus labour, either in this form or in the form of surplus value.
There is a constant tendency within the capitalist enterprise to
reduce the number (and pay) of those agents who perform the work of
control and surveillance (especially at the bottom of the hierarchy).
Whatever money is paid to the supervisor is not available for capital accumulation. Yet, to perform the global function of capital
means to be in a position of privilege (including level of income)
vis-à-vis those who perform the function of the collective worker.
Thus, the process of devaluation of the new middle class' labour
power is coupled with a constant erosion of the time during which
the global function of capital is performed. This class is subjected to an attack on a double front. As far as the function of the
collective worker is concerned, the devaluation of this class'
labour-power reduces the wage component. As far as the global function of capital is concerned, its constant and tendential reduction
reduces the revenue component. Therefore, the tendential decrease
in the incomes of the new middle class (93) (or at least of large
sections of it, especially of technicians and employees) is a result
of this double movement. As far as capital is concerned, the double
result is achieved of, 1, reducing the value of the labour-power
employed and, 2, increasing the time during which this labour-power
provides surplus-labour (surplus value).
    We now have all the elements necessary for an understanding of
the proletarianization of the new middle class. This process takes
place at the bottom of that section of the corporation which performs both functions, i.e. it means, in terms of production relations, the disappearance of the global function of capital in order
to make room exclusively for the function of the collective worker,
a function which is performed by agents whose labour-power has been
reduced to the average value. Of course, the two parts of this
double movement are strictly related. Take, for example, a chemist

who, beside performing quality control tests (function of the collective worker) is responsible for a number of technicians in the sense that he performs the work of supervision and management *in its double nature*. The moment these tests can be performed by someone with lower skills, perhaps by those same technicians he used to supervise,(94) 1, the value of his labour-power is reduced to that of a technician, 2, he loses his function as co-ordinator of the technicians' labour and, 3, consequently, there is no need to assign to him the work of control and surveillance of those technicians. In other words, a process has been started the final outcome of which will be not only the complete disappearance of the function of capital but also the reduction of the labour-power to an unskilled level. *In short, proletarianization is the limit of the process of devaluation of the new middle class's labour-power, i.e. the reduction of this labour-power to an average, unskilled level coupled with the elimination of the global function of capital.*(95) There is thus a difference between devaluation of labour-power and proletarianization: the latter is only the limit of the former. This definition of proletarianization allows us to use this term not indiscriminately. For example, while we can talk of the proletarianization of the card-puncher (because her function is only the performance of the function of the collective worker and her labour-power has been reduced to the unskilled level), we should talk about the devaluation of the chemist's labour-power, if he must perform simpler and simpler functions thus giving up progressively the global function of capital (e.g. the control and overseeing of the technicians working under him). There are thus, two reasons for introducing a new term (proletarianization) to refer to what at first could look like an old familiar concept (the devaluation of labour-power). First of all, we refer to the limit of that process of devaluation, thus giving the term proletarianization an exact meaning. Secondly, when used with reference to the new middle class, i.e. those who perform both the global function of capital and the function of the collective worker, this process of devaluation of labour-power implies also (and this is merely the other side of the coin) the disappearance of the global function of capital.(96) We can now see that all the phenomena which are usually associated with proletarianization and which are summarized in Piccone-Stella's 'definition' (the lowering of the level of living, the down-grading of functions, the tendency to approach the culturally determined subsistence minimum, the vulnerability to unemployment, etc.)are all corollary manifestations of the process of devaluation of labour-power; a process which implies also, as far as the new middle class is concerned, the progressive disappearance of the function of capital.(97) Only when proletarianization, as defined above, has taken place: only then, will all the corollary phenomena reach the degree of intensity characterizing the proletarian condition. A final remark: we should be careful not to confuse proletarianization with 'becoming proletariat'. The former term only refers to the economic sphere which, as we know, is not enough to classify groups and strata within one or another class. When the process of proletarianization has been completed we have only the objective conditions for a certain stratum to become part of the proletariat.(98) There are, however, also political and ideological

conditions which must be met before that stratum or group will
actually become part of the proletariat.

NOTES

1 First published in 'Economy and Society', vol. 4, no. 1. This
   chapter differs from the original article due to some technical
   changes, to the addition of some notes and paragraphs, and to
   the elimination of the 'Addendum' which is reproduced in chapter
   4. The additions have been placed within square brackets.
2 One of the passages that seem to lend justification to the
   interpretation of the middle classes as unproductive workers is
   the following: 'What he [i.e. Ricardo, G.C.] forgets to emphasize is the constantly growing number of the middle classes,
   those who stand between the workman on the one hand and the capitalist and landlord on the other. The middle classes maintain
   themselves to an ever increasing extent directly out of revenue,
   they are a burden weighing heavily on the working base and increase the social security and power of the upper ten thousand'
   ('Theories of Surplus Value', vol. II, p. 573). This passage is
   divided into two parts. In the first part Marx states, 1, that
   the middle classes stand between the working class and the capitalist class (they stand in between not in terms of distribution
   relations, i.e. income, etc. but, at least in my opinion, in
   terms of production relations, because in these terms they are
   spurious), and, 2, that the middle classes are growing (but I
   think only in absolute, not relative, terms). In the second
   part of the passage, Marx says that those who make up the middle
   classes, those who are unproductive, because paid out of revenue,
   are increasing. Moreover, Marx seems to indicate that he is
   thinking here of the police, the army, etc., i.e. all those who
   increase the social security of the capitalist class. Now, it
   is one thing to define (very generally) the middle classes as all
   those standing between the two basic classes, adding that among
   the middle classes those who are paid out of revenue (who, by the
   way, are not only the unproductive workers participating in the
   unproductive process as, e.g., the commercial workers) are
   increasing. It is quite another thing to read into this a definition of middle classes as those who are paid out of revenue.
   Among those who subscribe to the view identifying the middle
   classes with the unproductive workers, we can mention P. Walton
   and A. Gamble, 'From Alienation to Surplus Value', London, 1972,
   pp. 220 and ff. and N. Poulantzas, On Social Classes, 'New Left
   Review', no. 78, pp. 27-54.
3 We abstract from the theories denying the existence of the middle
   class, (either new or old), a standpoint taken by Marxist authors
   as well as others. J.F. Becker, for example, identifies the
   working class with productive labour and the capitalist class
   with unproductive labour (Class Structure and Class Conflict in
   the Managerial Phase, 'Science and Society', Fall 1973, pp. 259-
   77 and Winter 1973-4, pp. 437-53). To do so, this author must
   abandon the Marxist labour theory of value and define productive
   labour as all the labour which 'aids in the reproduction of

social labour through its contributions either to production or
to the co-ordination of production — and all of it would be
technically useful and reproductively necessary even outside
the confines of the capitalist mode' (p. 244). Thus, even
women bringing up children are (or could be) productive
labourers! (*ibid.*). As section 3 will show, there is a basic
difference between the unproductiveness of the unproductive
labourer and that of the production agent performing the global
function of capital.

4 In this paper the term employees will be used as opposed to
worker.

5 What follows in this section is only an outline of the theoretical tools needed for our analysis. A somewhat more detailed
discussion would require a paper in itself. We must therefore
rest content with what is practically a summary of the theoretical framework used in this paper.

6 For sake of brevity, under 'means of production' I include all
the material conditions of production, including raw materials
etc.

7 There is, thus, a difference, as Althusser and his school correctly point out, between the relations among the agents of production and means of production (which I call *production relations*) and the relations between the agents of production
(which I call *social relations*) and which can be economic, political, and ideological social relations. See, e.g., N. Poulantzas, 'Political Power and Social Classes', London, 1973, pp.
64-5. By agents of production I understand here persons as
carriers of certain production relations.

8 The relation between production and distribution relations is
one of determination in the sense to be explained below.

9 By unity in determination I mean here the fact that the mode of
production determines the production process. The latter, however, has a relative autonomy in the sense that the direction
of domination within the former does not necessarily correspond
to the direction of domination within the latter. These remarks
cannot be developed and are only meant to give an indication of
the complexity of the economic structure even at the highest
level of abstraction. A more detailed discussion of these problems will be provided in another paper.

10 Italian translation: 'Il Capitale, Libro I, Capitolo VI Inedito',
Florence, 1969. Whenever I will quote from 'Resultate...', I
will add also the number of the page in the original manuscript
within square brackets.

11 N. Poulantzas defines the production process as the unity of the
labour process and the relations of production (On Social
Classes, 'New Left Review', no. 78, p. 28 and p. 30). The dis-
advantage of doing so is that one fails to stress that the production process is always the unity of the labour process in
general and a particular way to produce, a particular way to
carry out productive labour. Under capitalism this particular
way to produce is the surplus value producing process.

12 Usually, in the definition of the capitalist production process,
the domination element is forgotten. E.g. W. Wygodski defines
the capitalist production process simply as 'The unity of labour

process (concrete labour) and value- and surplus-value producing process (as the result of the application of abstract
labour under capitalist conditions)'. See 'De ontwikkeling
van het ekonomies denken van Marx', SUN, Nijmegen, 1974, p. 25.
13 These two sets of relations might remind the reader of Balibar's relations of real appropriation and relations of property
(see L. Althusser and E. Balibar, 'Reading Capital', London
1970, p. 215). There is no room within the limits of this
article to examine and criticize Balibar's contribution, important as it is. It will suffice to point out that a close analysis will show a radical difference between Balibar's two sets
of relations and the two types of relations used in this paper.
14 Since these relations are combinations and not combinatories in
the sense given to these terms by Althusser, it will be clear
that we do not have here the simple addition of one element.
When all three, instead of only two, elements are considered,
also the content of the relation between producer (labourer)
and means of production changes. In short, if we consider only
producer and the means of production, their relation (i.e.
relations underlying the labour process) is one of subordination of the latter to the former. If, on the other hand, we
consider the relation between these two elements as a sub-set of
the relations between all three elements, i.e. including also
the non-labourer (relations underlying the surplus value producing process), then it is the latter which subordinates the
former to itself (Marx's 'reign of dead labour over living
labour'). See 'Resultate...', p. 17 [465.] [See also H. Braverman, 'Labor and Monopoly Capital', Monthly Review Press, 1974,
p. 193. However, Braverman 1, conflates labour process and
capitalist production process and, 2, talks about the control
of the labour process over humans whereas he should talk about
the control of the means of production over the labourer.]
15 For an indication of the proof that this is so, see footnote
above. This justifies the opening statement of this section.
In fact, the relations among the three elements mentioned there
(those underlying the surplus value producing process) are only
one of the two sets of relations binding together the elements
of the capitalist production process. Since, however, they are
the dominant set, we are justified, as a first approximation, in
focusing only on them.
16 A more detailed analysis of the capitalist mode of production
would have to include the social, economic, and technical conditions underlying *both* aspects of this mode of production.
This will be done in section 3 below.
17 The relation within these two elements is, as we have seen, one
of domination.
18 Balibar's limits of variation. See 'Reading Capital', p. 305.
19 Marx, 'Grundriss...'. ''. 99-100. Marx clearly gives the same
word two different meanings: the determination of the production
relations by the distribution relations is not the same thing as
the determination of the latter by the former. In short, while
to be overdetermined means to be modified and affected, to be
determined means to be called into existence as a precondition
for the existence of the determinant instance. These remarks

and quotations show clearly the insufficiency of regarding distribution as a simple expression of production. For an example
of such an insufficient approach, see Wygodski, op. cit., p. 47.

20   E.g. certain strata of the working class which, from the point
of view of production relations belong to proletariat, i.e. the
labour aristocracies, become part of the petty bourgeoisie on
political and ideological grounds (and almost inevitably also
on grounds of distribution relations). Thus, the proletariat
is first of all economically identified (see next section).
This economic identification, the basis for a complete definition in terms of all three levels, is already overdetermined
because it corresponds to that class of agents who are the producers, the labourers. For example, under monopoly capitalism
it is the class of agents who perform one of the functions of
the collective worker, who make up the collective worker, rather
than being individual labourers. But this economic identification (already overdetermined) is also directly modified by the
class struggle in the sense that strata of the proletariat
become part of the petty bourgeoisie. This is the direct overdetermination; the changes in the contours of the economic
identification due to the superstructure and the class struggle.

21   According to A.L. Harris (Pure Capitalism and the Disappearance
of the Middle Class, in 'Journal of Political Economy', June
1939, pp. 328-56) the first person to have used the term 'pure
capitalism' was Henryk Grossman in his 'Das Akkumulations-und
Zusammenbruchsgesetz des Kapitalistischen Systems', Leipzig,
1929. As Harris Says: 'As employed here the term denotes the
simplified conditions and assumptions under which Marx projec-
ted his theory of economic development. These conditions and
assumptions help to reveal the laws of capitalist production in
their ideal form' (p. 336). And also, 'This assumption that
the laws of capitalist production evolve in their pure form is
fundamental in Marx's method of analysis. The validity of the
assumption is based on the fact that all the non-capitalist
spheres of production tend either to be eliminated by the
expansion of capitalist production or to be subordinated to it'
(p. 337). Thus, to assume that, on the highest level of abstraction, the laws of capitalist production evolve in their pure
form is a valid procedure because, as a first step in the analysis, we focus on what is essential. The proof that we concentrate on what is essential is given by the fact that all the
non-capitalist modes of production tend either to disappear or
to be incorporated in, dominated by, the capitalist mode of
production.

22   Poulantzas, op. cit., chapter II and ff.

23   In order to avoid any misunderstanding, let us make clear that
the process of shifting to more and more concrete levels of
abstraction is not a process of approaching reality. This
would be, as Althusser correctly says, an idealist mistake, it
would mean to regard the real as the product of thought. To
shift to more concrete levels, means to reproduce the concrete,
to add new elements to the analysis. This 'is by no means the
process by which the concrete itself comes into being'. (Marx,
'Grundrisse...', op. cit., p. 101).

24   Written in 1914 and published in the 'Collected Works', vol. 29,
     p. 421.
25   Actually, instead of 'groups of people' it would be more cor-
     rect to speak of 'production agents'.
26   In the above mentioned pamphlet Lenin does not provide a dis-
     cussion of the elements of this definition and of their inter-
     relations. What follows, then, is to a great extent my own
     interpretation. However, the discussion will have to be res-
     tricted only to what is essential for the purpose of this
     paper. Discussion of the determinant role of ownership and the
     function of distribution relations, both elements in the defi-
     nition would require two separate sections and must thus be
     postponed to another time.
27   N. Poulantzas, On Social Classes, 'New Left Review', no. 78,
     p. 29. Balibar defines economic ownership of the means of pro-
     duction as 'the power to consume them productively, depending
     on their material nature, on their adaptations to the condi-
     tions of the labour process, as means of appropriating surplus
     labour', 'Reading Capital', p. 231. Bettelheim points out that
     even some Marxist authors, e.g. O. Lange, fail to distinguish
     economic from juridical ownership. This mistake also influen-
     ces the analysis of 'the real content of socialist ownership
     and of its various forms'. See C. Bettelheim, 'La transition
     vers l'economie socialiste', Italian translation, 'La transi-
     zione all'economia socialista', Jaca Books, Milano, 1969, pp.
     129 and ff.
28   Moreover, the third element, i.e. the social division of labour,
     is important in the treatment of classes because it provides
     the possibility of internally stratifying classes by sections
     of the economy (e.g. the commercial worker or finance capital),
     by branches of the economy (steel industry or coal miners), by
     professional qualification (skilled, semi-skilled, unskilled
     workers), by basic sections of the economy (production or con-
     sumption goods). And, most important, this element provides
     the basis for distinguishing between those who perform the
     function of labour and those who perform the function of capital
     and, within the former, between productive and unproductive
     labourers.
29   See 'Capital', vol. II. The following texts might be profitably
     read in this connection: V.I. Lenin, 'A Note on the question of
     the market theory', 'Collected Works', no. 4, pp. 55-64; V.I.
     Lenin, 'Once more on the theory of realization', 'Collected
     Works', no. 4, pp. 74-93; V.I. Lenin, 'The development of capit-
     alism in Russia', Moscow, 1967, pp. 31-70; R. Luxemburg, 'The
     Accumulation of Capital', New York, 1968, pp. 76-138; E. Mandel,
     'Marxist Economic Theory', New York, 1968, pp. 305-41;
     P. Sweezy, 'The Theory of Capitalist Development', New York,
     1968, pp. 75-95 and 162-4; J. Valier, Les Théories de l'impéria-
     lisme de Lénine et Rosa Luxemburg, in 'Critique de l'Economie
     Politique', no. 4-5, July-December 1971, pp. 34-114; Balibar,
     'Reading Capital', pp. 268-9, holds that these schemes, or
     better said the structural conditions expressed mathematically
     in these schemes, are not specific to the capitalist mode of
     production. See also Luxemburg, op. cit., pp. 84-5.

30 This addition will become useful in section 3 below, when we
    will see that not only the bourgeoisie but also sections of the
    proletariat (the unproductive labourers) live off the surplus
    value produced by the productive labourers. Even serious
    students of Marx, as e.g. T. Kemp, are led into confusing the
    origin of a class' income with its nature: '...the bourgeoisie —
    using this term to comprehend all those whose income comes
    directly from surplus value — ...' (T. Kemp, 'Theories of
    Imperialism', London, 1967, pp. 71-2).

31 [The reader will notice the difference between this clearly
    insufficient concept of capitalist mode of production and the
    more articulated one expounded in the Introduction and sum-
    marized in figure 2.] The difference between the view expounded
    above and Althusser's view should be obvious. According to
    Althusser, the labour process makes up the material conditions
    of the production process while the production relations make up
    its social conditions: 'We have thus arrived at a new condition
    of the production process. After studying the material condi-
    tions of the production process which express the specific
    nature of the relations between men and nature, we must now turn
    to a study of the social conditions of the production process:
    the social relations of production' (Althusser, 'Reading Capi-
    tal', p. 174). The fact is that the labour process has social
    conditions itself i.e. the relation producer/means of production,
    as well as the figure of the producer. Not only, but the labour
    process has economic and technical conditions as well. Without
    going into an analysis of the conditions of the labour process
    and of the surplus value producing process, we only point out
    that just as the social conditions of the two processes are not
    the same (and actually the production relations upon which the
    surplus value producing process rests dominate the production
    relations upon which the labour process rests), so the technical
    and economic conditions of the two processes differ. Let us
    give only a couple of examples. We know that, with the growth
    and expanded reproduction of the capitalist mode of production,
    with the process of concentration and centralization, which is
    one of its inevitable tendencies, the minimum amount of capital
    necessary to start a business must grow as well. This is an
    economic condition dictated by competition and thus it is an
    economic condition pertinent to the surplus value producing pro-
    cess. The same economic conditions might be quantitatively dif-
    ferent with respect to the labour process because the minimum
    amount of capital needed is now determined technically and can
    be lower than the one mentioned above. For example, the minimum
    size of steel-works is determined technically while its economic
    minimum size is determined by the laws of competition, if this
    enterprise must be a (capitalist) viable one. Let us take
    another example. When the capitalist starts a capitalist pro-
    duction process, he starts, as we know, both a labour process
    and a surplus value producing process. To start a labour pro-
    cess he needs means of production. When he buys means of pro-
    duction, he is interested in their qualitative characteristics:
    a machine is bought, with reference to the labour process, only
    because it is a use value. But the capitalist starts a labour

process only because this is the only way to start a surplus
value producing process. Therefore, when he buys a machine he
must be careful not to buy a machine which, irrespective of its
use value, has incorporated in it a quantity of labour-time
higher than the socially necessary one. If the value of that
particular machine happens to be higher than the average, the
capitalist will not buy it, even if that machine would fit
particularly well into the labour process. These two examples
show that the economic and technical conditions of the labour
process, just as the social conditions, are subordinated to the
corresponding conditions of the surplus-value producing process.
In other words the mode of production upon which the labour process rests is subordinated to the mode of production upon which
the surplus-value producing process rests and this is the reason
why, in examining the capitalist mode of production, for practical purposes, it is sufficient to examine the dominant mode of
production.

32 Another example: labour must be provided more regularly and more
    intensively. See 'Resultate...', p. 59 [473.]
33 What said above can be summarized as follows: the elements and
    general nature of the labour process are indifferent to the
    social, economic and technical conditions in which this process
    takes place. While these conditions change, the elements and
    general nature of the labour process do not change. Under
    capitalism, these conditions (the mode of production upon which
    the labour process rests) change due to their subordination to
    the conditions upon which the surplus value producing process
    rests. Therefore, to refer to the labour process as the 'tech-
    nical conditions of labour' as Poulantzas does, is mistaken.'
    ... the labour process (concerning the material and technical
    conditions of labour, and in particular the means of production)
    ...', 'Political Power and Social Classes', p. 65.
34 For example, the Italian branch of IBM lists more than 1200 dif-
    ferent functions in which its personnel, numbering 6,400, is
    subdivided. See FIM, FIOM, UILM, 'Impiegati '72', p. 217 and
    p. 220.
35 The rationale for the choice of the terms 'formal and real sub-
    ordination' is clearly stated by Bettelheim as follows: 'The
    formal mode of appropriation in the transitional phase towards
    capitalism is already the capitalist form of ownership, i.e. the
    separation of the worker from the ownership of his means of pro-
    duction; on the contrary, the real mode of appropriation is not
    yet the one characteristic of capitalism, i.e. big industry'
    ('La transition vers l'économie socialiste', p. 16).
36 The need to shift from formal to real subordination of labour to
    capital is dictated by the need to shift from the production of
    absolute surplus value (lengthening of the working day) to the
    production of relative surplus value (reduction of the value of
    both constant and variable capital). See 'Capital', vol. 1,
    pp. 310, 314, 315 and J. Bischoff, H. Ganszmann, G. Kümmel, G.
    Löhlein, 'Produktieve en onproduktieve arbeid als kategorieën
    der klassenanalyse, in 'Karl Marx over produktieve en onprodukt-
    ieve arbeid', Nijmegen, 1970, pp. 5-36.
37 It should be pointed out that Balibar interprets this double

movement as an extension to the collective labourer and a
limitation only to those who are wage labourers (see 'Reading
Capital', pp. 240-1). Actually, as we have seen, this double
movement is: limitation to production of surplus value and
extension to the collective labourer. As we will see soon,
Marx considers, side by side the pure capitalist production
process, a capitalist production process which does not produce
surplus value, i.e. the commercial enterprise. A bank employee
is both a wage worker and a member of the collective worker who
takes part in the production of the bank's services, i.e. in
the bank's labour-power. According to Balibar, then, this
worker, by being both a wage worker and a member of the collective labour power, should be a productive labourer.

38 This term is borrowed from: I Quaderni di Avanguardia Operaia,
'Lotta di Classe nella Scuola e Movimento Studentesco', Milano,
1971, p. 13.

39 We disregard here situations of monopoly capitalism, e.g. the
investment in unproductive activities (the sales-effort) as a
means to prevent a fall in the monopolistic sector's profit
rate.

40 Thus, one should not make the mistake of thinking that concrete
labour determines the technical aspect of a function and abstract labour determines its social aspect.

[41 A more complete and more detailed analysis of the nature of a
position will be provided in chapter 4.]

42 This hypothesis is a-historical because, as we have seen above
in scheme 2, the introduction of the technical division of
labour within the labour process and thus the need for some
agents to perform a function of co-ordination of that process,
is a result of a mode of production based on antagonistic
production relations.

43 This work need not be the typical work of the foreman. Take a
project leader who carries out a feasibility study. Inasmuch
as he determines the technical content of each sub-phase of the
project, he performs the function of the collective worker.
Inasmuch as he determines *how long* each technician should spend
on these sub-phases, he performs the global function of capital. The determination of the length of each sub-phase usually
makes it unnecessary for the project leader to perform the work
of control during the actual carrying out of the project. The
length will be determined in such a way that the technician
will provide labour at a certain speed, with a certain intensity, etc. These remarks will become clearer after a complete
reading of this section.

[44 H. Braverman, 'Labor and Monopoly Capital', p. 90.]

45 'This labour is then productive', 'Capital', vol. III, p. 383.

[46 H. Braverman, 'Labor and Monopoly Capital', p. 61.]

47 This is why the manager, even though he must sell his 'labour
power'; even though he is paid a 'salary', even though he
expends energy, just as everybody else taking part in the production process, cannot be considered as a labourer.

[48 Thus, H. Braverman, in discussing the unproductive capitalist
industries (which, however, he lumps together with productive
capitalist industries under the misleading name of clerical

industries), seems to consider all those working in those industries as performing the function of capital. 'In all these
industries, the development of capital has transformed the
operating function of the capitalist from a personal activity
into the work of a mass of people.' 'Labor and Monopoly
Capital', p. 301.]

49 See E. Mandel, 'Marxist Economic Theory', Merlin Press, 1968,
pp. 539-40.

50 The fact that the top managers might, and usually do, share in
the legal ownership by owning a certain amount of stocks,
obviously does not invalidate the distinction. We will return
to this point later.

51 For example, in the Italian branch of IBM, employing a total
personnel of 6,400, there are 640 'heads' who perform either
exclusively or to a great extent only the function of capital.
The connection between centralization of capital and the generation of bureaucratic functions is stressed by A. Illuminati,
'Sociologia e Classi Sociali', Turin, 1967, p. 82. But this is
only a tendency, one of the major counter-tendencies of which
being the process of proletarianization of the new middle
class (sections 4 and 6 below). This process implies the disappearance of the global function of capital in many of the
positions in which this function is combined with the function
of the collective worker.

52 This should not be interpreted as meaning that under private
capitalism the capitalist carries out the function of capital
completely alone. He can have, of course, a few employees to
help him. But they are not performing the global function of
capital. This position in the social division of labour gives
the employee under private capitalism a position of privilege
vis-a-vis those performing the function of the collective
worker, something which bourgeois sociology seems unable to
explain. Typical of bourgeois sociology also is its inability
to see the difference between the 'old' employee and the new
one, the agent which has a double function, i.e. the agent who
not only performs the global function of capital (rather than
the function of capital) but who also performs this function
together with the function of the collective worker, For
example, A.L. Mok and H. de Jager say, in their 'Grondbeginselen der sociologie', Leiden, 1971: 'De employee wordt vanouds
geidentificeerd met de ondernemer, in wiens directe nabijheid
hij doorgaans werkte. Hij droeg een 'witte boord' en was een
'heer' al deed hij het nederigste klerkenwerk, in tegenstelling
tot de handarbeider die een 'blue collar' droeg en een 'werkman'
was, ook al deed hij het ingewikkeldste vakwerk' (p. 260).
This inability to understand the nature of the employee's function in different stages of capitalism is of course strictly
related to the inability to grasp the nature of the working
class and thus of the process of proletarianization (see section 6 below). For the evolution of the figure of the employee
(even though the theoretical frame is quite different from the
one adopted here) see G. Baglioni, 'Il conflitto industriale e
l'azione del sindacato', Il Mulino, Bologna, 1966, pp. 152-73.

53 See M. Godelier, 'Rationality and Irrationality in Economics',

London, 1972, p. 75. Godelier's book provides also an excellent demonstration of the limited, or better, non-scientific usefulness of these theories and disciplines.

54   The fact that he provides both concrete and abstract labour in the sense just mentioned must not be confused with the fact that, e.g., the machine he buys is both a use value and exchange value; he does not provide concrete labour by buying a use value an abstract labour by buying an exchange value as we will see.

55   This seems to be implied also in the following quotation: 'no business will be founded on the principle that it can sell its products with *greater difficulty* than another. If this resulted from the smaller size of the market, then not a larger — as presupposed — but a smaller capital would be employed there than in the business with a larger market'. 'Grundrisse', p. 521.

56   The implications of this analysis for a truly radical sociology of labour are important. Let me hint at only one example. When Marx was writing The Communist Manifesto, it was quite clear who was a labourer and who was a non-labourer. The former was a wage earner, while the latter was not. Nowadays, with the extension of the wage payment also to those who perform the function of capital (e.g. the managers, the new middle class inasmuch as it performs the function of capital), there is no immediate identification between being a wage earner and being a labourer, a worker. Nowadays, the labourer is every agent who performs the function of the collective worker, while the non-labourer is every agent who performs the global function of capital. Having provided an exact definition of the two types of functions (definition worked out on the basis of Marx's analysis of the capitalist production process), it is now possible to prove scientifically that the manager, even though he expends human activity, does not work. The capitalist of individual capitalism and the manager of monopoly capitalism, irrespective of under what form they get their payment, have this feature in common: they both do not work because they both do not take part in the labour process. Thus the concept of *work* must be distinguished from that of *activity*. Under capitalism, the concept of work coincides only with the performance of a definite function, the function of labour, either of the individual or of the collective labourer.

57   Something which has nothing to do with the 'multiplicity of criteria of definitions', a favourite bourgeois criticism of the Marxist standpoint, as T. Dos Santos correctly points out, in his The Concept of Social Classes, 'Science and Society', Summer 1970, pp. 166-93.

[58   This formulation can be confusing. If we consider only the functional element of the production relations, then the non-labourer (the agent performing the global function of capital) cannot be oppressed. However, as shown in the Introduction, an agent, whenever performing the global function of capital while not owning the means of production, is both oppressed and oppressor (or exploiter).]

[59   In subsequent chapters, the term 'individual capitalism' will

be substituted for the term 'private capitalism'.]
60 Needless to say, it would be possible to provide a more
detailed periodization. For example, space limitations forbid
me to consider the reproduction of the capitalist system (and
thus the study of the capitalist production process) on an
international scale and thus the reproduction of classes under
imperialism. This means that in the present phase of development of capitalism both the collective worker and the global
capitalist are spread over a number of countries. In other
words, the stage of private capitalist characterized by real
subordination of labour to capital is the stage of the socialization of the labour process, the stage of monopoly capitalism
is the stage of socialization of the surplus value producing
process (and thus of the socialization of the capitalist production process but on a national plane), while the present
stage of imperialism is the stage of the *international* socialization of the capitalist production process. The omission of
these elements, however important they may be for the theory
submitted, is justified in the light of the fact that the
three-stage periodization is the minimum (and yet the sufficient) basis for the purposes of this essay. Moreover, we
should not regard these stages as if they followed each other
always in the same order. These are logical as well as historical categories. This means that two or even all three stages
can co-exist or even present themselves in inverted order.
Marx shows in 'Resultate des Unmittelbaren Produktionsprozess'
(p. 70 [478]) how formal subordination can co-exist with or
even follow real subordination.
61 We skip here any discussion of the so-called 'managerial revolution' the ideological description of the emergence of the
global function of capital. The reader is advised to turn to
R. Blackburn's The New Capitalism, in R. Blackburn, ed.,
'Ideology in Social Science', 1973, pp. 164-86, for an up to
date critique of the managerial revolution thesis. However,
even Blackburn while stressing that the manager does not behave
differently, basically, from the owner entrepreneur,
(a) fails to develop the concept of what it means to perform
    the function of capital, and
(b) fails to see that there is a stratum of the middle class
    (the new middle class) which performs both the function
    of the collective worker and the global function of capital.
Poulantzas, on the other hand, in his review of Milliband's
book 'The State in Capitalist Society', stresses, very rightly
the non-essential character of the manager's behaviour as an
element of class collocation but mentions only in passing that
'the manager exercises only a functional delegation' of capital
(see The Problems of the Capitalist State, in Blackburn, op.
cit. p. 244). Here too, however, there is no analysis of the
function of capital and of the fact that, at certain managerial
levels, this function is combined with the function of the collective worker. Therefore, Poulantzas cannot see that, even in
purely economic terms, the manager does not necessarily belong
to the capitalist class but can belong to the new middle class
when the social content of his function is double, i.e. when he

performs both the global function of capital and the function
of the collective worker.

62 It is in the light of these considerations that one should read
Mandel's remarks on the managers and his argument for placing
them within the bourgeoisie. He says: 'The decisive question
is whether the managers behave in their social role in a different way from the bourgeoisie, whether they are indifferent
to private property or even fight against it, whether they
engage in struggle with the leading circles of big capital,
whether they mostly spring from the bourgeoisie or from the
working class' ('Marxist Economic Theory', p. 540).

Of course these remarks are right but they do not constitute
the 'decisive question'. They are not the decisive question
simply because Mandel focuses on sociological, psychological,
political and ideological considerations without mentioning
that these elements must rest upon an economic basis, i.e. on
production and distribution relations. The decisive point is
that the managers have the real ownership of the means of production and thus are part of the hierarchical and bureaucratic
complex which performs the global function of capital and consequently either exploit or economically oppress the proletariat.

63 The distribution relations, i.e. the income of the middle
classes, will be considered in the next section.

64 The statement that this capitalist presents elements of both
the exploiter and the exploited should be compared with Marx's
treatment of independent farmers and handicraftsmen. 'According to Marx, the independent farmer and handicraftsman possess
a twofold productive character in capitalist society. [It
should be stressed that this is so *in capitalist society* and is
an example of the subordination of other modes of production to
the capitalist one. G.C.] As the owners of their means of
production, they are capitalists. As the owners of their
labour power, they are wage-earners. Thus, they pay themselves
wages as capitalists and derive profits from their capital.
In other words, they exploit themselves as wage-labourers and
pay themselves the tribute in surplus products which capital
customarily appropriates from labour.' In A.B. Harris, Pure
Capitalism and the Middle Class, in 'Journal of Political
Economy', June 1939, p. 340. See also K. Marx, 'Theories of
Surplus Value', vol. 1, pp. 407-9.

65 Or the proletariat and bourgeoisie if we consider the economic
identification, i.e. if we consider classes on the socio-
economic system level of abstraction.

66 Space does not allow me a discussion of similarities and differences between this and other concepts of the new middle
class. I will only mention that, to the two traditional
theories of the new middle class as, 1, an extension of the
proletariat and, 2, an extension of the bourgeoisie, Dahrendorf
('Class and Class Conflict in Industrial Society', Stanford
University Press, 1959) adds his own theory according to which
the new middle class is not a homogeneous whole but is made up
of two parts. 'The bureaucrats add to the bourgeoisie, as the
white-collar workers add to the proletariat' p. 56. I disregard

here a fourth type of theory which regards the employees as
oscillating between the proletariat and the bourgeoisie
(mentioned by G. Baglioni, 'Il Conflitto Industriale e
l'Azione del Sindacato', Bologna, 1966, p. 179). What matters
is to avoid confusing Dahrendorf's position with mine. The
translation of Dahrendorf's concept of the new middle class
into my terminology would sound as follows: the new middle
class is made up of two sections, the former performing only
the global function of capital, the latter only the function
of the collective worker. This somewhat simplifying statement
is useful for stressing the difference with my own view according to which the agents making up the new middle class perform
both functions.

67 The discussion of the figure of the foreman requires some additional remarks on the relationship connecting the three elements of the capitalist production relations. As the reader
might recall, in section II above I indicated that the relation
among the three elements of the production relations (i.e. the
labourer, the non-labourer, and the means of production) is
three-fold because it should be regarded *from the point of view
of ownership* (who owns the means of production and who does
not?), *from the point of view of production* (who is the producer and thus the exploited and who is the non-producer, and
thus the exploiter?), and *from the point of view of the function performed* (who is the labourer, i.e. who performs the
function of labourer, and who is the non-labourer, i.e. who
performs the function of capital?) Since I had to devote a
great deal of attention to the functional element (a basically
unexplored terrain in Marxist literature) I might have conveyed
the impression that I consider this aspect as the fundamental
one. This is not so. Let me state schematically my point (a
detailed analysis must be postponed to another occasion). In
section 3 I pointed out that a function has always a technical
and a social aspect. This is so because the capitalist production process is divided into a number of fractional units which,
just because they are parts of the production process, and
given that the production relations are the relations in which
the agents of production enter when they participate in the
production process, cast upon the people who carry out those
fractional units the attribute of being carriers of production
relations. Thus, each fractional unit implies that the agent
carrying it out, 1, either owns the means of production or not,
2, either is the producer/exploited or the non-producer/
exploiter, 3, either performs the function of capital or the
function of labour (and this is why each fractional unit, considered from the functional viewpoint, i.e. considered as a
function, has always a social content, i.e. is either the function of capital or the function of labour). In each of these
fractional units there can be correspondence between the *ownership* element (*which is determinant*) on the one hand, and the
production and functional elements (which are determined) on
the other hand. Or, conversely, there can be no correspondence,
i.e. contradiction. Correspondence means that the ownership of
the means of production implies performing the function of

capital and being the non non-producer (and vice-versa for the
non-ownership of the means of production). Thus, we have
correspondence in the economic identification of the proletariat and of the bourgeoisie (we consider only the production
relations). The middle classes, on the contrary, are definable in terms of non-correspondence. For example, we have
fractional units (and thus agents) defined in terms of non-
ownership on the one hand and performance of both the function
of capital and the function of labour on the other (i.e. the
new middle classes). This is why the definition of classes
must take place in terms of all the three elements of the production relations, because there can be contradiction among
them. Thus, it would be misleading to consider scheme 10 as
depicting the subdivision of the production agents into the
three primary classes. This scheme does so but *only in terms
of the functions performed*. But, as mentioned above, to identify a class economically, all three elements of the production
relations (plus also the distribution relations) are necessary.
Therefore, the fact that in this scheme the foreman is placed
with the capitalist class because he only performs the function
of capital, does not mean that, in terms of production relations as a whole, he really belongs to this class. Since he
combines elements of both primary classes, i.e. since his position is contradictory in terms of production relations, he must
be classified as middle class. In this sense the definition of
new middle class which I give above is insufficient, even
though it covers by far the greatest and most important part of
all the agents making up the new middle class. On the other
hand, the advantage of this definition resides in the stress
given to the existence of agents of production who, while not
owning the means of production, perform both functions.
Another definition, in terms of non-correspondence between
three elements of the production relations, would be more encompassing but would perhaps lose its didactical quality of
focusing on the possibility of an agent performing both functions. Such a definition of the new middle class would encompass all those agents who, while not owning the means of production, perform the global function of capital (either alone
or in combination with the function of collective worker) and
thus can be either only the non-labourer/non-producer/exploiter
[but he is also oppressed, since he does not own the means of
production] or both the non-labourer/non-producer/exploiter
[and exploited] and the labourer/producer/exploited.

68 For the sub-division of the total labour-time between productive labourers and unproductive labourers, see Mandel, 'Marxist
Economic Theory', pp. 202-4: 1, in 1948, in the US, in the
petroleum industry, 55 per cent of all wage-earners were
employed in all forms of distribution and sales and, 2, in the
car industry, in the same year, there were almost 1 million
wage-workers in the production sphere as against 1.5 million in
the sale and distribution sphere. [See also 'Der Spätkapitalismus', p. 363.] The subdivision by functions has been made
somewhat arbitrarily because of the total lack of empirical
studies (to the best of my knowledge) based on the concepts of

function of collective worker and global function of capital,
as defined in section 3. Even in the Marxist literature and in
the trade unions publications, the usual distinction is between
those who give orders and those who carry them out. (See,
e.g., FIM, FIOM, UILM, 'Impiegati '72', p. 198, see also
E. Mingione, 'Impiegati, Sviluppo Capitalistico e Lotta di
Classe', Rome, 1973, pp. 64-5.) But to give orders can mean
both to co-ordinate the labour process and to help perpetuate
the system based on exploitation. Similarly, to carry out
orders can mean both to perform the function of the collective
worker and to perform the global function of capital, as in the
case of a middle-manager carrying out orders from the top
management (it should not be forgotten that this last function
is performed by a complex organized hierarchically and bureaucratically). In the absence of empirical studies using my
framework, it is possible to gather only indications of the
extent to which both functions are combined into the same position and of the number of such positions. Of course, there is
a host of variables which should be considered when trying to
generalize as above, in scheme 10: the size of the enterprise,
the technical nature of its production process, etc. Here are
some indications taken from the first of the two above-
mentioned publications. 1, At the FIAT (Mirafiori) plant in
Turin not many sections were found where the employees perform
also the global function of capital. However, some of the sections not studied are those 'where undoubtedly this function is
much more common' (p. 21). Moreover, as far as the *global*
function of capital goes, it was found that the 'despotism' of
the section heads was particularly visible at the 'Customs
office' (p. 19-20). 2, The IBM enterprise in Milan has a total
personnel of about 6400, 640 of whom are 'heads'. Thus, the
ratio is 1 : 10. Since, of the total 6400 only 680 are workers, the ratio of 1 : 10 could only be extrapolated to popula-
tions of employees. Moreover (a) no data are given about the
number of the top managers and (b) the professional technicians
probably perform also the global function of capital, even
though to a limited extent, (p. 215 and p. 217). We can mention examples also for smaller plants. 3, The EMANUEL plant in
Turin employs 280 workers, 100 employees and 80 heads for both
categories. 4, At the SAE plant, after the 1968-9 wave of
strikes, out of 318 employees a hierarchical structure of 115
heads was created, 20 of whom at a managerial level (p. 86).
We can assume that these 20 only perform the global function of
capital while the remaining 95 perform both functions. It is
interesting to note that this structure has a two-fold function:
(a) it makes the performance of the global function of capital
more efficient, and (b) since these heads introduce the enterprise's ideology among the employees, it is also a powerful
ideological instrument and thus indirectly a way to increase
productivity. An analogous point, concerning the political and
ideological functions of the division of labour, is made by C.
Bettelheim in his 'Calcul économique et formes de propriété',
Italian translation, 'Calcolo economico e forme di proprieta',
Jaca Books, Milan, 1970, p. 150. But to go back to our scheme

10, even though the subdivision in the scheme between those who only perform one of the two functions and those who perform both of them might no reflect accurately a typical concrete situation, the data mentioned above point out clearly that the discrepancy would never be of such a proportion as to invalidate the theory.

69 This vertical notion describes the hierarchy within the capitalist production process only when the relation of subordination of the labourer to the capitalist is considered.

70 Let me repeat once more that I am here only economically defining the middle classes, i.e. providing the economic basis upon which to build a definition of the petty bourgeoisie; a definition which would encompass the ideological and the political also. When all three dimensions are taken into consideration, then some parts of the middle classes (i.e. some parts of the petty bourgeoisie economically identifiable as such) will become part of the proletariat on political and ideological grounds (I think principally of those sections which are about to be proletarianized, in the sense to be explained in section 6) and some parts of the proletariat will become part of the petty bourgeoisie, again on political and ideological grounds (see, e.g. the labour aristocracies). There are, of course, also sectors which at the level of the production relations belong to the working class while in terms of distribution relations (income) belong to the middle classes and thus cannot be considered as part of the working class (e.g. the system engineers). In other words, there can be a discrepancy between the first three and the fourth element of Lenin's definition. Thus, even at the economic structure level, the middle classes are far from being made up only of what I have called the old and the new middle class. But it is important to distinguish between those parts of the middle class which are already such, on the level of production relations, and the other parts. The following two sections will prove this point.

[71 It should be kept in mind that here the analysis is restricted to, 1, the socio-economic system level of abstraction and, 2, the developed capitalist countries (central capitalism). Without these two restrictions the analysis would have to be expanded and integrated. For example, S. Amin carries out an analysis of the reasons, both economic and not, determining wage differentials among wage earners in some underdeveloped countries (peripheral capitalism) on a level of analysis which, according to my terminology, can be placed at the concrete structure level of abstraction even though what is missing in Amin's book is a detailed analysis of the structure of the economy at this level of abstraction. See 'Accumulation on a World Scale', Monthly Review Press, New York and London, 1974. For example, the summary of the reasons underlying wage differentials in the Maghreb is given at p. 279.]

72 E.g., 'the commercial worker, in the strict sense of the term belongs to the better paid class of wage workers' 'Capital', vol. III, p. 300). I.e. the value of this worker's labour power is higher than the average (due to the knowledge of languages necessary, etc.) and thus he belongs to the 'better paid'

section of the working class (here considered purely in terms
of production relations). It might be worth pointing out that
we are dealing with deviations of wages from the value of
labour-power *on the aggregate level*. On the level of the individual worker, as Marx points out ('Resultate...', p. 65 [476])
his wage can fluctuate above or below the subsistence minimum
(e.g. he can be only partially employed). Moreover, different
individual workers have different degrees of ability, etc. and
all these factors are reflected in his wage.

73 Both the income of the unproductive worker and that of the capitalist derive from surplus value. But only the former can be
called wage because, whether it is surplus value or not, it is
the income of an agent of production who allows the capitalist
to share in the redistribution of surplus value; it is the income of an agent whose labour is directly appropriated (rather
than in the form of value) and in a quantity higher than the
labour equivalent to his labour-power.

74 The fact that the salaries of the technicians are much higher
than (sometimes ten times as high) the average wage has created
much theoretical confusion. Both E. Mallet and A. Gorz have
mistaken a particular situation, valid for a section of the
working class, for a generalized one (see P. Rolle, 'Introduction à la sociologie de travail', Italian translation pp. 210
and ff.). E. Mingione ('Impiegati, sviluppo capitalistico e
lotta di classe', Rome, 1973, p. 23) slips into the bourgeois
problematic of the 'economics of education' by stating that the
technicians' higher salaries are a 'rent, even though a limited
one, on the money and energy invested in many years of study'.
In fact, the technicians' salaries are higher than the average
wage because, 1, the value of their labour power is higher,
2, they might perform also the global function of capital and
thus have an economically privileged position, 3, of political
and ideological reasons (e.g. the systems engineer must also
'sell' a certain image of the corporation for which he works),
4, of conjunctural reasons (e.g. relative, temporary scarcity
of a certain type of technician, the dominant position of a
certain enterprise which allows it to attract qualified labour
power by paying higher salaries, etc.). All these elements,
however, are only a modification and not a supersession of the
basic relationship between the value of labour power and wages.

75 The income of the new middle class cannot be called, as in the
case of the private capitalist, wages of supervision and
management because this work encompasses, as far as the function of the collective worker is concerned, only the work of
co-ordination and unity. The new middle class, on the other
hand, takes part to a much wider range of functions within the
labour process.

76 Let us hint at two fundamental points. First of all, contrary
to what M. Mauke seems to imply ('Die Klassentheorie von Marx
und Engels', Italian translation, 'La teoria della classi nel
pensiero di Marx e Engels', Milan, 1971, p. 115) Marx and
Engels regarded the labour aristocracy as much more than a
simple matter of income distribution within the proletariat.
They focus principally on production relations (imperialism)

and political and ideological considerations (for a good selection of their articles and letters in which they analyse
this problem, see:('On Colonies, Industrial Monopoly and
Working Class Movement', FUTURA Publishing House, Copenhagen,
1972). Secondly, it should be clear from what follows that the
term labour aristocracies is not used here to indicate a supposedly integrated proletariat in the capitalist system, a community of interests between the former and the latter. Given
the great number of variations on this theme, it is impossible
here even to sketch a criticism of this view.

[77 The following statement by S. Amin indirectly supports this
point: 'It is possible to construct a valid model of development of a capitalist economy without bringing international
relations into it. The theoretical model is perfectly correct
because capitalist economy forms a coherent whole which is
logically self-sufficient. A model like this is out of the
question for an underdeveloped country, which, by definition,
cannot be isolated from the international market. The forms of
its international integration condition the pace and direction
of its development. The underdeveloped economy does not constitute a coherent whole in itself. It does not make sense
apart from the world capitalist market which shapes it.'
'Accumulation on a World Scale', p. 560.]

78 This, of course, only explains the possibility of certain parts
of the working class to entering the ranks of the labour aristocracy. The actual emergence of concrete labour aristocracies, however, must be explained by reference to the particular
social, historical, etc. conditions within which this possibility becomes a reality. As T. Nairn says in his The English
Working Class, in R. Blackburn, ed., 'Ideology in Social
Science', 1973, the element of 'bribe', imperialism, etc. are
factors external to the English working class. However, one
has to examine 'the internal history that gave to such factors
their true meaning and effects', (p. 204).

79 Take system engineers, for example. Their position within the
computer factory and their relatively small number (about 400
out of a total personnel of 6400 at the IBM in Milan; see FIM,
FIOM, UILM, op. cit., p. 217) give them a strategic position.
This means that, even if the system engineer only performs the
function of the collective worker, there must be no difference
ideologically speaking between him and the manager. He is,
then, an extreme example of labour aristocracy, of someone who
is, on the level of production relations, a member of the working class but, on the level of distribution, political and
ideological relations, is a member of the petty bourgeoisie.
This is, incidentally, a good example of how the determinant
role reverts always to the economic while the dominant role can
revert also to either the ideological (as in this case) or the
political. In this case, the economic has the determinant role
because it is the position this technician has within the production process which determines his importance, his strategic
position. But it is the ideological which has the dominant
role because the performance of this strategic function is
ensured by the role played by the ideological. In other words,

it is the conditions determined by the economic which assign
the ideological its dominant role.

80 In other words, as far as the economic level goes, the labour
aristocracy belongs to the petty bourgeoisie only on the level
of distribution relations, while the new middle class belongs
to the petty bourgeoisie already at the level of production
relations.

81 The original article, dating back to 1942, by K. Davis and
W.E. Moore as well as some of the most relevant contributions
to the theoretical controversy started by it, can be found in
M.M. Tumin (ed.), 'Readings on Social Stratification',
Prentice-Hall, 1970, pp. 367-428.

82 '...the need to control, rather than the need for efficiency
and productivity, leads the capitalist to break down all functions, to create fictitious qualifications, to divide workers
and tasks in ever increasing categories.' E. Mingione,
'Impiegati, sviluppo capitalistico e lotta di classe', Rome,
1973, p. 43.

83 This is an example of the determining role of production relations and of the relative autonomy of the distribution relations. Just as the former determines the latter and is modified by it, so the identification of the proletariat on the
basis of production relations is modified when distribution
relations are considered.

84 Robert Davies, The White Working Class in South Africa, 'New
Left Review', no. 82, pp. 40-59, points out that the white
workers in South Africa are a labour aristocracy in terms of
distribution relations (they are paid more not only than the
value of their labour power but also than the value they produce) and of political and ideological relations. Their privileged economic position is determined by their political
importance for the settler bourgeoisie (but this political
importance in turn is a function of the need to maintain a certain mode of production). Thus, this section of the South
African working class seems to belong to the petty bourgeoisie
not on account of production relations. However, Davies remarks that '"civilized labourers" no longer perform manual
labour in gangs of subsidized erosion preventers, *now the white
worker is increasingly a supervisor* or at least a skilled operative' (p. 48, emphasis added). It would be interesting to
know to which of the two aspects of the work of supervision
Davies refers. If the white worker starts performing also the
function of capital, then this would be a case of a passage
from the working class to the middle class on ground of production relations.

[85 Piccone Stella's approach is essentially the same than C.W.
Mills's. See 'White Collar', Oxford University Press, 1951,
pp. 295 and ff.]

86 We do not have time to elaborate on this point. It suffices to
say that the inability to see the process of proletarianization
rests on the (non-Marxist) presupposition of a fixed, and non
culturally determined, subsistence minimum.

87 That is, the part of the total value produced (a total which
increases constantly) going to variable capital tends to

decrease in percentage terms while the part going to surplus
value tends to increase. In absolute terms, both parts increase. Marx is very clear on this point in several of his
writings. For example, in 'Wage-Labour and Capital' (International Publishers, New York), Marx states very clearly that
minimum wages are of a social, i.e. relative, nature (p. 33)
and that real wages may rise (together with nominal wages) and
relative wages fall contemporarily (p. 36). I.e. Marx does not
talk about absolute but only about relative impoverishment of
the workers (p. 39). See also 'Theories of Surplus Value',
vol. II, p. 572. While bourgeois sociologists like to point at
the rise in real wages as a 'proof' for the 'embourgeoisification' theory, bourgeois economists like to point at the same
fact to show that Marx is inconsistent on this point. 'It is
now well known that Marx expected the relative rather than the
absolute deprivation of the working class. What is perhaps
less well known is that the tendency of wages to rise as a
constant proportion of national income is built into his model
of capital accumulation. For, as Joan Robinson shows, if s/v
is constant and c/v is rising, then s/c + v must be falling,
but at the same time real wages must be rising as productivity
increases. Labour receives a constant proportion of a rising
total. Robinson believes that this analysis is based on a
simple inconsistency in Marx and that he really wants to argue
what he holds elsewhere, namely that real wages do not rise.
She therefore proposes to get rid of the tendency of the rate
of profit to fall, which she never liked. But it seems much
more sensible to argue that the assumption of constant real
wages was an assumption Marx made for a specific analysis, and
that it is the assumption of rising real wages that fits his
model of capital accumulation best because it means that one of
the central features of this model, the tendency of the rate of
profit to fall, does not have to be abandoned'. P. Walton and
A. Gamble, 'From Alienation to Surplus Value', London, 1972,
p. 226.

88 '...in every process of creating value, the reduction of skilled labour, e.g. one day of skilled to six of unskilled labour,
is unavoidable' (Marx, 'Capital', vol. I, p. 198). [Pollock
provides the example of the introduction of the feedback system
in the testing of chemical products. We will use this example
to illustrate the loss of the global function of capital undergone by the chemist in charge of testing as a result of this
technical innovation. Let us subdivide Pollock's example into
three phases. In phase a 'the tests are made by the chemists
and their assistants in laboratories at each successive stage
in production. The necessary information is passed on to the
operator in charge of the control room. By adjusting the
appropriate dials this operator makes the necessary correc-
tions in the process.' Here the chemist, in so far as he controls his assistants and participates in the labour process
(also by co-ordinating the work of the assistants), performs
both the global function of capital and the function of the
collective worker. Phase b sees 'the introduction of a series
of automatic devices at each stage of production to test the

quality of the product'. Finally, in phase c, automation is introduced also in the control room and 'the functions formally performed by the man in the control centre are taken over by a device which will automatically correct the working of the machines.' What interests us here is the transition between phases a and b. Before testing becomes completely automated (i.e. before phase b) new machines can be introduced which will simplify the testing process so that at first only the chemist will be necessary to do the job. By loosing his assistants, and thus by loosing the double aspect of his supervisory work, he looses also the global function of capital. Now he performs only the function of the collective worker, even though he does not carry out any more the work of co-ordination and unity of the labour process. Successively, when new machines will further simplify testing, his job can be given to one of the former assistants. Of course, either one or both of these intermediate steps can be skipped and automated testing directly introduced in the production process. The quotations above are taken from F. Pollock, 'The Economic and Social Consequences of Automation', Oxford, 1957, p. 15. At page 171 of the same book, we can find an example of how automation dequalifies the labour of technicians in charge of testing: '... for instance, automatic testing equipment was designed recently to check the reliability of military electronic devices. One girl with no technical training is able to run the new equipment. It took seven technicians with a high degree of specialization and fourteen semi-skilled workers to do the same testing job before.']

89   The introduction of the computer is justified by the greater productivity of labour achieved through (a) a reduction in manpower and (b) a devaluation of the labour-power employed. This is what has happened, just to mention one example, at the FIAT's administrative sector since 1960. See FIM, FIOM, UILM, 'Impiegati '72', p. 33. The interpretation that the computer does not cause unemployment because this would be contrary to the capitalist's interests (given that only labour power creates value and thus surplus value) is pure nonsense and betrays an amazing lack of understanding of Marxian economics. For such an 'interpretation', see Gruppo di studio IBM, 'IBM: Capitale imperialistico e proletariato moderno', Milan, 1973, p. 34.

[90   'For a short time in the 1940's and early 1950's the dataprocessing occupations displayed the characteristics of a craft. This was during the period when tabulating equipment based on the punched card dominated the industry. Installations were small and the tabulating craftsman worked on all machines: the sorter, collator, tabulator, calculator, etc. ... The development of a data-processing craft was abortive, however, since along with the computer a new division of labor was introduced and the destruction of the craft greatly hastened. Each aspect of computer operations was graded to a different level of pay frozen into a hierarchy: systems managers, systems analysts, programmers, computer console operators, key punch operators, tape librarians, stock room attendants, etc. It soon became characteristic that entry into higher jobs was at the higher level of the hierarchy, rather than through an all-round training.' Braverman, 'Labor and Monopoly Capital', p. 329.]

[91 The creation of these new, highly qualified functions has dazzled many authors inducing them to see the working class under monopoly capitalism through the optical illusion of the 'new working class'. The foremost protagonist of this tendency is of course S. Mallet. I will mention here only some of the many criticisms that can be moved to Mallet. This authors uses a three-phase scheme. Phase A corresponds more or less to the stage of formal subordination of labour to capital; phase B to the stage of real subordination of labour to capital; and phase C to the sub-stage of monopoly capitalism which starts after WWII and which is characterized, among other things, by the introduction of automation. First of all, Mallet assumes big industry to extend itself into monopoly capitalism without any qualitative changes and then considers only a sub-stage, that characterized by automation. Secondly, Mallet considers the collective worker of stage B as made up only of the unskilled workers. Thus he concludes that the (collective) worker has been dispossessed of his knowledge. Thirdly, his notion of the collective worker is nothing more than the mechanical, arithmetical summation of individual workers. In fact, in phase C he sees the collective worker regaining his technical knowledge because each worker becomes, through automation, a scientist. Fourthly, and this point is explicitly connected with the previous one, Mallet has a completely mistaken idea of the effects of automation on the social structure. For Mallet, automation is 'the dialectical negation of the fragmentation of labour' (La nouvelle classe ouvrière', Editions du Seuil, 1969, p. 74). On this point see 'Sunschrift 14', Nijmegen, 1970 and N. Poulantzas, 'Les classes sociales dans le capitalism aujourd'hui', Paris, 1974, pp. 258-261. Fifthly, concerning the vanguard's role supposedly played by the 'new working class' (i.e. technicians, scientists, etc.) Mallet's technological determinism and his economicism are only two sides of the same coin. The Italian experience shows, e.g., that in the 'hot autumn' of 1969 and afterward the vanguard has been the 'traditional' working class and that the technicians, employees, etc. have sided with the traditional working class basically because (a) the latter had reached very high levels of combativeness and thus had become a reference point for the 'new' working class and (b) the technicians, etc., had already gone through a process of dequalification (and thus of devaluation of their labour power) which — in case these agents had performed both the global function of capital and the function of the collective worker — resulted also in the proletarianization, in their becoming part of the proletariat already at the level of production relations.]

92 See, as far as the Italian scene is concerned, M. Lelli, 'Tecnici e lotta di classe', Bari, 1973, pp. 47-86; C. Baglioni, 'Il conflitto industriale e l'azione del sindacato', Bologna, 1966, pp. 150-215; G. Martinoli, I laureati nell' industria in

'I laureati in Italia', Bologna, 1968, pp. 147-209; the
interpretation of the material and the perspective are of
course quite different from the ones of the above-mentioned
authors.

93 Decreasing, that is, in relation to the average wage, i.e.
approaching this average wage.

94 This is what seems to have happened in the chemical industry
where many of the functions which used to be performed by university graduates are now performed by technicians with only a
high-school diploma. These technicians might make more mistakes than the university graduates and thus cause more losses,
but these losses are more than offset by the saving in variable
capital.

95 To the best of my knowledge, the only publication relating the
disppearance of the global function of capital to proletarianization is 'Lotta di classe nella scuola e movimento studentesco', Quaderni di Avanguardia Operaia, Milan, 1971, p. 26.

96 Of course, one should not forget the counteracting factors.
We have said that proletarianization means the disappearance
of the function of capital. In the example above, the chemist,
now a technician, himself becomes the object of control and
surveillance. This work must now be performed by someone else.
That is, the proletarianization of employees and technicians
calls for a 'multiplication of middle-level managers' to control the former (see FIM, FIOM, UILM, op. cit., p. 133 and p.
149). In turn, middle-management undergoes changes (something
already anticipated by H.J. Leavitt and T.L. Whisler in their
article Management in the 1980's, in 'Harvard Business Review',
Nov.-Dec. 1958) and becomes an increasingly thinner section of
the corporation's total personnel. In the intermediate steps
which remain, the global function of capital becomes almost
the only function and the function of the collective worker
tends to disappear because taken over by the computer (see,
e.g., the Rank Xerox in Milan employing about 1200 persons only
40 of which are workers, as quoted in FIM, FIOM, UILM, op.
cit., p. 84). The function of these middle-managers becomes
almost exclusively one of 'political function of control over
the employees' (ibid.). And this, after all, could not be
otherwise. If the function of the collective worker is
increasingly taken over by the computer, the survival of those
positions is justified only in so far as they are useful as
'political control over the employees'. The counteracting tendencies are originated also by the conjuncture. The example of
the SAE plant in Milan given above in note 68, shows how
heavily political and ideological reasons might weigh in the
creation of positions combining both functions.

97 Let us repeat that the analysis provided in this chapter is not
a conjunctural one. It is quite clear that the ups and downs
of the business cycle will influence wages, unemployment, etc.
This holds not only for the working class but also for the
middle classes. However, in the case of the latter classes,
one has to have, first of all, a theory of proletarianization
in terms of value (and thus also in terms of functions). Only
then can one see how the basic trend and the conjuncture

interact. The tendency to see proletarianization exclusively
in conjunctural terms is common to many authors, including
Marxist writers. See, e.g., the following: 'In like manner
a contraction of the market and a slowing up of production
throw the superintendents, the salesmen, and the office staff
"on the pavements"' in A.L. Harris, Pure Capitalism and the
Disappearance of the Middle Class, 'Journal of Political
Economy', June 1939, p. 353.

98   As far as the employees are concerned, among the ideologies
which hinder their becoming conscious of their objective situation, the myth of 'career making' is one of the most powerful
and well known. What is not so well known is the fact that it
is the employees lowest in the hierarchical scale, those who
have been proletarianized, who fall more easily prey of this
myth. As E. Mingione puts it: 'The wide gap among the real
salaries of those employees who do the same job in the same
enterprise confirms how the hope to make a career can be strong
for the employee, if he faithfully serves the firm for which he
works. It is likely that the mirage of a career still plays a
role which is the more relevant the more a position is dequalified and devoid of any real technical and professional content'
('Impiegati, sviluppo capitalistico e lotta di classe', p. 174).
Quite clearly, capital concentrates its efforts to prevent the
rise and development of a proletarian class consciousness in
the potentially more dangerous areas of social stratification.
This fact explains, according to Mingione, why Italian typists,
card-punchers, and book keepers were at the tail of the great
wave of strikes of 1969-70. However, it should be added, other
sectors of the employees did participate in the class struggle
and have reached a certain degree of class consciousness. An
ideology must sooner or later fade away if its material (economic) basis has disappeared.

Chapter 2

THE ECONOMIC IDENTIFICATION
OF THE STATE EMPLOYEES

INTRODUCTION

In chapter 1, I have put forward a theory for the economic identification of social classes under capitalism, with particular reference
to monopoly capitalism and the new middle class. In this chapter
(1) I will use the theoretical framework worked out so far in order
to study the class collocation of the state employees. This chapter
has been subdivided into three sections. Section I draws a distinction between capitalist and non-capitalist state activities and
reaches the conclusion that the class analysis provided in chapter 1
applies tout court to the agents employed in capitalist state activities. Section II analyses the particular nature of the non-
capitalist state activities and reaches the conclusion that the economic identification of the agents employed by these state activities follows the same lines than those of the agents employed in an
unproductive capitalist enterprise. Finally, in section III I make
explicit some of the political implication of my theory by setting
it against a different approach.

I CAPITALIST AND NON-CAPITALIST STATE ACTIVITIES

What is the relevance of chapter 1 for an analysis of the state
employees? First of all, the methodology followed. Let's look
quickly at how social classes have been determined. The starting
point has been the study of the capitalist production process (both
productive and unproductive). Secondly, this first step has allowed
us to analyse the capitalist production (and distribution) relations. Thirdly, on the basis of this analysis, an economic definition, or identification, of classes has been provided. To put it in
other words, classes are defined in terms of production and distribution relations which, in their turn, are defined in terms of the
nature of the process of production. In the essay, the production
process considered has been only the capitalist one, both the typical, productive, one and the unproductive (e.g. commercial) one.
Capital personified has been considered in the form either of the
individual or of the global capitalist. In the latter case, I have

limited myself to those joint-stock enterprises economically owned
by a limited group of 'private' capitalists and legally owned by a
large group of stock owners. On the basis of the study of the production process taking place in these enterprises, and thus on the
basis of the study of the production relations engaged into by the
production agents, we have been able to define the working class,
the middle class and the capitalist class, but only with reference
to those agents which are engaged in a capitalist (either productive
or not) production process. But what about the state, or 'public',
enterprises? What about the class collocation of those working in
state enterprises? If the methodology followed in the essay is
correct, then the same itinerary must be followed. To repeat, we
must start, first of all, from a study of the production process
taking place within the state enterprises, from there we must come
up to the production relations and finally, on the basis of this
knowledge, we can collocate the state employees within the class
structure. Now, state enterprises can be subdivided between capitalist and non-capitalist ones. I will call them capitalist state
activities and non-capitalist state activities respectively.(2)   A
first, important conclusion can be drawn: if a criterion can be
found discriminating the capitalist from the non-capitalist state
activities, the analysis, provided in chapter 1, of the new middle
class and also of the working class and of the capitalist class,
can be applied *in toto* to the capitalist state activities. I.e.
state employees cannot be categorized a priori as one or the other
class. First of all, we must consider whether they, in their role
as production agents, take part in a capitalist or in a non-
capitalist production process. If the former is the case, then
they will be subdivided among the three major classes according to
the criteria provided in chapter 1. Those state employees participating in non-capitalist state activities, on the other hand, will
have to be dealt with only after an analysis of the production process and of the production relations they engage in has been carried out.(3) Therefore, the task is two-fold. First of all, to
provide a criterion discriminating the two basic types of state
activities. Secondly, to provide an analysis of the production process and production relations which will allow us to identify economically those agents engaged in non-capitalist state activities.
Since it would be difficult to separate the discussion of each of
these two problems, in what follows the analysis of the production
process and production relations typical of a non-capitalist state
activity will help also in our search for a criterion separating
those activities from the capitalist state activities.
  Before starting the analysis, however, let me go back for a
moment to the question of the levels of abstraction. As we will
see later on, a proper understanding of which level of abstraction
is involved in carrying out our analysis of non-capitalist state
activities is essential for the class collocation of the state
employees. Let me give an example of what I consider as a non-
capitalist state activity, which, for sake of brevity, from now on
I will abbreviate as non-CSA (the abbreviation for capitalist state
activities will be CSA): a state hospital. To put the question in
more concrete terms: on what level of abstraction do we move when
placing the doctor or the nurse, working in a state hospital, in

the class structure? First of all, we are not on the pure capitalist mode of production level because on this level classes are defined in relation to the pure (productive) capitalist production process and the doctor, not taking part in this process, cannot be part
either of the capitalist or of the working class. In terms of the
definition in chapter 1, the doctor meets two of the requirements
for being part of the working class (distribution relations aside).
In fact (a) he does not own the means of production and (b) he is
part of the collective labourer, which, in a state hospital, carries
out the labour process by providing health services. However, the
doctor in question (as opposed to the doctor working in a private
clinic) is not hired by capital, does not participate in a pure
capitalist production process and thus cannot be the producer/
exploited. Yet he, and much more so the nurse, has on the face of
it a capitalist relation with the employer. We will see soon why,
and what is the nature of this relation. Secondly, we are not on
the socio-economic system level either because on this level we
still consider classes which, even though defined in terms of all
the three instances (the economic, the ideological, and the political), are objectively identifiable exclusively in relation to the
capitalist production process, either productive of surplus value
or not (e.g. the commercial capitalist production process). Again,
the doctor in question meets two of the requirements for being classified on this level of abstraction but does not meet the third
requirement because, not being employed by capital, cannot be considered either as a productive or as an unproductive worker. Both
the objective identification of the proletariat, of the bourgeoisie,
and of the petty bourgeoisie (i.e. the middle classes) takes place
in terms of the capitalist process (both productive and not) and
relations so that there is no place on this level for classes which
are not objectively identifiable in these terms. We are then on the
level of the concrete society (where we consider several socio-
economic systems and their relations to the dominant one) because
the doctor in question is working in a production process other than
the capitalist one (as we will see soon): he provides (produces),
with the other members of the collective worker, services but is not
employed by capital (either productive or not). The important point
to be made for the purposes of our analysis is that on this level
not only we consider production processes and production relations
other than the capitalist ones but also how these processes and
relations are modified by the fact that they exist in a society
dominated by the pure capitalist production process and relations.

We can now start our search for a criterion with which to separate the CSA from the non-CSA. Let us begin by subdividing the
state-owned activities in
  (a) those which spend their money in order to increase it, and
  (b) those which do not, i.e. which spend the money allocated to
      them basically in order to meet needs.
I submit that there is no difference between (a) and the 'privately'
owned enterprises. Take a state-owned steel-works. This factory is
not owned by an individual capitalist, but neither is the joint-
stock company. While in the individual enterprise the legal ownership belongs to the individual capitalist, and in the joint-stock
company it belongs to the stock-holders, in the state-owned

enterprise the legal ownership belongs to the whole of the bourgeoisie, rather than to a very limited part of it. This can be seen
from the fact that, *since it is the legal ownership which determines
the appropriation of revenue,* while the individual capitalist (who
has both legal and economic ownership) appropriates to himself the
whole of the surplus-value (part of which is accumulated and part is
revenue, i.e. spent unproductively, for himself), in the joint-stock
company the revenue is appropriated by the stock-holders (the other
part of the surplus-value being accumulated by those who have the
real ownership), and in the state-owned company the revenue goes to
the state, i.e. to the bourgeoisie as a whole (while the other part
of the surplus-value is accumulated by the real owners, just as in
the joint-stock company). As far as the real ownership is concerned,
it belongs to the managers both in the joint-stock company and in
the state-owned enterprise. In both forms of enterprise, it is the
manager who is the non-labourer/exploiter/non producer/real owner.
In both enterprises, the manager, as capital personified, is opposed
to the labourer/exploiter/non-owner/producer. In terms of production relations, then, there is no difference between these two types
of enterprises. But why is this so? Because both behave according
to the laws of capitalist competition and accumulation, both produce
commodities in order to produce surplus-value rather than use values,
both re-invest the surplus value produced according to criteria of
profitability rather than of the customers' needs to be met, in
short, *both advance money in order to increase it.* In other words,
and if we abstract for the time being from state enterprises acting
in the non-productive spheres of the economy, as e.g. a state-owned
commercial enterprise or bank, both engage in a production process
in which the production of surplus-value dominates the labour process, i.e. both are engaged in the production of surplus-value.(4)
As Marx says, money is capital 'only because utilized or spent in
order to increase it....If this, in relation to the amount of money
or of value, appears as its destination — its internal impulse, its
tendency —, in relation to the capitalist who owns it and in whose
hands this amount of money must carry out such a function, appears
as objective, as aim.'(5) This means that we can define concisely
the pure (productive) capitalist production process both as production *of* surplus value (if we consider the objective function of
capital, 'its internal impulse, its tendency', the fact that it is
money which expands itself) and production *for* surplus value (if we
consider the aim of the capitalist, whose only aim as capital personified is to produce and realize surplus value, who thus produces
use values only as a means to produce exchange values). It is clear
then, that both the private capitalist enterprise and the state-
owned enterprise which advances money in order to increase it, are
essentially similar, are essentially *production for and of surplus
value.* We can thus define the CSA as the state-owned enterprise
whose production process is production both of and for surplus-
value, where production of surplus-value means to advance M and to
get M' at the end of the production process, and production for
surplus-value refers to the aim of the real owners, the managers, in
carrying out the production process.

   It is useful, for the purpose of our discussion, to compare the
productive capitalist production process with the unproductive one.

Both of them are production *for* profit because in both cases the capitalist has advanced money in order to increase it. But only the former process is also production *of* surplus-value; the latter is not, since here we have only a formal transformation. Thus, the unproductive capitalist production process can be defined concisely as *production for, but not of, surplus value*. The same can be repeated for the state enterprise acting in a non-productive (e.g. financial) sphere of the economy. Let us now compare the CSA (both productive and not) with a basically different type of activity: that which advances money not in order to increase it but in order to meet needs. Take, to begin with, a private and a state hospital. The former is a capitalist (productive) enterprise; it provides use values (health services) only as a means to produce surplus-value. The latter is basically concerned with meeting needs, e.g. it tends to expand when the number of patients grows (at least in principle, i.e. disregarding from the government's investment policy, etc.); the former, on the other hand, might or might not expand if the number of patients grows, depending upon the profitability (getting M' out of M) of doing so. *The latter is neither production of surplus-value nor production for surplus-value*. It is this type of activity which we define as the non-CSA. Having thus provided a criterion for distinguishing the CSA from the non-CSA, we can substantiate our *first conclusion*: the class analysis provided in the first chapter (and thus also the analysis of the new middle class) applies tout court to the CSA, i.e. to those state-owned enterprises whose production is either both of and for surplus-value, or only for surplus-value.

II   NON-CAPITALIST STATE ACTIVITIES AND STATE EMPLOYEES

The reader may recall that the problem to be solved in order to identify economically the state employees was two-fold. Having provided an answer to the first aspect of the problem, i.e. having provided a criterion for defining which state activities are capitalist and which are not, we can now proceed to an analysis of the non-CSA. As already mentioned above, the procedure must be such that, starting from an analysis of the production process characteristic of a non-CSA, through an examination of the relations to it corresponding, we can come up with the economic identification (class collocation on the economic plane) of the non-CSA's employees. Let us begin with the nature of the non-CSA's production process.
　　As already pointed out, we place our analysis on the concrete society level. On this level, we have the coexistence of several production processes and relations, all subordinated to the pure capitalist production process and relations. It is instructive to compare:
1　a pre-capitalist production process, e.g. the medieval artisan surviving in a capitalist setting;
2　an unproductive capitalist production process, e.g. the commercial enterprise;
3　the production process taking place in a non-CSA.
　　Process 1 can be considered as the unity of the labour process and of the value producing process. We talk about value, and not

surplus-value, producing process because there is no exploitation
or oppression: since the artisan owns his means of production, the
non-labourer has no place in the production process. There is indeed appropriation of value produced by the artisan by other sectors of the economy since, as a general rule, the productivity of
the former is lower than the latter's.(6) However, this appropriation of value takes place on the exchange and not on the production
level. In the feudal artisan's production process 'not the exchange
value as such, not enrichment as such, are the aim and result of the
exploitation of other people's labour...', here 'dominates, as a
law, the limitation of production within the boundaries drawn a
priori by consumption and not within the boundaries set by the
value of capital.'(7) In other words, we could say that in this
production process the value producing process does not dominate the
labour process but is dominated by it.

In 2, as the reader might recall from chapter 1, section III, the
production process is the unity of the labour process and of the
surplus-labour producing process. There is, here, economic oppression — rather than exploitation — i.e. there is here direct extraction, on the part of the capitalist, of human labour as a means for
the appropriation of surplus-value produced in the productive
sphere of the economy. Since, as we know, this production process
is unproductive of surplus value and yet it is production for surplus-value, we can say that here the labour process is dominated by
the surplus-labour producing process.

In 3 too there is appropriation, extraction, of surplus-labour.
To put it differently, the employee of the non-CSA is paid, tendentially, the full value of his labour power but certainly not the
equivalent of the labour provided by him. Let us make the example
of a primary school. The teacher in this school is not employed by
capital (to repeat, the production of services is production neither
for nor of surplus-value) and yet there is no difference between him
and his colleague working the same hours, under the same conditions,
at the same pay, etc., in the privately owned school (capitalist and
productive); if anything, the teacher in a private school gets a
better treatment (for reasons other than economic) than his colleague employed by the state. Thus, just as in 2, there is direct
appropriation (this time on the part of the state rather than of the
individual capitalist) of surplus labour, so that in 3 like in 2 the
production process can be thought of as the unity of the labour process and of the surplus labour producing process. We can thus extend the concept of economic oppression to the employee of the non-
CSA, provided all the above mentioned qualifications are kept in
mind. But here the similarities end. The production process in an
unproductive capitalist enterprise is production for surplus-value
(even though not production of surplus-value), i.e. in such a production process the surplus labour producing process dominates the
labour process. The commercial capitalist engages in his activities
first and foremost because he wants to make a profit. Therefore he
produces a *capitalist commodity,* which is defined as goods and services, 1, which are both use values and exchange values and, 2, in
which the use value is produced only as a means to produce exchange
value. Succinctly, then, a capitalist commodity can be defined as
the unity in domination of exchange value and use value.(8)

The non-CSA, on the contrary, spends its money not in order to increase it but in order to meet needs. Its production process is neither production for nor of surplus value. Therefore, the commodity produced by the non-CSA has only one of the characteristics of the capitalist commodity: it is the unity of use value and exchange value (9) but now the aim of production is not so much the exchange value but the use value. Primary education is provided by the state not according to criteria of profitability but, generally speaking, because the state wants to provide the population with certain services. The emphasis is on the use value rather than on the exchange value. This means that in the production process of a non-CSA it is the labour process which dominates the surplus labour producing process: *the extraction of surplus labour* (and we will see soon why there has to be such an extraction) *is not the primary reason for the provision of the non-CSA's services*. The opposite is true for the unproductive capitalist enterprises. To sum up what has been said so far, we can say that there are two points of similarity and two points of difference between the production process of an unproductive capitalist enterprise and that of a non-CSA. The similarities are that both processes, 1, are characterized by appropriation of surplus labour and, 2, are the unity of labour process and surplus labour producing process. The differences are that in the former process, 1, the surplus labour producing process dominates the labour process (while in the non-CSA the opposite is true) and, 2, as far as the product is concerned, the exchange value dominates the use value (while in the non-CSA the opposite is true). Note also the similarity between the non-CSA and the feudal artisan. In both production processes it is consumption which limits production (rather than capital), the difference — in this respect — being that in the latter it is the individual producer and in the former it is the state, which limits production to needs.(10)

Having determined the nature of the non-CSA's production process, we can now proceed to the analysis of the production relations upon which this process rests. The fact is that the nature of the product (not only in the sense underlined by Marx, i.e. whether it is one use-value or another, but also in the sense whether it is a completely capitalist commodity or not) is totally indifferent to the labourer, just as it is totally indifferent to him whether he is economically oppressed by an individual capitalist, by a joint-stock company, or by the state. In all three cases he gets, tendentially, only the value of his labour power. The employee of a non-CSA takes part in a production process which is dominantly production of use values. But since this non-capitalist production takes place in a capitalist economic structure, i.e. in a structure dominated by the capitalist production process and relations, it is dominated by this structure and thus takes place according to capitalist criteria, i.e. *it produces use values just as capitalist commodities are produced, i.e. by the extraction of surplus labour*. In other words, the non-CSA produces use values just as exchange values are produced, it produces non-capitalist commodities just as if capitalist commodities were produced. Therefore, both the unproductive labourer and the employee of a non-CSA are expropriated of surplus labour, are economically oppressed. But the similarities do not end here. Just as the unproductive worker, the state employee, e.g. the

primary school teacher, is the non-owner of the 'means of production', is the labourer (i.e. performs the function of the collective
worker whereas the school master performs the equivalent of the
function of capital) and is paid the equivalent of his labour
power's value. *Therefore, in terms of production and distribution
relations there is no difference between the unproductive worker
and the employee of a non-CSA,* even though there are differences as
far as the production process in which they participate is concerned. Therefore, and this is our *second conclusion,* the economic
identification of all those working in a non-CSA follows the same
lines than the economic identification of those working in an unproductive capitalist enterprise.

If we sum up what said so far about the state, we can come up
with a general conclusion. The economic identification of all those
working both in the CSA and in the non-CSA follows the same pattern
than the one provided in chapter 1. To put it in an extremely concise way: state activities, both capitalist and non-capitalist (and
in the case of the former, both productive and unproductive), employ
production agents who, from the point of view of their economic
identification, belong to the capitalist class, or to the new middle
class, or to the working class. This identification is based on· the
application, at the several levels of abstraction, of the definition
of classes provided in chapter 1, section II and on the interpretation and discussion of this definition in the subsequent sections.
To give just an example, the nurse, the teacher, etc. employed by
the state are objectively identifiable as proletariat inasmuch as,
1, they do not own the means of production, 2, they are expropriated
of surplus labour (economically oppressed), 3, they perform the
function of the collective worker, and, 4, they receive a wage (a)
tendentially equal to the value of their labour power, (b) produced
in the productive sphere of the economy, and (c) paid to them by the
state after part of the surplus-value originating in the productive
sphere of the economy has been distributed among the various unproductive sectors of the economy (including the state). The only difference between the nurse or the teacher employed in a capitalist
(productive) enterprise and the nurse or the teacher employed in a
non-CSA is that the former can be classified as working class
already at the pure capitalist mode of production level while the
latter can be economically identified as proletariat only at the
concrete society level of abstraction. It should be clear, then,
that if these wage-earners belong objectively speaking, to the proletariat, it is not because of a superficial equation wage-
earners = proletariat but because of the production relations of
which they are the carriers.

III   SOME POLITICAL IMPLICATIONS

In this third and last section I would like to make explicit some of
the political implications which can be drawn from my treatment of
classes. In order to keep the discussion within reasonable limits,
I will deal almost exclusively with the class collocation of the
state employees. Moreover, in order to bring in sharp relief such
implications more easily, I will set my approach to the state

employees against that of G. Armanski.(11)

If I understand Armanski's thesis correctly, the state employees (Staatliche Lohnarbeiter) would belong to the middle class on account of two reasons. First of all, they cannot belong to the working class because they are — just as the commercial worker — unproductive. The reason why unproductive workers cannot belong to the working class is that they, by not reproducing capital, do not reproduce capitalist relations either. The second reason is that the state employees, having been excluded from the working class, present the peculiar feature of deriving their income both from profits and from wages, thanks to the appropriation by the state of part of the income of the capitalist and of the working class. Therefore, an important conclusion concerning the class conscious-ness of the state employees, a conclusion to which however Armanski subscribes only with qualifications, is that this sector of the middle class has interests which are contrary both to those of the capitalist and to these of the working class.

The reader will notice immediately how my analysis differs from Armanski's. To begin with, Armanski only hints at the existence of a productive state sector (by mentioning the state's non-productive sector) but offers no criterion for separating productive capital-ist state activities from unproductive capitalist state activities, nor a criterion for separating CSA from non-CSA. As pointed out above, the unproductiveness of the former state activities is dif-ferent and only apparently similar to the latter unproductiveness. The former is production for but not of surplus-value while the latter is production neither for nor of surplus-value. Or, in the former production process the surplus labour producing process dominates the labour process (and thus produces a capitalist commo-dity in which the exchange value dominates the use value) while in the latter the reverse is true. Therefore, the state employees are expropriated of surplus labour, i.e. are economically oppressed, just as the commercial worker. But we should not forget that the term economic oppression can be extended to the state employees only by analogy with the commercial workers and only if the differ-ences in the two production processes are kept in mind. If these qualifications are not considered, then the term economic oppesssion, or expropriation of surplus labour, only serves to gloss over impor-tant differences as far as the production process is concerned. Therefore, not all state employees are expropriated of surplus labour but only those who satisfy both of the following conditions: 1, they must work either in non-CSA or in unproductive CSA and, 2, they must belong either to the working class or to the new middle class (and in the latter case only in so far as they perform the function of the collective worker). In more general terms, the de-marcation line does not place the state employees *en bloc* either on the side of the working class or on the ·side of the new middle class but divides them within the three primary classes. This difference with Armanski's view, all-important as we will see soon as far as political implications are concerned, can be ascribed basically to two important methodological and analytical differences. First of all, I distinguish in my analysis several levels of abstraction and proceed from the highest to the lowest. This allows me to analyse several production processes and production relations, as e.g. the

productive (capitalist) production process, the unproductive capitalist production process, the production process of the non-
capitalist state activity, etc. Secondly, when analysing a production process (including the capitalist one) I emphasize the functional element and not only the ownership and productiveness elements. This lack of analysis of the several production processes
and thus of the several types of production relations makes it so
that in Armanski's view the state employees are different from the
commercial worker only on the level of distribution relations,
since their income is made up both of wages and of profits. In my
view, on the contrary, there are parts of the state employees whose
income is both wages and revenues (see chapter 1, section V). But
this is not the element characterizing them as middle classes. They
are middle classes and thus have a mixed income only because they
are such already at the level of production relations, i.e. because
they, even though not owning the means of production, perform both
the global function of capital and the function of the collective
labour.

The result of all this is that, instead of deriving production
relations from production processes and then deriving an economic
identification of classes from production relations, in Armanski's
article the economic identification (actually, economic definition,
but on this point I will come back shortly) of classes is directly
tied to the study of the production process (and to a study which in
my opinion is insufficient).(12) In Armanski's view the unproductive labourer cannot be part of the working class because he does
not reproduce capital. But there is a difference between being
productive labourers (reproducing capital) and reproducing capital
relations. Of course, as long as we remain on the highest level of
abstraction, as long as we consider only the typical, productive
capitalist production process, the labourer (by definition productive) reproduces both capital and its relations. But as soon as we
move to lower levels, when e.g. we analyse the unproductive capitalist production process, we see that the unproductive labourer reproduces capital relations by being economically oppressed rather than
exploited (if only this element of production relations is considered). Our study in this section has shown that there is no complete identity between a production process and production relations
in the sense that two similar sets of production relations can
spring from two different production processes (i.e. the capitalist
unproductive process, and the non-CSA's process). But, *basic for
class collocation* (on the economic level, i.e. abstracting from the
ideological and the political), *are the production relations and
not the production process*. This is why e.g. the unproductive
labourer, both in a capitalist enterprise and in a non-CSA, reproduces capitalist production relations while not reproducing capital:
he reproduces capital production relations by being economically
oppressed.

We have now all the elements necessary to bring up some political
conclusions by contrasting them to the political implications which
can be drawn from Armanski's approach. *First,* it should be clear by
now that the thesis according to which the state employees' interests are contrary both to the working class and to the capitalist
class is at best incomplete. State employees are capitalist class

or new middle class, or working class already on grounds of production relations. Since they are internally stratified, their interests are too. Therefore, objectively speaking, their interests can
be those of the capitalist class, or those of the working class or
they can be opposite to both. Thus, and this is my *second point,*
only what I call the new middle classes in the CSA and in the non-
CSA have contrasting interests. It is only with reference to this
specific part of the state employees that I agree with Armanski
about their nature as new middle classes. But the ways travelled
to reach this similar conclusion are of course quite different.

Thirdly, it seems to me that Armanski's view is rather static.
Even if we restrict our analysis to that part of the state employees
identifiable with the new middle class, we have to take into consideration their process of proletarianization as analysed in chapter
1, section VI. Such a process, as explained above, becomes intelli-
gible only with reference to the laws of capital accumulation. On
the one hand, already existing strata of the new middle class become
proletarianized. This means that, objectively speaking, their
interests become closer and closer to those of the working class.
This means, in turn, that even when strata of the state employees
have interests contrary to both fundamental classes, the incidence
of one type of interest vis-a-vis the other is not fixed but varies
according to that process the outcome of which is to push a large
part of these strata towards the working class (so that their interests become more and more those of this class), and another smaller
part toward the capitalist class (so that their interests become
more and more those of this class). On the other hand, changes in
the production forces and thus in the process of production (e.g.
the introduction of the computer), originate new functions which
bourgeois sociology limits itself to study only from the technical
point of view but which must be studied also from the social point
of view (i.e. whether they are functions of labour or of capital).
New strata of the middle class come thus to life, with 'mixed'
interests. *The two basic components of these spurious interests
will be mixed in various and changing degrees.* To sum up, then,
to say that the state employees have mixed, contrasting interests
is only true, in my opinion, if, 1, we limit this statement to that
part of the state employees which can be identified as new middle
class and, 2, we qualify this statement in a dynamic sense, i.e. by
considering, how, thanks to the process of proletarianization, the
balance for certain sectors of the state employees between the two
contrasting interests can change up to the point where only one
interest, either that of the working class or that of the capitalist
class, is left.

Fourthly, and lastly, it seems to me that implicit in Armanski's
article is a direct equation between objective interests and class
consciousness or, in other words, that there is no mention of the
relatively autonomous role played by the political and the ideological in creating class consciousness. Armanski mentions the following three points: (a) The state employees, being paid by the
state rather than by the capitalist, have the illusion that the
state is above class interests and only cares for the interest of
society as a whole. (b) The state employees sell their labour power
for a wage, just as the productive labourers do, but do not directly

experience exploitation because, given that the efficiency of the
state services is not checked on the market, what is important is
the use value of their labour power. (c) Even though it is the use
value of the state employee's labour which is important, the possibility of an increasing pressure on his wage is built into the
'wage-form'. This pressure leads to a position more and more similar to that of the rest of the wage workers.

A number of objections can be moved to these political conclusions which are the logical outcome of Armanski's analysis. To
begin with point (a). The state employee, not being able to see
the source of his income paid to him by the state, considers the
latter as above classes. But this does not explain why large sectors of the working class or of the middle class share the same myth
of the state's neutrality. An explanation of this phenomenon must
be sought in a detailed analysis of the function of ideology. To
give only one indication of what I mean, I would like to refer the
reader to Poulantzas' discussion of ideology as an extremely useful and fruitful approach.(13) As to point (b) above, my analysis
has shown the need to differentiate (and analyse in their specifi-
city) the production process and production relations both in the
CSA and in the non-CSA. If we single out the non-CSA, we find out
that in their production process it is indeed the labour process
(use value) which dominates the surplus labour producing process.
But in terms of production relations this fact makes little difference for the labourer who is expropriated of surplus labour just
as, and in the same measure as, the unproductive labourer. The
state employee has indeed no experience of exploitation but does
have a direct experience of economic oppression. It is this experience which explains (partly, of course) the combativeness of the new
middle class (including the state employees) in Italy since 1968.
Thus, the state employees do experience the equivalent of exploitation. However, as said above concerning point (a) and as I will
elaborate further in a second, this subjective experience is not
enough to explain the greatly increased militancy of the new middle
classes: what is needed is also an analysis of the political and
ideological conjuncture. Finally, concerning point (c). The pressure on the state employees' wages, i.e. their reduction to the
average, is not so much implied in the wage-form but rather in that
process of devaluation of labour power and proletarianization as
described in chapter 1. Wage decreases are only a reflection of the
process of proletarianization. These remarks are not pedantic. In
Armanski's words: 'the use of the concept "state wage-workers" — in
spite of all the mentioned limitations — means a scientific and a
political programme inasmuch as, behind the apparent movement, the
significance can be discovered of the wage-form for the real situation of the workers employed by the state and, besides, inasmuch as
this concept of "state wage-workers" can clarify the link between
them and the working class.'(14) In my opinion, the link between
the new middle classes (including those employed by the state) and
the working class (or better said, the proletariat) is given not
only by the wage-form, i.e. on the level of the distribution relations, but first and foremost by the type of production relations
which these classes bear. The new middle classes will be identifiable with the working class when (given that they already are the

non-owners of the means of production and disregarding from whether
they are productive or unproductive workers) the global function of
capital will have disappeared to make room exclusively for the function of the collective worker. Only then will they get a wage, i.e.
the equivalent of the value of their labour power. But this will
not necessarily transform them in proletarians, will not necessarily
create a proletarian class consciousness. Important conjunctural
political as well as ideological factors must be present before such
a qualitative change can take place. Consider, for example, the
mounting consciousness and participation to the class struggle of
the Italian employees — both in the state and in the private
sector — and thus their increasing militancy, since 1968.(15)
Purely economic considerations are totally insufficient to explain
this phenomenon. (16) Such an explanation must go back to the
1960s and to the significant internal changes this sector underwent.
Just to mention, in a highly schematic fashion, some of the most
relevant factors: on the one hand the weight of the technicians
within this sector grows while that of the administrative personnel
decreases. On the other hand, this sector undergoes a process of
proletarianization, as a result of an intense mechanization introduced by the capitalist class. This fact determines, just as it
had happened in the working class, a drop in the average age of the
employees and thus the ommission in this sector of people who are
politically inexperienced but also relatively free from the ideological domination of the reformist parties. All this, together with
the general crisis of bourgeois ideology (due to the counter-attack
on an international level of the proletarian ideology: the Vietnam
War, the Cultural Revolution, the May events in France, etc.) , with
the direct and indirect influence of the student movement (direct
influence: students take part in picketing, in assemblies of workers, etc.; indirect influence: former students with political
experience become employees, etc.) and, last but not least, with the
high combativeness of the working class (which becomes a reference
point for the employees) , determines a wide participation, for the
first time, of large strata of the employees to the class struggle,
their setting up of unions, their gaining a proletarian consciousness.
     This is the sense of my distinction between identification and
definition of classes. To draw political implications from a purely
economic identification of classes, to deny the importance of the
political and the ideological for a definition of classes, to establish a non-mediated relationship between objective economic interests and class consciousness, in short, to establish a mechanicist
rather than a dialectical relation of determination among the various levels of a society, can only have a negative effect on the
growth and qualitative development of the proletariat.

NOTES

1 First published in 'Social Praxis', vol. 2, no. 3. The first
   section of this paper, summarizing the content of chapter 1, has
   been omitted and partly incorporated in the Introduction. Only
   technical changes have been made.

2 When I speak of state activities (both capitalist and non-
capitalist) I refer to those activities the basic function of
which is technico-administrative (e.g. schools, hospitals,
public works, industries, etc.). I disregard, therefore, those
activities the basic function of which is the domination of the
working class. I owe this distinction to Marta Harnecker, 'Los
Conceptos elementales del materialismo historico', Siglo XXI editores, Mexico, 1971, p. 115. Harnecker derives this distinction, correctly in my opinion, from the following quotation:
'On the one hand, all labour in which many individuals co-
operate necessarily requires a commanding will to co-ordinate and
unify the process, and functions which apply not to partial
operations but to the total activity of the workshop.... On the
other hand,... this supervision work necessarily arises in all
modes of production based on the antithesis between the labourer,
as the direct producer, and the owner of the means of production.... Just as in despotic states, supervision and all-round
interference by the government involves both the performance of
economic activities arising from the nature of all communities,
and the specific functions arising from the antithesis between
the government and the mass of the people.' 'Capital', vol. III,
pp. 383-4. Therefore, the double nature of the work of supervision and management — one of the basic points in the analysis
of the nature of the new middle class — is extended also to the
state the role of which is both oppression of the working class
(this oppression is carried out both in the economic, in the
political, and in the ideological spheres) and technico-
administrative. A. Giddens is therefore mistaken when he thinks
that Marx's writings are ambiguous on this point: 'Marx's
writings on the nature of the relationship between the state and
the society contain a definite ambiguity. On the one hand, the
theory is advanced that the state is nothing more than the vehicle whereby the interests of the dominant class are realized:
the state is merely an agency of class domination. On the other
hand, many of Marx's comments upon the capitalist state show an
awareness of the administrative significance of the state as the
"supervisor" of the operations of capitalist production.' See
'The Class Structure of the Advanced Societies', London, 1973, p.
51.

3 To avoid confusion, let me state clearly that a *production* process is not necessarily a *productive* process. In a capitalist
economic structure considered at the concrete society level there
is a variety of *production* processes, all dominated by the *capitalist productive process*.

4 As Marx says in vol. II of 'Capital', p. 97, the state, in these
instances, 'performs the function of the industrial capitalist'.
Engels, in his 'Anti-Dühring', (New York, 1970, p. 303) goes as
far as saying that 'At a certain stage of development even this
form [i.e. the form of exploitation taking place in the joint-
stock company, G.C.] no longer suffices; the official representative of capitalist society, the state, is constrained to take
over their management.' 'But neither the conversion into joint-
stock companies nor into state property deprives the productive
forces of their character as capital' (ibid., p. 304).

5 'Resultate...', p. 4.
6 See E. Mandel, 'Marxist Economic Theory', New York, 1968,
   p. 306.
7 'Resultate...', p. 64. See also 'The German Ideology', pp.
   70-4, and 'Theories of Surplus Value', vol. 1, pp. 407-9.
8 The domination element is often forgotten in the Marxist
   literature. According to Godelier ('Rationality and Irrationality in Economics', London, 1972, pp. 226-7), 'for Marx, a
   commodity is an object characterized by two properties
   (a) It is useful; and so, a commodity has a use value
   (b) It is exchanged in a certain proportion for goods of a
       different utility. It has an exchange value, and has this
       only because it first of all has a use value for someone
       else.'
   But a capitalist commodity is not only the unity of a use
   value and an exchange value (and not necessarily an object, it
   can be also a service), but also a unity in which the latter
   element dominates the former.
9 Objections could be raised against the thesis that the product
   of a non-CSA is a commodity on grounds that such a product,
   inasmuch as produced in the absence of competition, cannot have
   an exchange-value. What Engels says in the 'Anti-Dühring' (see
   note 4 above) should be enough to take care of this objection.
10 The differences are, of course, much more important that this
   similarity. What has been said above about the limitation of
   production by consumption applies also to a society in transition to socialism as, e.g. in the contemporary People's
   Republic of China. There too there is production of commodities in which, just as in the products of the non-CSA, the use
   value dominates the exchange value (see C. Bettelheim, 'Revolution culturelle et organisation industrielle en Chine', Maspero,
   1973, p. 73). But, of course, the non-CSA is subordinated to a
   capitalist production process, production relations, and productive forces (in short, to a capitalist economic structure)
   and to a superstructure which is dominated by the capitalist
   one. The production of commodities in China, on the other hand,
   is immersed in a totally different structural and superstructural (i.e. socialist) context.
11 See G. Armanski, Staatliche Lohnarbeiter — Teil der Lohnarbeit-
   erklasse oder neue Mittelklasse? Zum Verhaltnis von Akkumulation des Kapitals und unproduktiver Arbeit, in 'Probleme des
   Klassenkampfs', no. 14, 1974. I would like to stress that what
   follows is not meant to be a 'well balanced' review of Armanski's article. The many positive aspects as well as some points
   of disagreement are not dealt with here. I only want to present
   his central thesis, which is also shared by other authors (even
   though there are of course differences among them), as a convenient starting point for my discussion.
12 This lack of analysis of several production processes leads
   Armanski to assert that, to study the capitalist mode of production, one should start from the division of the social product,
   division which originates different forms of wages (Armanski,
   op. cit., p. 5). Since there is complete identity between product and production process and since there is a lack of

analysis of the various production processes and thus of the
various production relations making up a concrete capitalist
economic structure, the state employees' wages are differenti-
ated in terms of distribution and not of production relations.

13 See N. Poulantzas, 'Political Power and Social Classes',
    London, 1973, especially chapter III. What I just said, how-
    ever, should not be taken to mean that I subscribe completely
    tó all of Poulantzas' theses. I have serious doubts, e.g.,
    concerning his treatment of classes.

14 Armanski, op. cit., p. 20.

15 See I Comitati Unitari di Base, in 'I Quaderni di Avanguardia
    Operaia', no. 6, Sapere Edizioni, Milan, 1973, pp. 35 and ff.

16 A similar point, even though the theoretical basis differs from
    mine, is made, with reference to the West German technicians,
    by H. Lange, L. Peter, F. Deppe, De technies-wetenschappelijke
    revolutie en de theorie van be 'nieuwe arbeidersklasse',
    'Sunschrift 14', Nijmegen, 1970, pp. 13-28.

Chapter 3

ON DIALECTICAL DETERMINATION:
AN OPERATIONAL DEFINITION

One of the central problems a social scientist has to solve in analysing a society is that of the relationship connecting its various elements. General agreement seems to exist on the two following propositions:

1 every instance contributes to the overall determination of society, and

2 every instance, in turn, is determined by the global structure. However, this scheme, useful as it is inasmuch as it stresses the interaction among the various instances of a society, and the need to see this interaction as taking place within a definite global structure, is insufficient because it omits to mention the existence of a determinant instance and thus disregards the analysis of what type of relationship ties this instance to the other; determined instances.

In this chapter (1) I will submit a concept of dialectical determination, the aim of which is first of all to discuss the nature of the determinant instance/determined instances relation and, secondly, to present this relation split up into several statements, which can be seen also as logical steps in the analysis, in order to facilitate its use in concrete inquiries. Since my aim is to intervene in the class struggle waged on the ideological plane at the present stage of capitalist development (late capitalism), all the examples used to support my argument will be taken either from the capitalist system or from a system in transition between capitalism and socialism. (2)

1 The concept of dialectical determination I would like to submit can be conveniently subdivided into the following three statements. First, *the determinant instance* (e.g. the economic structure vis-à-vis the superstructure, or within the economic structure, the mode of production vis-à-vis the production process, or within the mode of production, the production relations vis-à-vis the productive forces or the distribution relations, etc.) *determines the determined instances* (superstructure, production process, productive forces, distribution relations, etc.) *in the sense that the former calls into existence the latter as a condition of its own existence.* For example, the capitalist economic structure, being based as it is on antagonistic production relations

(exploitation) generates class antagonism. Since this class antagonism would jeopardize the reproduction of the capitalist economic
structure itself, a political and ideological structure is generated
which limits the class struggle.(3)

   2   Second, *the determined instances react upon (modify) the*
determinant instance, i.e. the determinant instance is over-
determined by the determined instances. For example, conflicting
economic interests generate class struggle not only on the economic
but also on the political and ideological level. This class
struggle makes it necessary to introduce production processes (the
non-capitalist state activities) which are basically different from
the capitalist production process. I.e. the provision of services
by the state is made possible by the redistribution of surplus
value among all the non-productive sectors of the economy but is the
outcome of the struggle waged by the working class. The provision
of these services (e.g. schools, hospitals etc.) takes place according to laws which are basically different from the laws moving the
production of capitalist commodities.(4)   Thus, the capitalist economic structure is modified, due to the class struggle (the determined instance) in the sense that this structure is not a pure capitalist structure any more but is the unity (a unity in domination)
of several production processes and production (and distribution)
relations.

   As another example of determination and overdetermination we can
choose a society in transition between capitalism and socialism. If
we consider the case of the People's Republic of China, we see that
here we have an economic structure which is not a capitalist one any
longer but which is not a completely socialist one yet. Therefore,
there is a constant clash within China between two basic types of
ideology: the socialist one which puts politics in command, i.e.
politics above production (and therefore stresses moral rather than
material incentives) and the essentially capitalist one (revision-
ist) which gives priority to production and which therefore fosters
a type of accelerated development along capitalist lines.(5)   Which
type of development predominates at different times depends upon a
series of factors the analysis of which is extremely complex. The
important point, as far as overdetermination is concerned, is that
the predominance of the economicist type of ideology will tend to
push China's economic development in the capitalist direction, while
the predominance of the socialist ideology will tend to foster a
socialist type of development.

   We will see in a while how the concept of overdetermination I am
submitting differs from Althusser's.(6)   What has to be stressed at
this juncture is that my concept of overdetermination implies the
following three points.

   2A   The determined instances have a relative autonomy vis-à-vis
the determinant instance; but it is the determinant instance which
circumscribes the degree of autonomy.(7)   This explains why, e.g. as
far as classes are concerned, the old and the new middle classes
defined in terms of production relations, can give rise to similar
ideologies and political practices.(8)   However, there are limits
beyond which the ideology of the middle classes cannot go, and these
limits depend upon the production relations identifying these
classes. For example, the new middle class, as long as it remains

such, i.e. as long as it is not completely proletarianized,(9) cannot develop a full proletarian consciousness.

How are we to explain the determined instance's relative autonomy? Take, for example, the case of computer-science. Its rise and development is tied to a series of factors, not only economic but also political (e.g. the needs of the military establishment) and ideological,(10) i.e. to the development of capitalism in all its aspects and not only in its economic aspects. Thus, computer science is determined, in the strict sense of the word, by the capitalist economic structure (determination in the last instance) but in reality is determined by the development of the whole system and by each of its component parts. This holds for all determined instances. The concept of dialectical determination submitted here serves to explain only the determination in the last instance, the (mediated) tie between the economic structure and each of the determined instances. This tie, this relation is never immediate because in reality each component part of society is determined by all other instances, both determinant and determined. It is this fact which explains the determined instances' relative autonomy. If there were an immediate relation (determination) between the two orders of instances there could be no autonomy at all. On the other hand, if all instances were given a status of complete autonomy, i.e. if we would deny the determinant role which reverts only to one instance, we would leave the realm of Marxism to fall into the structuralist morass.

2B The dominant role can revert also to the determined instance and not only necessarily to the determinant instance; but it is the latter which determines which determined instance has a dominant role. Let us take, as an example, the definition of social classes. Classes are defined always in economic, in political, and in ideological terms. The economic definition of classes (in terms of production relations) is always the fundamental one but a complete definition can be given only when also the two other dimensions are considered. Thus, we define the working class, in terms of production relations, as all those agents of production who (a) do not own the means of production, (b) are exploited (or economically oppressed) and (c) perform the function of labour.(11) This is a purely economic definition. However, a complete definition, a definition of the proletariat — I use the two terms 'working class' and 'proletariat' to emphasize the difference between a purely economic definition and a complete definition of this class — encompasses also the ideological (i.e. we consider as proletariat only that part of the working class which has developed a proletarian class consciousness) and the political (i.e. we consider only that part of the working class which has joined the worker's party and which joins in proletarian political practice). Thus, e.g. that part of the working class known as labour aristocracy cannot be considered as part of the proletariat, even though from the point of view of production relations it belongs to it, because its ideology and political practices are essentially petit bourgeois. In other words, in this case it is the ideological and the political which are dominant; the determinant role, on the contrary, reverts always to the economic. Moreover, it is the economic which determines which instances must be dominant. In the case of the labour aristocracies, it is the economic which assigns the dominant role to the ideological because the capitalist economic structure, in order to reproduce itself, needs to introduce within the working class several types of bourgeois ideologies (e.g. reformism). It can be useful to notice that, just as the determinant instance need not be also the dominant one, so the principal (determinant) aspect of a contradiction between two socio-economic systems, co-existing and struggling in a concrete society (i.e. in a society in transition), i.e. the contradiction between two types of production relations, need not be the dominant aspect of that contradiction. Thus, in China, where two types of production relations (the capitalist and the socialist production relations) co-exist and struggle, the principal (determinant) contradiction (or the principal aspect of the contradiction between capitalism and socialism) is the one between capitalist and socialist production relations. However, the dominant aspect of the contradiction is on the political plane. The dominant instance is the political. As C. Bettelheim says: 'Le déplacement de l'aspect principal de la contradiction entre les rapports sociaux capitalistes et les rapports sociaux communistes s'effectue de façon inégale. L'instauration de la dictature du prolétariat amène un déplacement de l'aspect principal de la contradiction en faveur du prolétariat sur le plan politique et partiellement sur le plan idéologique, mais, dans une première phase, tant que le prolétariat ne domine pas au sein de chaque unité de production, ce déplacement ne s'accomplit pas ou que très partiellement dans le base économique elle-même, c'est-à'dire au niveau des rapports de production'.(12)

2C   There can be either correspondence or contradiction between the determinant and determined instances. There is correspondence when the determined instance helps in the process of reproduction of the determinant instance and there is contradiction when the opposite is the case. For example, capitalist production relations determine capitalist distribution relations in the sense that the former cannot exist without the latter. Thus, the income of the working class is tendentially equal to the value of labour power. As long as this is the case, we have correspondence. A situation of contradiction arises when sectors of the working class (the labour aristocracies) get an income (for the above mentioned ideological and political reasons) higher than the value of their labour power. (13)   It is important not to mistake relative independence for contradiction. For example, in the nineteenth century in England, while the bourgeoisie dominated economically and politically, the dominant ideology was aristocratic in nature. From this analysis, P. Walton and A. Gamble draw the following conclusion: 'which is to say that the bourgeoisie dominates at every level of practice',(14) a conclusion which, of course, destroys the claim that the superstructure is relatively autonomous. However, the fact that the dominant ideology is that of the aristocracy and that it serves the interests of the bourgeoisie, does not mean that the bourgeoisie dominates on the ideological level. Under certain conjunctural circumstances the bourgeoisie must leave the ideological domination to another class (in this case the aristocracy) in order to retain economic and political domination. In this particular case, we have both correspondence and relative independence. Correspondence because the ideological helps reproduce the capitalist production relations. Relative independence because this correspondence takes place through a type of ideology which is not capitalist but aristocratic in nature. What Walton and Gamble do here is, 1, to conflate the concepts of correspondence and relative independence, 2, to mistake a situation of correspondence for one of relative independence and, 3, to deduce that there is, in this specific case, no relative autonomy.

3 We now come to the third point of the concept of dialectical determination: *the determinant instance sets the limits of variation to its own overdetermination*. To return to our example concerning the labour aristocracies: production relations determine distribution relations, i.e. wages are tendentially determined by the value of labour power. Some sectors of the working class (the labour aristocracies) can be paid wages higher than the value of their labour power and conceivably also wages higher than the value of the commodities produced by them.(15) However, this could never be the case for the working class as a whole, i.e. the distribution of the new value produced could never go beyond certain limits set by the production relations because there would be then no expropriation of surplus value, i.e. no profits, and thus no capitalist production relations.

The point on limits of variation should not be interpreted as if the determinant instance always manages to keep its own overdetermination 'within limits'. The contradiction between determinant and determined instances can lead to a point where the latter becomes one of the basic causes of change in the former (of course, in this case we have an antagonistic contradiction). It is not my intention to attempt even a sketch of a theory of the limits of variation. All I can do here is to indicate a possible point of departure for such an analysis by referring to Godelier's valuable contribution. (16) Godelier starts from a distinction between contradictions within a structure and contradictions between two structures. As far as the latter is concerned, Godelier examines the contradiction between production relations (determinant instance) and productive forces (determined instance). Godelier points out that, as far as the development of capitalism goes, at the beginning of this system there is correspondence between productive forces and production relations, in the sense that capitalist production relations develop a certain type of productive forces (collective worker, big business) and in turn these capitalist productive forces reinforce the capitalist production relations. At a later stage of capitalist development, however, the emphasis shift to the contradiction between these two elements of the capitalist economic structure. Finally, the development of the productive forces will not possibly be contained any longer within the limits imposed by the capitalist production and distribution relations (objective conditions for a revolutionary change) and will thus cause a radical change in the latter. *Thus, it is the determined instances (productive forces, class struggle, etc.) which ultimately cause a transition to a different type of society.*(17)

One fundamental criticism that can be moved to Godelier is that his approach focuses exclusively on the structural aspects of social change, thus disregarding the obvious fact that it is the agents of production who are the carriers of certain (antagonistic) social relations and who, therefore, become the agents of social changes. (18)   The contradictory nature of the capitalistic production relations (exploitation) is reflected in the consciousness of the working class (given certain objective and subjective conditions).   When the capitalist production relations and the capitalist productive forces become contradictory, the objective conditions are created for the conscious, organized class struggle, for the struggle for the establishment of new production relations.(19)   While the capitalist production relations are defended by the capitalists and their allies, the new socialist production relations are fostered by the proletariat and its allies.   Thus, the class struggle originates from the contradictory nature of capitalism.   The only way to destroy the old production relations is a social revolution, i.e. a conscious and organized process of destruction of the capitalist system.   However, in such a system, it is impossible for the socialist production relations to come to life and to develop themselves up to the point when they become dominant (as the capitalist production relations did within the feudal system).   The characteristic element of the transition from capitalism to socialism is that the socialist production relations can be established only through a revolution which gives first of all the political and ideological power to the proletariat.   There is no automatic transition from capitalism to socialism at the level of the economic, contrary to the case of the transition from feudalism to capitalism, where the capitalist production relations grew spontaneously within the feudal system and anticipated the capitalist political and ideological relations.   In the transition between capitalism and socialism it is the political and the ideological that get ahead of the economic, it is the determined instances (political and ideological socialist relations) which, by being the conditions for the existence of the determinant instance (the socialist economic or production, relations) reinforce the latter until when it becomes dominant.

From what was said above, it follows that the fact that the productive forces explode the limits of variation imposed by the production relations and thus are one of the causes of a radical change in the latter, does not imply that the determinant role reverts to the productive forces.   F. Engels, in his 'Anti-Dühring'(20) assigns the determinant role to the productive relations.   To do otherwise, would mean to fall into technological determinism (21) and to consider both the productive forces and the production process under capitalism as neutral.(22)

Historically, we see that the development of the capitalist production relations (stage of formal subordination of labour to capital) precedes that of the capitalist productive forces (stage of real subordination of labour to capital).   This fact, however, cannot be taken as an argument for assigning the determinant role to the production relations.   Such a role must be assigned on grounds of a logical and not of an historical analysis.   This remark calls for a few comments on the difference between these two types of analysis. As C.J. Arthur puts it:

> the order of categories used to correctly analyse a given system, e.g. capitalism, may be different from the order in which they appeared in history.   This raises also the whole issue of the

relation between systematic and genetic analysis. It is one thing to say how the elements of a given structure condition one another: it is another thing to explain whence the elements arose and combined. Neglect of this distinction in Marxist theory may lead to technological determinism, extrapolating unwisely from such Marxian dicta as 'the handmill gives you society with the feudal lord, the steammill society with the industrial capitalst'. In this example, it should be understood that 'gives' is not an historical category but a structural one · about the social relations appropriate to a given productive force. The analysis of the *change* from a feudal to a capitalist mode of production is another question altogether.(23)

Given, thus, that there is a difference between logical and historical analysis, the question arises as to the nature of the connection between them. Engels deals with this problem:

> The logical method of treatment ... is nothing else than the historical method, only divested of its historical form and disturbing fortuities ... (it) will be nothing else than the mirror image of the historical course in abstract and theoretically consistent form.(24)

In commenting on the above-given quotation, Walton and Gamble point out that historical analysis would then account for the 'accidents'. This is true, provided that 'accidents' are not considered as chance elements: if this were the case, Walton and Gamble would be right in saying that dialectics would not be of much help in analysing historical situations. 'Accidents' are to be understood as those factors which account for the discrepancy, the displacement between the rhythm of development of the various instances of a concrete society considered at various conjunctural moments. These accelerations and delays are the way the relative independence of the determined instances, so far examined only from the point of view of logical analysis, manifests itself in historial analysis.

Thus, while the two types of analysis are different, and yet related to each other in the above mentioned way, they both share one basic characteristic: they both must be dialectical. This fact, in turn, throws light on the fact that there cannot be one type of analysis without the other. A logical analysis (an analysis of determination, overdetermination, correspondence and contradiction, etc. among the various instances of society) can be carried out at various levels of abstraction, while an historical analysis is always an analysis on the conjunctural level. An historical analysis, then, is the logical outcome (on the most concrete level of abstraction) of an analysis (logical) which necessarily must begin on the highest level of abstraction only to descend to more and more concrete levels. This is why there can be no historical analysis without a logical one. But the reverse is also true. Without a study of history, a logical analysis falls immediately in ideological traps such as the functionalist-structuralist view in Sociology or the 'homo-economicus' in Economics.

Thus, the distinction between historic and logical analysis is a valid and a necessary one (there is no contradiction but complementarity between the two of them because both are aspects of scientific inquiry),(25) but also an insufficient one. An inquiry, once it has been carried out, must also be presented in the most suitable and convenient way. As Marx says:

> Of course the method of presentation must differ in form from
> that of inquiry. The latter has to appropriate the material in
> detail, to analyse its different forms of development, to trace
> out their inner connection. Only after this work is done, can
> the actual movement be adequately described. If this is done
> successfully, if the life of the subject-matter is ideally ref-
> lected as in a mirror, then it may appear as if we had before
> us a mere a priori construction.(26)

M. Nicolaus, in his Foreword to the 'Grundrisse' (27) provides an
excellent discussion of the 'question of where to begin' and how
Marx worked out this problem. Whereby Marx starts the 'Grundrisse'
with a discussion of material production (also as a reaction against
Hegel's idealism), just as he had started 'The German Ideology', at
the end of the 'Grundrisse' he reaches the conclusion that the
starting point must be the commodity: '(the commodity) is a beginning which is at once concrete, material, almost tangible, as well
as historically specific (to capitalist production); and it con-
tains within it (is the unity of) a key antithesis (use value v.
exchange value) whose development involves all the other contradictions of this mode of production'.(28)

To conclude, we must distinguish between logical and historical
analysis. Moreover, once the inquiry (which depends on both types
of analysis) has been completed, a distinction must be made between
method of presentation and method of inquiry. The question concerning which instance plays the determinant role cannot thus be decided
on account of the method of presentation or of historical analysis
but only on account of a logical analysis.

Having cleared the way through some theoretical confusion, i.e.
having decided on what ground the production relations must be
assigned a determinant role, we can now provide some concrete
examples of how productive forces are determined by production relations. Let us examine here, as an aspect of the productive forces,
both the technical and the economic conditions of production. Let
us first of all see how the capitalist production relations and the
socialist production relations determine their respective conditions
of production and after this has been done, let us see what is the
effect of either correspondence or contradiction between a certain
type of production relations and certain conditions of production.

The capitalist relations of production determine their own economic conditions in the sense that, for example, at the beginning of
capitalism, primitive accumulation is necessary; or that there is a
continuous tendency to increase the size of the enterprise. That
the socialist production relations determine their own economic conditions (29) can be seen from the fact that at the beginning of
socialism (the transition period) primitive accumulation, even
though still necessary, plays only a seconday role. The primary
role goes to the socialist development of the productive forces,
i.e. to the process of political and ideological development of the
masses; or from the fact that emphasis is placed on the development
of small and medium-sized enterprises. The same holds for the
technical conditions of production. Capitalist production relations
need fragmentation of tasks, subordination of manual to intellectual
work, restricted management, etc. Socialist production relations

require de-fragmentation of tasks, parity of manual and intellectual work, mass management, etc. Moreover, under capitalism the
introduction of new techniques depends on their profitability;
under socialism this obstacle has been removed: here new techniques
are introduced when they save labour, when they make labour safer,
more pleasant, etc. It should be noticed that in China the removal
of this obstacle has opened up an immense field to innovations.
These examples could be multiplied.

We have seen above, in point 2C, that there can be either correspondence or contradiction between the determinant and the determined
instance, in this case between the production relations and the productive forces. We have seen also that correspondence means fos-
tering the reproduction of the determinant instance and that contradiction means the opposite. Let us now provide an example taken
from a society in transition to socialism, Socialist China. Here,
even if the socialist production relations are dominant, there exist
still capitalist production relations in the sense that there relations disappear only slowly *and only when all the conditions for
their existence have disappeared*. If the technical and economic
conditions of production (productive forces) develop in a capitalist
direction (e.g. a capitalist technical division of labour) then
there is contradiction between the socialist production relations
and the productive forces and, conversely, correspondence between
the capitalist production relations and the productive forces. Thus,
those production relations with which the development of the productive forces is in correspondence tend to be reinforced while those
production relations (the socialist ones, in this example) with
which the nature of the productive forces is in contradiction tend
to be weakened. (30)

We can now draw four important conclusions from what was said
above. *First,* there must be correspondence between the determinant
and the determined instances in order for the former to reproduce
itself on an enlarged scale. However, correspondence and contradiction must be understood here in qualitative, rather than in quantitative terms, i.e. in terms of their nature. For capitalism, e.g.
the contradiction which emerges between the capitalist productive
forces and the capitalist production relations is summarized in the
formula: social nature of production, private appropriation.
Second, the relation between the determinant (productive relations)
and the determined instances (productive forces) can be and usually
is one of both correspondence and contradiction. The question is,
then, which aspect is dominant. For the capitalist stage of real
subordination of labour to capital, e.g., the element of contradiction is given (as a constant aspect of the capitalist system) by the
above-mentioned formula (social nature of production, private
appropriation). The element of correspondence, however, (the collective worker, the big industry, etc.) still dominates the contradictory element because the basic function of the productive forces
is still that of helping in the enlarged reproduction of the system.
Third, a distinction must always be made between a logical and an
historical analysis. As far as the latter is concerned, relative
autonomy means that the determinant and the determined instances do
not have to come to life and to disappear at the same time (displacement). We have seen that the capitalist production relations

come to life first, and capitalist productive forces only later. Also, the capitalist production relations tend to disappear first (in a transitional society) while the capitalist productive forces (and also the bourgeois ideology, etc.) tend to disappear later. Since the capitalist production relations have not completely disappeared yet, i.e. since the socialist production relations are not yet fully dominant in the first period of transition to socialism, and since the conditions for the existence of the capitalist production relations still exist, there is always the possibility that the capitalist production relations might gain strength if the conditions of their existence are not constantly stifled. One of the points Althusser fails to make clear in his discussion of determination is the distinction between concepts which apply to a logical (structural, in his case) analysis and concepts which apply to an historical analysis.(31)   Relative autonomy, e.g., is a concept which applies to both types of analysis while displacement applies only to historical analysis and domination applies only to logical analysis.

Fourth, we can now understand why a technique can never be neutral. According to Bettelheim (32) this is so because it is always the class struggle which determines the nature of the technique by imposing transformations on both the process of production and on the production relations. This is certainly so, but this is how and not why it happens. Just as there is a difference between explaining the need capital has for self-expansion (the why, i.e. M -M') and explaining how this happens, i.e. through which mechanism (i.e. competition), in the same manner there is a difference between explaining *how* a technique is never neutral (i.e. through class struggle) and *why* this must be so. A technique can never be neutral because its nature (as an element of productive forces) is either in correspondence or in contradiction with the dominant production relations; or, to be more precise, because its dominant element is either in correspondence or in contradiction with the dominant production relations.(33)

Before proceeding to the examination of some of the characteristics of the concept of dialectival determination submitted here, it might be useful to hint at the relationship between this concept and the concept worked out by Althusser and his school. It should be obvious to the reader that the present discussion owes much to Althusser, Balibar, Godelier, Poulantzas, etc. But it should be also obvious that there are points of radical difference. Some of these points have already been hinted at and others will emerge shortly.(34) Rather than going into a lengthy comparison between Althusser's concept of determination and mine, I will limit myself to stressing the different content given to the word overdetermination. For Althusser

> there is not one simple economic contradiction, that between
> the forces and relations of production, which governs everything.
> There is rather a multiplicity of contradictions existing at all
> levels of the social formation and constituting a kind of hier-
> archy of effectivity within it. So, determination is never
> simple but always complex and multiple, and this Althusser en-
> capsulates in the concept of overdetermination.(35)

For Althusser, then, overdetermination means complex or multiple

determination in which the economic plays a primary role.   In my
approach, on the other hand, a distinction is made between the way
the determinant instance determines the determined instances (the
former calls into existence the latter as a condition of its own
existence) and the way the determined instance determines the determinant instance (the former reacts upon, modifies the latter).
It is only in this latter case that we can talk of overdetermination.   In short, while determination means to call into existence
as a condition of its own existence, overdetermination means to
react upon, to modify.   The reason behind giving two different names
to the relationship between the determinant and the determined
instance, according to whether this relationship is considered from
the point of view of the former instance (determination) or of the
latter instance (overdetermination), is that Marx himself while
using the same word (determination) both to indicate determination
and to indicate overdetermination, gives this word two completely
different meanings.   The following two lengthy quotations are necessary to prove the point:

> The relations and modes of distribution thus appear merely as the
> obverse of the agents of production.   An individual who partici-
> pates in production in the form of wage labour shares in the pro-
> ducts, in the results of production, in the form of wages.   *The
> structure of distribution is completely determined by the struc-
> ture of production.*   Distribution is itself a product of produc-
> tion, not only in its object, in that only the results of produc-
> tion can be distributed, but also in its form, in that the speci-
> fic kind of participation in production determines the specific
> forms of distribution, i.e. the pattern of participation in dis-
> tribution.... In the shallowest conception, distribution appears
> as the distribution of products, and hence as further removed
> from and quasi-independent of production.   But before distribu-
> tion can be the distribution of products, it is, 1, the distribu-
> tion of the instruments of production, and, 2, which is a further
> specification of the same relation, the distribution of the mem-
> bers of the society among the different kinds of production....
> If it is said that, since production must begin with a certain
> distribution of the instruments of production, it follows that
> *distribution* at least in this sense *precedes and forms the pre-
> supposition of production,* then the reply must be that production
> must indeed have *its determinants and preconditions* which form
> its moments.(36)

Thus, the economic structure is not a simple but a structured unity
(37) in which only one element, the production relations, play the
determinant role in the sense that it determines the other elements
as conditions of its own existence.   The determined elements, in
turn, determine the determinant element but in quite a different
way, as the following quotation shows clearly:

> The conclusion we reach is not that production, distribution,
> exchange and consumption are identical, but that they all form
> the members of a totality, distinctions within a unity.... A
> definite production thus determines a definite consumption, dis-
> tribution, and exchange as well as *definite relations between
> these different moments.*   Admittedly, however, *in its one-sided
> form,* production is itself determined by the other moments.   For

example, if the market, i.e. the sphere of exchange, expands, then production grown in quantity and the division between its different branches becomes deeper. A change in distribution changes production, e.g. concentration of capital, different distribution of the population between town and country, etc. Finally, the needs of consumption determine production. (38)

We can now close this chapter by examining some of the characteristics of the concept of dialectical determination submitted here. First of all, *the concept submitted here encompasses both simple and dialectical determination*. To understand why this is so and what is the difference between the two types of determination, let us start from the remark that dialectical determination implies always a relationship of domination (either the determinant or the determined instance must play the dominant role) while the reverse is not true. In a relationship of determination there is always an instance to which the dominant role reverts. However, a relationship of domination does not imply a relationship of determination. To prove this point, let us consider the capitalist production process. Marx has shown (39) that, 1, this process is the unity of the labour process and of the surplus value producing process, and, 2, that the latter process dominates the former. Synthetically, it can be said that the capitalist production process is the unity in domination of the labour process and of the surplus value producing process. Neither one of the two aspects of the capitalist production process determines the other.

We have said that the capitalist production process is the unity in domination of the labour process and of the surplus value producing process. If we now examine the outcome of this process, i.e. the capitalist commodity, we see that it too, 1, is the unity of a use value and of an exchange value, and, 2, is a unity in which the exchange value dominates the use value. Thus, we can say that the capitalist commodity is the unity in domination of use value and exchange value. It can be seen that the fact that the capitalist commodity is the unity in domination of use value and exchange value is due to the fact that the capitalist production process is the unity in domination of the labour process and of the surplus value producing process. The relationship between the producing process and the product is a relationship of *simple determination*. In this kind of determination there is no reacting of the determined instance upon the determinant instance (no overdetermination) and thus no relative autonomy, no domination of one instance over the other, and no correspondence or contradiction between the determinant instance (the production process) and the determined instance (the commodity). That we are dealing with determination in this particular case can be seen from the fact that the direction of domination within the production process (the surplus value producing process dominates the labour process) determines the direction of domination within the commodity (the exchange value dominates the use value). That we are dealing with *simple* determination can be seen from the fact that a capitalist production process turning out a commodity in which the use value would dominate the exchange value is totally inconceivable. Thus, we should not make the mistake of reducing all determinations to simple (or mechanical) determinations, a mistake made both by economicists and by spontaneists when dealing with the relationship between economic structure and superstructure (or class struggle). But we should not make the opposite mistake either, that of considering all determinations as dialectical ones. Only concrete study can tell us with what type of determination we are dealing in each single case. But the important point, for the purpose of our discussion, is that we can now prove our statement to the effect that the concept of determination submitted here encompasses both simple and dialectical determination. When we must limit our analysis only to the determined instances as a condition for the existence of the determinant instance, we deal with the concept of simple determination. When we extend our analysis also to encompass the aspects of overdetermination and of the limits of variation, then we deal with dialectical determination. It follows, therefore, that economicism is not considering a relationship of determination as simple when its nature is such, but it is considering only the first aspects (determination) when also the other two aspects (overdetermination, limits of variation) should be considered.

Secondly, *dialectical determination,* as here defined, is a theory of both correspondence and contradiction among the various instances of a society and thus *is a theory both of stability, of change within the boundaries of the existing society, and of revolutionary change.* As long as, and inasmuch as there is correspondence between the determinant and the determined instance, the latter is one of the conditions for the reproduction of the former; the extent to which it does so is directly related to a situation of complete correspondence. If, on the other hand, there is contradiction between the two elements of the relation, the determined instance becomes one of the conditions for the determinant instance's suppression. When contradictions push the determined instances beyond the limits of variation compatible with the determinant instance, then the conditions are created for a revolution within the determinant instance.

To put it differently, my notion of dialectical determination makes it possible to explain stability, change within the boundaries of an existing society, and revolution. A stable system is one in which there is correspondence between the determinant instance (the economic structure, and within it the relations of production) and the various determined instances. In this case the former instance is constantly reinforced. Overdetermination goes in the direction of reinforcement. Particularly important is of course the question whether there is correspondence or not between the production relations and the productive forces. Correspondence in this region implies also correspondence with all other determined instances in the sense that contradictions between structure and superstructure cannot arise as long as the productive forces are in correspondence with the production relations. Thus, a stable society is not one in which there is no movement but one in which the movement of all its various parts goes in the direction of strengthening the basic nature of that society (production relations). Capitalism, in the period of correspondence between productive forces and production relations, was a stable system but also a vigorously expanding one. The concept of stability, just as that of change, should be a dynamic one.(40)

But this situation of correspondence is bound to come to an end. Production relations and productive forces enter in contradiction. The conditions are thus created for a contradictory relation between structure and superstructure:

But even if this theory, theology, philosophy, ethics, etc. comes into contradiction with the existing relations, this can only occur because existing social relations have come into contradiction with existing forces of production. (41)

We have then a situation of change, which can be both change within the boundaries of the existing society (e.g. from individual to monopoly capitalism), or to put it concisely, overdetermination within the limits of variation; or revolutionary change, due to the accumulation of contradictions which makes possible for the determined instances to explode those limits of variation. (42)   As E.J. Hobsbawn puts it:

It is equally important that internal tensions may sometimes be reabsorbed into a self-stabilizing model by feeding them back as functional stabilizers, and that sometimes they cannot. Class conflict can be regulated through a sort of safety-valve...but sometimes it cannot. The state will normally legitimize the social order by controlling class conflict within a stable framework of institutions and values, ostensibly standing above and outside them... and doing so perpetuate a society which would otherwise be riven asunder by its internal tensions....Yet, there are situations when it loses this function. (43)

The concept of dialectical determination submitted above encompasses all these various possibilities.

One additional point should be made in order to avoid misunderstandings. We have talked about revolutionary change as an explosion, as the breaking of the limits of variation due to the accumulation of contradictions. In reality, if we left the matter here, we would identify the revolutionary change with its ruptural moment. (44)   Not only, but we would dangerously underestimate the subjective element, the agents making the revolution. (45)   It is basically through the proletariat, as the organized revolutionary force, that these contradictions explode those limits, that a sudden qualitative change in the basic structure of a society takes place. And a revolutionary change, as the change fostered by the proletariat and its vanguard, starts of course far earlier than the ruptural point and continues much longer after it.

NOTES

1 First published in 'Amsterdams Sociologisch Tijdschrift', vol. 2, no. 2. Only technical changes have been made.

2 For the justification of the terms 'system in transition between capitalism and socialism', see the exchange of letters between P. Sweezy and C. Bettelheim in 'Monthly Review': P.M. Sweezy, Czechoslovakia, Capitalism and Socialism, October 1968; C. Bettelheim, On the Transition between Capitalism and Socialism, March 1969; P.M. Sweezy, Reply, March 1969; C. Bettelheim, More on the Society of Transition, December 1970; P.M. Sweezy, Reply, December 1970.

3 We talk about limits to, and not abolition of, the class
   struggle. 'Dire par exemple qu'il existe une classe ouvrière
   dans les rapports économiques, cela implique *nécessairement*
   une place spécifique de cette classe dans les rapports idéolo-
   giques et politiques, *même* si cette classe peut, en certain
   pays et en certaines périodes historiques, ne pas avoir une
   "conscience de classe" propre ou une organisation politique
   autonome. Cela veut dire que, dans ces cas, même si elle est
   fortement contaminée par l'idéologie bourgeoise, son existence
   économique se traduit par des *pratiques politico-ideologiques
   matérielles spécifiques,* qui percent sous son "discours"
   bourgeois.... Tout cela, qui s'inscrit en faux contre la série
   d'idéologies de l'"intégration" de la class ouvrière, veut dire
   finalement une chose: que point n'est besoin d'une "conscience
   de classe" propre et d'une organisation politique autonome des
   classes en lutte *pour que la lutte des classes ait lieu, dans
   tous les domaines de la realite sociale.'* N. Poulantzas, 'Les
   Classes sociales dans le capitalisme d'aujourd'hui', Paris,
   1974, p. 19.
4 The reader will recall the following points: 1, the capitalist
   economy is made up as far as the production process is concerned, not only by one production process (the pure, productive, capitalist production process as analysed by Marx) but by
   a number, a variety of production processes; 2, these production processes are all dominated by the pure capitalist production process, the way this domination reveals itself being different for each dominated production process; 3, each production process should be analysed at a certain level of abstraction, e.g. at the highest level of abstraction we consider only
   the pure capitalist production process.
5 For the difference between capitalist and maoist economics, see
   J.G. Gurley, Capitalist and Maoist Economic Development, in
   'America's Asia', New York, 1971; for the relationship between
   types of economic development and ideological and political
   struggle, see E.L. Wheelwright and B. McFarlane, 'The Chinese
   Road to Socialism', New York, 1970, and C. Bettelheim,
   'Revolution culturelle et organisation industrielle en Chine',
   Maspero, 1973.
6 See L. Althusser, 'For Marx', Vintage Books, 1970 and L.
   Althusser and E. Balibar, 'Reading Capital', London, 1970.
7 The other side of the coin is of course the relative dependence
   among instances. As P. Walton and A. Gamble put it: "we must
   avoid thinking that contradictions arise only because of uneven
   development between structures that otherwise are quite independent of one another." 'From Alienation to Surplus Value',
   London, 1972, p. 132.
8 See, e.g., N. Poulantzas, 'Political Power and Social Classes',
   London, 1973; On Social Classes, 'New Left Review', no. 78, and
   'Les Classes sociales dans le capitalisme d'aujourd'hui'.
   Poulantzas' writings are certainly an important contribution to
   the field. However, his treatment of the new middle class at
   the level of production relations seems to me to be unsatisfactory. A criticism of Poulantzas' approach will be found in the
   following chapter.

9   For the concept of proletarianization of the new middle class, see chapters 1 and 4.

10 See, e.g., M. Janco and D. Furjet, 'Informatique et Capitalisme', Maspero, Paris, 1972.

11 The terms 'economic oppression' and 'function of labour' are defined in chapter 1, section III.

12 Bettelheim, 'Révolution culturelle...', p. 108.

13 This is an example of non-antagonistic contradictions. For the difference between antagonistic and non-antagonistic contradictions, see Mao Tse-Tung, On Contradiction, 'Four Essays on Philosophy', Foreign Languages Press, Peking, 1966. Failure to see the connection between production and distribution in the proper light can lead to serious theoretical mistakes, as e.g. in the case of Habermas. 'For the time that Marx was writing, Habermas concedes that the subsystem of work was "embedded" in the institutional framework. But he argues that in modern capitalism the two have become autonomous. There no longer exist any reactions on the development of the productive forces, because modern industry has discovered a new source of surplus value that is independent of the labor time of workers. This is the "scientisation of technology". This is the *reductio ad absurdum* of Habermas' argument, for as we shall show, it removes production from man as such. It suggests that the process of production can be understood without the system of distribution.' Walton and Gamble, 'From Alienation to Surplus Value', p. 46.

14 Ibid., p. 138.

15 This is what R. Davies seems to argue in The White Working Class in South Africa, 'New Left Review', no. 82, pp. 40-59.

16 See M. Godelier, 'Rationality and Irrationality in Economics', London, 1972, pp. 77 and ff.

17 We abstract, of course, from the subjective conditions for a revolution.

18 [Of course, to recognize the obvious fact that it is the agents of production, in their role as carriers of economic, political and ideological relations, who are the agents of social change, does not mean to fall into the false dilemma of historical determinism vs. the role of personality in history.] See V.I. Lenin, What the 'Friends of the People' Are and how they fight the Social Democrats, 'Collected Works', vol. 1, Moscow, 1963, p. 159.

19 In what follows, I rely heavily on M. Harnecker, 'Los Conceptos elementales del materialismo historico', Siglo SSI Editores, sixth edn, 1971, pp. 150-60 and p. 224.

20 Quoted in Walton and Gamble, 'From Alienation to Surplus Value', p. 60.

21 See M. Nicolaus, The Unknown Marx, in R. Blackburn, ed., 'Ideology in Social Science', Vintage Books edn, 1973, p. 324. Yet H. Braverman, while rightly rejecting technological determinism, assigns the 'primacy' to the forces of production. See 'Labor and Monopoly Capital', Monthly Review Press, 1974, p. 19.

22 See Poulantzas, 'Les Classes sociales...', p. 247.

23 C.J. Arthur, 'Introduction to K. Marx and F. Engels, 'The German Ideology', New York, 1970, p. 33.

24 Marx-Engels, 'Selected Works', 1, p. 339, quoted in Walton and

Gamble, op.cit., p. 73.

25   Thus E.P. Thompson creates a false problem when he states 'I
     do not see class as a "structure", not even as a "category",
     but as something which in fact happens (and can be shown to
     have happened) in human relationships.' See 'The Making of
     the English Working Class', Penguin edn, 1963, p. 9.

26   K. Marx, 'Capital', vol. 1, International Publishers, New York,
     1967, p. 19. The mirror, however, is a very special one. It
     'reflects' reality with various degrees of comprehensiveness
     and with an increasing richness of details, depending upon which
     level of abstraction is being used for the analysis.

27   Penguin edn, 1973, pp. 35 and ff.

28   Ibid., p. 38.

29   All the examples used to support my argument are taken from
     Bettelheim, 'Revolution culturelle...', passim.

30   A similar point is made by A. Gorz with reference to the capit-
     alist mode of production: 'it is the technology of the factory
     which imposes a certain technical division of labor, which in
     turn exacts a certain type of subordination, of hierarchy and
     of despotism... one does not see how "collective appropriation"
     of the means of production carrying the imprint of *this* techno-
     logy would be able to change anything in the regimen of the
     factory, in the "stuntedness" and the oppression of the workers.'
     A. Gorz, Their Factories and our People, 'Telos', no. 18, Winter
     1973-4, p. 152.

31   In fact, Althusser does not even deal explicitly with the dif-
     ference between the two types of analysis.

32   'Revolution culturelle...', p. 93.

33   Moreover, these remarks allow us to tackle the question of what
     is rational and what is not in a certain society or system.
     From the point of view of the system, the determined instances
     which are in contradiction with the determinant instance are
     irrational. A proletarian, revolutionary ideology is irrational
     in the context of a capitalist society. It can become again
     rational, from the point of view of the capitalist system, *only*
     if subordinated to it, e.g. only if de-natured into reformist
     ideology. The view that considers technology as a neutral,
     external factor of development tends to slip into even serious
     Marxist works as, e.g., 'Accumulation on a World Scale'. As
     S. Amin himself remarks in the afterword to the second edition,
     p. 595, 'I did not pay enough attention to this theme, for I
     tended to see technology as a factor external to the problem, an
     independent variable. Within this narrow context it is clear
     that the (obligatory) choice of modern industries amounts merely
     to copying the technology of the West of today, following the
     example set in their time by Japan and Russia. However, we are
     beginning to see that technological research follows a direction
     that accords with the requirements of the system, and therefore,
     that technique is not an external factor.'

34   My differences with Althusser's scheme have only to a small
     extent originated from the discussion around his work. E.g.
     'Marxism Today' has published a highly critical article by John
     Lewis (January and February 1972), a Reply by Althusser (October
     and November 1972) and several comments on the Lewis-Althusser

debate (by G. Lock, June 1972; by J. Oakly, September 1972; By
M. Cornforth, May 1973; by C. Gray, July 1973; by D.D. Grant,
August 1973; and by J. Wrigley, September 1973). Unfortunately,
in all these articles, the whole question of the dialectical
nature of determination is almost completely disregarded. The
reader should also consult N. Geras, Althusser's Marxism: an
Account and Assessment, 'New Left Review', January-February
1972, no. 71, pp. 57-68; A. Glucksmann, A Ventriloquist Structuralism,'New Left Review', March-April 1972, no. 72, pp. 68-92;
and R. Blackburn and G. Stedman (eds), 'The Unknown Dimension',
Basic Books, 1972, pp. 365-87.

35 Geras, op.cit., p. 71.

36 Marx, 'Grundrisse...', pp. 95 and 97. Emphasis mine.

37 This is often forgotten since usually the determinant role is
assigned to the economic structure *tout court* rather than only
to the production relations. Actually, even this formulation is
not correct because, within the relations of production, only
one element (the ownership element) plays the determinant role.
The proof of this last statement will have to be postponed to
another occasion.

38 Ibid. pp. 99-100. These are only two examples but actually the
'Grundrisse', only to mention one work by Marx, is full of
similar examples. Just to mention one more example, concerning
overdetermination 'consumption certainly *reacts* on production
itself' (p. 283, emphasis added).

39 See chapter 1.

40 Thus we are miles away from bourgeois economics' favourite
interpretations of stability both as stagnation and as a situation characterized by various 'vicious circles'. For this
latter interpretation, see R. Nurkse, 'Problems of Capital
Formation in Underdeveloped Countries', Oxford University Press,
1967.

41 K. Marx and F. Engels, 'The German Ideology', New York, 1970,
p. 52.

42 What is said above should not of course be confused with G.
Myrdal's mechanical concept of 'cumulative movement' as set
forth in 'Asian Drama', New York, 1968, vol. III, pp. 1843 and
ff.

43 Karl Marx's Contribution to Historiography in R. Blackburn
(ed.),'Ideology in Social Science', 1973, p. 280.

44 This is one of the limits of Althusser's structuralism. See
N. Geras, Marx and the Critique of Political Economy, in R.
Blackburn (ed.), 'Ideology in Social Science', p. 303.

45 The relation between the agents and the system is a complex one
and must be left aside for the time being. As an indication of
the direction in which the answer should be sought, I will only
say that, 1, the reproduction of the system and the reproduction
of the agents are two distinct but related phenomena; 2, the
relation is one of determination in which the reproduction of
the system plays the determinant role, and, 3, it is in the
determined instance, as already mentioned above, that the more
immediate causes of a revolution must be sought. On the relation between agents and positions, see the following chapter.

Chapter 4

REPRODUCTION OF SOCIAL CLASSES AT THE LEVEL OF PRODUCTION RELATIONS

INTRODUCTION

In this chapter (1) I will examine the production and reproduction of classes under capitalism. Given the complexity of the problem I will limit my inquiry to the economic definition of social classes and, within this, to the definition in terms of production relations. This restriction should not be interpreted as meaning that social classes are identifiable only in economic terms, or only in terms of production relations. Classes must be defined in economic, political, and ideological terms. However, given the determinant role reverting to the economic,(2) it is essential that we start our inquiry on the production and reproduction of social classes at the level of production relations,(3) i.e. on the highest level of abstraction.

I THE NATURE OF THE PRODUCTION RELATIONS UNDER CAPITALISM

To begin with, let us examine the capitalist production relations. In chapter 1, I have shown that such relations bind together three elements; two types of agents of production and the means of production;(4) further, that these relations should be regarded from three different points of view: from the point of view of ownership, from the point of view of the expropriation of labour, and from the point of view of the function performed;(5) and that these three elements have a different connotation according to which point of view is chosen. When we consider the *ownership element*, we distinguish between the owner, the non-owner of the means of production and the means of production themselves. As far as the owner is concerned, it is important to distinguish between the legal and the real economic ownership of the means of production. While at the beginning of capitalism (stage of formal subordination of labour to capital, i.e. basically, before the advent of big industry) the individual capitalist enjoys both legal and real ownership, with the advent of the joint stock company, and under monopoly capitalism, we witness a dissociation between the legal ownership (which goes to the stockholders) and the real, economic ownership, i.e. the power

to dispose of the means of production and of the labour power
(which goes to the managers, or at least to the top managers). Also,
as Poulantzas (1974) has rightly point out, under conditions of
monopoly capitalism, the real ownership is fragmented in the sense
that it does not revert to an individual capitalist any more but to
a (small) number of managers (Braverman: 1973, 258-9).

As far as the non-owner is concerned, the distinction between
ownership and possession is of the utmost importance. Possession is
here defined as the ability to set in motion and to govern the means
of production. While in the stage of formal subordination of labour
to capital possession is characteristic of the individual worker, in
the stage of real subordination of labour to capital it is the collective worker,(6) thus including also technicians, engineers, etc.,
who have the possession of the means of production. In the stage of
monopoly capitalist and especially after the Second World War possession reverts to the collective labourer on an international
scale.(7)   In other words, while the ownership of the means of production (whether legal or economic, whether fragmented or not)
characterized the capitalists, the possession of the means of production is a characteristic of the non-owner (whether individual or
collective labourer), i.e. of the worker.

Let us now briefly consider the *expropriation of labour element.*
From this point of view we distinguish between those who are expropriated of surplus labour (which under capitalist takes character-
istically, but not exclusively, the form of surplus value) and those
who expropriate that surplus-labour, and the means of production.(8)
Only productive labourers produce surplus value, i.e. are expropriated of surplus labour in the form of surplus value. However, the
productive labourers are not the only labourers to be expropriated
of surplus labour. This is so because capitalism is not limited to
a single production process (the typical, productive one) but includes several production processes, all of them dominated by the
typical capitalist (productive of surplus value) production process.
For example, the commercial worker (as with all workers in the circulation sphere), being unproductive, does not produce surplus
value and thus, strictly speaking, cannot be exploited. However, he
is expropriated of surplus labour and is therefore economically
oppressed.(9)   From this analysis we can draw the following conclusion. First, it would be mistaken to identify the collective worker
with the production worker. In fact, while it is true that under
monopoly capitalism, for example, the productive worker is typically
a collective worker, the existence of the collective worker within
the commercial enterprise shows that the reverse is not true. Secondly, it would be a mistake to use the concept of productive worker
as a dividing line between the working class and the middle class.
Within the working class we find both productive and unproductive
workers, both workers who are exploited and workers who are economically oppressed.(10)

We come now to *the functional element;* that is to the function
performed by the agent of production (a term to be defined shortly)
within the production process. We have seen in chapter 1, that a
function always has a double content, i.e. a technical and a social
content. The former is determined by the technical division of
labour within the capitalist production process; in other words,

each agent must perform a certain function with certain technical
characteristics which depend on the technical division of labour.
The latter is determined by the social division of labour, by the
basic social division of labour which is also found within the
enterprise, within the capitalist production process: the division
between the labourer and the non-labourer. Under monopoly capitalism, the social content of a function is given by the fact that an
agent either performs the function of the collective worker or the
global function of capital.(11) The double nature of a function
derives from the fact that the capitalist production process is
never just a technical process but is based on production relations
which are antagonistic in nature. This process is based on the
division between the labourer and the non-labourer. Therefore, an
agent, by simply taking part in this process, automatically falls in
either one of these two categories and thus performs either the
function of the (collective) worker — and thus is a labourer — or
the (global) function of capital — and thus is a non-labourer. It
should be clear that performing one function excludes performing the
other in the sense that when an agent performs both functions, he
can never perform them *at the same time*. Moreover, whenever an
agent performs both functions, whenever, i.e. his working day is
divided into two parts, the one devoted to one function and the
other to the other function, the ratio between these two parts of
the working day is never a constant but changes over the time. This
is an important point for the understanding of the process of proletarianization of the new middle class (one characteristic of a section of this class being that of performing both functions), a process which I have interpreted as the devaluation of this class'
labour power and which, for most of those who perform both functions, means also the tendential disappearance of the global function of capital vis-à-vis the function of the collective worker.(12)

Essential for an understanding of what has been said so far and
of what will follow, are the following two points. First of all,
the capitalist production process is the unity of the labour process
(the combination of concrete labour and the means of production considered as necessary additions to labour-power; the combination
which creates the use value) and of the surplus value producing process (the combination of the abstract labour and of the means of
production considered as depositories of materialized labour; the
combination which creates the exchange value). Since under capitalism, the creation of exchange value dominates the creation of use
value (production for profit) we can say that *the capitalist produc-*
tion process is the unity in domination of the labour process and of
the surplus value producing process. Secondly, it should be remem-
bered that as far as the agents participating in this process are
concerned, they must be regarded not only from the point of view of
the ownership of the means of production and of the expropriation of
labour (whether in the form of surplus value or not), but also from
the point of view of the (social) function they perform within this
process. To repeat, an agent participating in the capitalist production process either performs the function of labour or the function of capital. Under monopoly capitalism, we talk of function of
the collective worker and global function of capital, since these
two opposite functions are not performed individually any longer,

but collectively.

At this point, a criticism of Poulantzas (1974) is in order.
According to Poulantzas (1974: 126 and ff) in the first stage of
capitalist development (formal subordination of labour to capital)
the possession of the means of production reverts to the direct producer (the proletariat). The second stage of capitalist development
(real subordination of labour to capital) is characterized by the
dispossession of the proletariat; possession going to the individual
capitalist. Finally, the stage of monopoly capitalism is characterized by the separation of legal and real ownership, a phenomenon,
the importance of which is not comparable to the dispossession undergone by the proletariat during the transition to the second stage of
capitalism. I disagree with Poulantzas on this point. In fact, the
possession, which in the first stage reverts to the individual labourer, in the second stage reverts to the collective labourer and
not to the capitalist.(13) The collective labourer is made up of
of all those agents who take part in the labour process, i.e. as
Marx says, not only by those who do manual work but also by those
who work 'with their head', by the technicians, engineers, etc. In
this stage, the individual capitalist performs both the work of co-
ordination and unity of the labour process (and inasmuch as he performs this function he is part of the collective worker) and the
work of control and surveillance (and this is the function of capital, his function as capital personified). In the stage of monopoly
capitalism the socialization of the labour process, which began with
the transition from the individual to the collective labourer but
had not yet reached the work of co-ordination and unity of the
labour process, proceeds further in the sense that this work is no
longer the task of the individual capitalist (as long as he was
performing this function, he was not a capitalist), but has become
the task of a collective; an ensemble of agents. Since the Second
World War this process of socialization of the labour process has
proceeded further in the sense that the collective labourer is no
longer restricted to a single country but extends itself to several
countries.(14)

My second point of disagreement with Poulantzas is that the characterizing distinction (at the level of production relations) between individual and monopoly capitalism is not the separation of
the legal from the real ownership of the means of production (if
this were the case Poulantzas would be right in considering this
fact as of secondary importance compared to the changes taking place
in the capitalist production process and dividing the first from
the second stage of capitalist development). The characteristic
element is that under monopoly capitalism we witness a similar process of socialization of the capitalist production process as far
as the surplus value producing process is concerned. In other
words, the characteristic element, in terms of production relations,
is the advent of the global capitalist, i.e. of that complex structure which performs collectively what, under individual capitalism,
used to be the function of the capitalist as capitalist. The work
of control and surveillance, the despotic organization of labour
under capitalism, is now performed by a great number of agents many
of whom do not even own the means of production. The so called
'managerial revolution' is only the ideological reflection of these

changes taking place at the level of production relations and in
this sense is much more than 'verbiage'. Thus, the changes taking
place under monopoly capitalism are just as important as those dividing the two stages of individual capitalism. From the point of
view of the labour process, these changes are a further socialization of this process in the sense that (a) the work of co-ordination
and unity of the labour process is also a collective task, and (b)
the collective labourer has now become an international entity. As
far as the other aspect of the capitalist production process is concerned, the surplus value producing process, these changes are even
more momentous since they are nothing less than the birth of the
global capitalis, i.e. the socialization of the surplus value producing process, the delegating of the work of control and surveillance to a complex structure, to a number of agents, the great majority of whom do not even own the means of production.(15) Moreover,
at the present stage of imperialism, we witness a parallel tendency
toward the inter-nationalization of the global capitalist.

It will have become clear by now that the inadequacies of Poulantzas' approach derive from a lack of analysis of (a) the capitalist
production process as the unity in domination of the labour process
and the surplus value producing process, and (b) the functional element at the level of production relations. His approach, makes it
impossible for him to see that:

1 There is a basic difference, at the level of production relations, between the second and the third stage of capitalist
   development (i.e. the birth of the global capitalist). The surplus value producing process as well as the labour process becomes socialized in shifting from the second to the third stage
   of capitalism.
2 The individual capitalist, inasmuch as he performs the work of
   co-ordination and unity of the labour process, is not performing
   his function as capital personified but is actually a labourer.
   (16)

Poulantzas' theoretical shortcomings also have other consequences.
Let us list some of them:

3 He talks about the domination of the capitalist production relations over the labour process (1974: 240) whereas it is the surplus value producing process which dominates the labour process.
   There are two levels of analysis, the production process and production relations. In chapter 2, section III, I have analysed
   some of the dangers inherent in confusing these two levels of
   analysis. Here I will only mention that *the concept of productive labour, while essential for an understanding of the capitalist production process, is of less importance for an analysis
   of the capitalist production relations and thus for an economic
   identification of classes at this level of abstraction.* This is
   also true at lower levels of abstraction when, for example, we
   also define classes ideologically and politically. In the explanation of ideological tendencies among the various types of
   agents of production who do not have the real ownership of the
   means of production, the functional element is just as important,
   and may be even more important, that the expropriation of labour
   element (whether in the form of expropriation of labour, as for
   the unproductive worker, or in the form of expropriation of

value, as for the productive worker).(17)

4   He fails to distinguish between the function of labour and the
    function of capital and thus does not identify classes in terms
    of the functions performed as well.(18)

5   He fails to see that an agent, when performing the function of
    capital, cannot, at the same time, also perform the function of
    labour (Poulantzas: 1974, 244).

6   He considers that all those who do not own the means of produc-
    tion and yet, in my terminology, perform the global function of
    capital are exploited because expropriated of surplus labour.
    He thus does not see that there is a difference between the ex-
    propriation of surplus labour of those who perform the function
    of labour (either exploitation or economic oppression) and of
    those who perform the function of capital.(19)

7   He cannot see the 'managerial revolution' as the ideological
    reflection of the advent of the global capitalist.(20)

8   He lacks a theory of the proletarianization of the new middle
    class, a theory which in my opinion rests on the two pillars of
    (a) devalutaion of labour power and (b) disappearance of the
    global function of capital. For example, according to Poulant-
    zas, the new middle class swings from a proletarian to a bour-
    geois position (1974: 318). This is so, but in the absence of
    an analysis of the changes taking place at the level of produc-
    tion relations, one cannot tell which parts of the new middle
    class are liable to tend towards the proletariat and which to-
    wards the bourgeoisie.(21)

II   REPRODUCTION OF CLASSES

The previous discussion of capitalist production relations was
necessary in order to introduce the concept of *position,* the first
of the two key concepts governing the reproduction of social classes.
We have seen that the capitalist production process is the unity in
domination of the labour process and of the surplus value producing
process. This process rests on definite production relations, i.e.
on the relations which bind together the agents of production and
the means of production. We have also seen that these production
relations are to be regarded from the point of view of ownership,
expropriation of labour, and function performed. If we now consider again the capitalist production process, we see that technically speaking it is subdividable in a great number of fractional
units the technical content of which is strictly determined by the
technical division of labour. Let us call these *fractional units
(regarded from the technical point of view) operations.* But, since
the production process rests on production relations, it follows
that each of the fractional units making up the production process
has not only a technical but also a social content, a content determined by the production relations. In the case of pure capitalist
production process, each fractional unit is characterized by the
fact that it, 1, either rests on the real(22) ownership of the means
of production or not; 2, either rests on the expropriation of surplus value or not; and, 3, either rests on performing the function of labour or on performing the function of capital. Let us

call these *fractional units, regarded from the point of view of both
their technical and their social content, positions.*(23)   Of course,
a position can imply the performance of more than one operation.
The same technical division of labour in two different enterprises
originates the same structure of operations but not necessarily the
same structure of positions.   As we will see, the latter structure
is also determined by political and ideological factors.   We can now
introduce the second key concept, that of the *agent of production.*
Everybody, simply by taking part in the capitalist production process, i.e. simply by occupying a certain position, automatically becomes a carrier of the capitalist production relations.   In other
words, an agent of production simply by filling a position, 1,
either owns (really, economically) the means of production or not;
2, either is expropriated of surplus value or not; and, 3, either
performs the function of capital or the function of labour.
    We can now introduce the following point: *the reproduction of
social classes depends on the reproduction of both positions and
agents of production.*   This fundamental thesis, already advanced by
Poulantzas (1974) will be one of the major themes to be worked out
in this chapter.   Before doing this, however, a few comments on the
relation between the three aspects of the production relations are
in order.   It was said above that social classes are to be defined
in economic, political and ideological terms.   However, the economic
definition, which in order to avoid being categorized as an economicist, I call economic identification, is determinant.   In turn,
within the economic identification, the identification in terms of
production relations is determinant.   Therefore, agents of production are distributed into classes, at the level of production relations, because each position has elements of the capitalist production relations.   To this, however, we must also add that within the
capitalist production relations, there is only one element which is
determinant, namely the ownership element.   A detailed proof of this
point will have to be left to another occasion.   Here I can simply
point out that ownership of the means of production also implies
performing the function of capital and expropriating surplus labour
(typically, surplus value).   Vice versa, the non-ownership of the
means of production implies the performing of the function of labour
and being exploited (or economically oppressed).   Thus, in terms of
production relations, we can define the capitalist as the agent of
production who occupies a position resting on ownership of the means
of production, on the expropriation of surplus value and on the performance of the function of capital.   Concisely, we can identify the
capitalist as the owner/non-labourer/exploiter.   Conversely, we can
identify the working class as the non-owner/labourer/exploited.   But
a relationship of determination also implies that the determined
instances (in this case the functional and expropriation elements)
are relatively autonomous and, thus, can be either in correspondence
or in contradiction with the determinant instance (the ownership
element).   There is correspondence in the identification of the capitalist and of the working class.   The middle classes, however are
only identifiable in terms of contradiction.(24)   For example, there
are positions, and thus agents, identifiable in terms of non-
ownership of the means of production and the performance of the
global function of capital.   This is one section of the new middle

class. At the lower steps of the hierarchical scale we find the
foreman or the line supervisor. But there are other positions, much
higher in the hierarchy, the nature of which is the same (in terms
of production relations) as that of the foreman. Let us quote an
example provided by J. Rasmus:

> Following this escalating conflict throughout 1971-72 and the
> explosion of 'mini-strikes' which began to occur, GM, in an
> effort to deal with the rising discontent over job cuts and
> working conditions, turned in a major way in early 1973 towards
> Job Enrichment. GM hired former Harvard Business School profes-
> sor Stephan Fuller, made him a vice-president, and gave him a
> staff of 144 plus a mandate to develop and experiment in what-
> ever manner was required to help quell the discontent and pro-
> tect and expand productivity.(25)

The nature of these agents' function is typically a capitalist one,
the devising of new forms of work of control and surveillance.
These agents, then, do not own the means of production and yet perform the global function of capital; they perform *collectively, in
a hierarchical structure, and in new forms,* what used to be the
function of the individual capitalist. The application of the
studies carried out by these agents, i.e. by all these 'social
scientists' engaged in the field of Job Enrichment as well as in
most other forms of worker participation, is to delegate aspects of
the global function of capital, which were previously carried out by
agents performing only this function (i.e. the foreman, the management at various levels, etc.) to the collective labourer, to those
agents who up to now were performing only the function of the collective worker (while at the same time not giving these agents any
fragment of real ownership). Let us again quote Rasmus extensively:

> Whatever the focus or emphasis, a central principle of job
> enrichment, like all participation arrangements, is to give
> workers greater *responsibility* for production without any real
> independent control over the decisions that determine that pro-
> duction. In turn, this greater responsibility serves to further
> subjugate workers more completely to the production process. By
> assuming responsibility for production, workers must also assume
> responsibility for eliminating work stoppages, absenteeism,
> tardiness, turnover, etc. In practical terms this leads to
> workers encouraging each other to work harder, recommending the
> elimination of 'unnecessary' jobs and the replacement of old jobs
> with new machinery and equipment, and workers disciplining each
> other. The work force as a group thus carries out voluntarily
> a number of tasks that were previously the responsibility of the
> management. By assuming these traditional management tasks
> workers become integrated into management functions without shar-
> ing in increased productivity and profits....This is strengthened
> by the fact that the integration reduces the need for traditional
> forms of line-management (i.e., foremen, line supervisors, etc.)
> which otherwise would be needed to force workers into accepting
> what they now voluntarily carry out themselves. But this elimi-
> nation of traditional line-management forms of authority is only
> apparent....In reality management's authority to ensure output
> and employee discipline is not diminished at all — it is only
> removed at a higher level in the management hierarchy where it is

exercised 'indirectly' so long as workers carry out their res-
ponsibilities to management's satisfaction.(26)

It should be mentioned that under monopoly capitalism (and especially after the Second World War) *some aspects of the global
function of capital are delegated by the company's management to
employers' associations and federations.* For example, in The Netherlands, one of the most important associations, the General
Employers Federation (in reality an association) provides a number
of services to its member firms such as assistance in collective
bargaining, 'legal advice, assistance in the establishment of company personnel departments, research in the personnel and labour
relations problems of a particular company, expert counsel on time
and motion study techniques, and guidance in the development of
modification of job classification systems, piece rates, and the
introduction of new work methods'.(27)   All these services are
among the *new, modern forms taken by the global function of capital;*
aspects of the work of control and surveillance when carried out
globally. The nature of this function does not change, whether it
is performed by the company's management or by experts hired by
employers' associations or federations. As far as the member companies are concerned, i.e. within their capitalist production process, these services are sophisticated ways to perform globally the
work of control and surveillance, to perform the global function of
capital. Aside from political and ideological considerations (which
vary from country to country), the establishment of employers'
federations has first of all an economic reason. On an aggregate
scale, the capital saved by the individual employers, which can thus
be devoted to productive use, is greater by far than the costs of
maintaining employers' federations. Moreover, more efficiency is
achieved in performing the global function of capital because the
federations can pull together top experts who might be out of the
reach of the individual firms and because even those companies
which could afford to have top experts on their pay-rolls might not
need their services full time (as in the case of renewal of collective agreements).

Thus, those agents who actually carry out the work of control and
surveillance within the enterprise are not the only agents performing the global function of capital. We can mention at least five
other ways of performing this function, either within or without the
enterprise; either by actually carrying out this function or by devising new ways of improving control and surveillance.

1 The study of the reorganization of the capitalist production process (in its aspect as surplus value producing process) within
   the enterprise. We think here, for example, of the various planning departments with the task of devising job enrichment
   schemes, etc. on which enough has been said above.
2 The delegation of the study of the capitalist production process's reorganization to organizations outside the enterprise.
   Clearly, the social significance of these agents' activity does
   not change simply because of this branching out.
3 The delegation of the performance of some aspects of the global
   function of capital to organizations outside the enterprise.
   Again, what said above about employers' organizations (e.g. about
   collective agreements) should suffice. Clearly, the activity of

these organizations falls under point 2 above as well as point 5 below.

4 The study, within the enterprise, not of the reorganization of the capitalist production process (in order to improve directly control and surveillance and thus labour's productivity) but of the 'conditions under which the workers may best be brought to co-operate in the scheme of work organized by the industrial engineer' (Braverman: 1974, 140). Clear examples are personnel and labour relations departments.

5 The delegation of the study (referred to in point 4 above) to institutions, organizations, etc. outside the enterprise. We can mention, again, the employers' organizations.

For sake of completeness, we should mention the indirect role played by the school system, especially at the highest educational level, in effecting improvements in the work of control and surveillance. Of course, here we cross the frontier into the realm of ideology, the study of which goes beyond the frame of this study. It is worthwhile, however, to quote at some length what H. Braverman has to say on this point:

The necessity for adjusting the worker to work in its capitalist form, for overcoming natural resistance intensified by swiftly changing technology, antagonistic social relations, and the succession of the generations, does not therefore end with the 'scientific organisation of labor', but becomes a permanent feature of capitalist society. As a result, there has come into being, within the personnel and labor relations departments of corporations and in the external support organisations such as schools of industrial relations, college departments of sociology, and other academic and para-academic institutions, a complex of practical and academic disciplines devoted to the study of the worker. Shortly after Taylor, industrial psychology and industrial physiology came into existence to perfect methods of selection, training and motivation of workers, and these were soon broadened into an attempted industrial sociology, the study of the work place as a social system.

The cardinal feature of these various schools and the current within them is that, unlike the scientific management movement, they do not, by and large, concern themselves with the organisation of work, but rather with the conditions under which the worker may best be brought to cooperate in the scheme of work organised by the industrial engineer. The evolving work processes of capitalist society are taken by these schools as inexorable givens, and are accepted as 'necessary and inevitable' in any form of industrial society. The problems addressed are the problems of management: dissatisfaction as expressed in high turnover rates, absenteeism, resistance to the prescribed work pace, indifference, neglect, cooperative groupd restrictions on output, and overt hostility to management. As it presents itself to most of the sociologists and psychologists concerned with the study of work and workers, the problem is not that of the degradation of men and women, but the difficulties raised by the reactions, conscious and unconscious, to that degradation. It is therefore not at all fortuitous that most orthodox social scientists adhere firmly, indeed desperately, to the dictum that their

task is not the study of the objective conditions of work, but only of the subjective phenomena to which these give rise: the degrees of 'satisfaction' and 'dissatisfaction' elicited by their questionnaires (Braverman: 1974, 139-41).
One should not overestimate, however, the weight of these institutions and theories as ideological means to force the workers to conform to the capitalist conditions of work. Socioeconomic conditions still play the principal role (Braverman: 1974, 146).

As implied in what said above, the other section of the new middle class, is made up of all those positions, and thus agents, identifiable in terms of non-ownership of the means of production and the performance of both the global function of capital and the function of the collective worker. I have dealt with this sector of the new middle class in some detail in chapter 1 and I will not repeat my analysis. The important conclusion to be drawn from these remarks is that, since there can be contradiction among the three elements of the capitalist production relations, an identification of classes must always take place in terms of all these three elements. And this is also the reason why the production relations are a relation among relations; a relation of determination between the relation of ownership on one side and the expropriation and functional relations on the other.

Having said this, we can now start the analysis of the reproduction of classes, at the level of production relations, under capitalism. First of all, we have to answer the following question: why is it necessary to distinguish between positions and agents of production and why do we have to consider both elements? If we only considered the agents, disregarding the positions occupied by them, we would make at least two major mistakes. First, we could not identify those agents in terms of production relations and thus could not collocate them in the social structure in terms of these relations. We would then be left in the position of the bourgeois sociologist who classified 'people' in terms of income (distribution relations, which are determined by production relations), status (ideological relations, determined by production and distribution relations), etc. Secondly, as Poulantzas correctly points out, we would identify the social system with the people making it up. Reasoning *ad absurdum,* even if all the capitalists suddenly disappeared, the nature of the capitalist system would remain the same because new people would fill up those positions conferring the quality of being a capitalist (1974: 37). On the other hand, if we considered only the production and reproduction of positions, so disregarding the agents we could not see structure 'as a product of human praxis' (Veltmeyer: 1974-5, 416) and would ultimately miss the connection between theory and praxis.

This, then, is why we must consider both positions and agents of production. But why do we have to distinguish them? The reason is that the production and reproduction of positions is not the same as that of the agents of production. The thesis I submit is that the production of positions is determinant vis-à-vis the production of agents. This thesis, to be proved in the following pages, should not be confused with the viewpoint which minimises the importance of the agents of production for social change. I have shown in chapter 3 that the categories 'determinant', 'determined', etc. are only

logical categories which do not correspond necessarily to the
weight a determinant or a determined instance might have when it
comes to social action. Actually, it is always 'the determined
instances (productive forces, class struggle, etc.) which ultimately
cause a transition to a different type of society'.

My thesis, then, is that the reproduction of positions and of
agents are not the same, and yet they are related by a relationship
of determination where the reproduction of positions plays the
determinant role. To prove this point, I will first examine what
determines the reproduction of positions and what determines the
reproduction of agents and why the two do not necessarily coincide.
Let us start with the reproduction of positions. It is clear, on
the basis of what has been said above, that there is a relationship
between positions and the capitalist production process.(28) As
long as no changes take place within the production process, we can
assume, as a first approximation, that the technical and social content of positions will remain unchanged. But this is only a first
approximation. Positions can undergo changes, for example, they can
be either fragmented or grouped together, as a result of political
and ideological factors. In a situation of heightened class
struggle, the internal organization of the production process can
be changed in order to strengthen capital's ideological domination
over the employees. In chapter 1, I have mentioned the case of an
Italian plant in which,

> after the 1968-69 wave of strikes, out of 318 employees a hier-
> archical structure of 115 'heads' was created, 20 of whom at the
> managerial level. We can assume that these 20 only perform the
> global function of capital while the remaining 95 perform both
> functions. It is interesting to note that this structure has a
> two-fold function: (a) it makes the performance of the global
> function of capital more efficient, and (b) since these 'heads'
> introduce the enterprise's ideology within the employees, it is
> also a powerful ideological instrument and thus indirectly a way
> to increase productivity.

Bettelheim makes a similar point in discussing the subdivision of
a production process into several technical units. He says:

> However, this 'subdivision' entails also some *social determin-
> ants:* in fact it can change according to the dominant ideologi-
> cal and political relations. This subdivision can be, e.g., a
> way to consolidate either the domination of the producers or
> that of the non-producers over the division of labour within a
> given economic unit. The 'technical units' thus perform essen-
> tially technical functions (of material production), but also
> political (of management) and ideological functions; consequently,
> the conditions in which they are subdivided are far from being
> 'purely' technical (Bettelheim: 1970, 150).

The same phenomenon is emphasized also by C.W. Mills concerning the
office work:

> The individual employee is a unit in an administrative hierarchy
> of authority and discipline....Within this hierarchy and mass,
> he is classified by the functions he performs, but sometimes
> there are also 'artificial' distinctions of status, position, and
> above all title. These distinctions, to which Carl Dreyfuss has
> called attention, arise on the one hand from the employee's need

to personalise a little area for himself, and on the other, they may be encouraged by management to improve morale and to discourage employee's 'solidarity'....A great deal has been made of such distinctions. Carl Dreyfuss alleged that they form 'an artificial hierarchy' which is encouraged and exploited by the employer who does not wish solidarity (Mills: 1951, 209).

However, these 'artificial' distinctions in so far as they are reflected in different wages for agents whose labour power's value is more or less the same, will tend to disappear. To quote C.W. Mills again:

> Only a sophisticated employer strongly beleaguered by attempted unionisation might see reason to make conscious use of prestige gradations. It would not, however, seem the most rational choice he might make and, in fact, the employer has been the leader of job descriptions and personnel work that reduce the number of complex functions and break down the work and hence lower pay (Mills: 1951, 211).

But let us for the moment exclude political and ideological factors and consider only changes in positions which are strictly determined by changes in the capitalist production process. One major source of change is the introduction of new techniques. This introduction will bring about a change in the technical content of functions and perhaps in their social content as well. This can be seen most clearly in the case of the proletarianization of a part of the new middle class, i.e. of those agents of production who, in terms of the function performed, perform both the global function of capital and the function of the collective worker. The devaluation of these agents' labour power, through the reduction of their labour from a skilled to an average level, usually takes place through the fragmentation of tasks, etc. (a change in the technical nature of the function performed). This reduces responsibility and originates a tendency to lose control and surveillance over other agents; a reduction (or loss) in the global function of capital (a change in the social nature of the function performed). It follows that changes in the technical division of labour also modify the social division of labour within certain positions.(29) The introduction of new techniques can thus bring about changes in the expropriation of surplus labour element and even in the ownership element if, for example, a lesser fragmentation of real ownership is required.

Let us now consider the reproduction of agents. Generally speaking, a member of the working class remains a member of the working class. The same applies to both the middle classes and to the capitalist class. In other words, there is no built-in mechanism that causes an upward (or downward) general movement from one class to another. Apart from social mobility (an exception as far as the agents are concerned, and of no significance as far as the positions, and thus changes in that structure, are concerned) the social structure under capitalism is fairly rigid. This means that the only way for an agent to change places in the social structure (again, vertical mobility aside, the only aspect on which, for obvious ideological reasons, bourgeois sociology focuses its attention) is through changes in the inner nature of the position he occupies. This is most evident in the case of the proletarianization of the new middle class where a change in the nature of the

positions making up the material substratum of this class causes a
change in the place those agents occupy in the social structure.
The complex relation between the changes in positions and the agents
of production will be examined shortly. Before doing this, however,
it is useful to examine very briefly why the agents are not strictly
determined by the positions they occupy. The point is that the reproduction of agents takes place only partly within the capitalist
production process, i.e. within the enterprise. The political and
ideological apparatuses as well as the class struggle on all levels
also contribute to their reproduction. But since these other elements are relatively independent vis-à-vis the economic structure, it
is possible that for some agents the opportunity is created for vertical mobility.(30)   There is, therefore, no identity; rather there
is a relative autonomy, under capitalism, between agents and positions as far as the social origin of the agents is concerned. In
short, *the social origin of the agents is relatively autonomous of
their position*. But it is clear, from what said above, that it is
the positions and their reproduction which play the determinant role.

III   TWO TYPES OF DEVALUATION OF LABOUR POWER AND THE
      PROLETARIANIZATION OF THE NEW MIDDLE CLASS

So far, the relative autonomy of the agents vis-à-vis the positions
has been explained in terms of the effects of the superstructure
(the ideological and political apparatuses) on the reproduction of
agents. Moreover, since as we have seen the superstructure and
class struggle can influence the reproduction of positions, one more
reason can be added to the contention that the reproductions of
positions and of agents do not necessarily have to coincide. But,
aside from the effects of the superstructure, *there can also be a
discrepancy between positions and agents at the level of the economic; there can be a discrepancy between the value of an agent's
labour power and the value of the labour power required by a position*. To be concise, let us call the latter the *value required*.
The computation of the value required depends upon the value of
wage goods. Only when the latter is known can we compute the value
required by a certain position, considering, for example, how much
education, training, etc. of a certain type are necessary to perform the technical content of a position. Let us, then, examine the
discrepancy between the value required and the value of an agent's
labour power. The starting point must be the double nature of a
position, its technical and its social content.
    We have seen that the social content of a position regulates the
agents' collocation in the class structure. To repeat, the social
content of a position is given by the ownership, expropriation, and
functional elements. In terms of the last element, the functional
one, it should be clear that it is only the social aspect of a function (i.e. whether an agent performs the function of capital or the
function of labour) which enters into the social content of a position. But a position, through the technical content of a function,
also has a technical nature. Since the technical content of a position is given only by the technical content of one of its elements,

the functional aspect, from now on we can talk interchangeably about either the technical content of a position or the technical content of a function. Given the technical content of a function, it follows that a position is characterized by certain technical requirements. These requirements determine the qualities, training, education, etc., necessary for an agent to fill that position, i.e. the technical content of a function requires a certain type of labour, of *concrete* labour. The requirement of a certain concrete labour goes hand in hand with the requirement of a certain level of skill and thus with the amount of labour time necessary to acquire those skills. This means that the technical content of a function requires that an agent's labour power must be of a certain value if that agent is to be capable of filling that position (assuming the value of the wage goods as given). In short, it is the technical content of a function which determines the value required, once the value of the wage goods and the composition of the basket of goods making up the culturally determined subsistence minimum are known.

We must be clear on this point. On the one hand, the value of an agent's labour power is given by the culturally determined subsistence minimum, i.e. by the value of all those commodities culturally deemed necessary for his production and reproduction. I.e. to know the value of labour power, we must know, 1, the composition of the basket of wage goods and, 2, the value of each one of those wage goods. When we talk about the value of labour power we usually refer to that of the average, unskilled labourer. Skilled labour counts as a multiple of simple labour.(31) On the other hand, we have the value required by a certain position, the value which is determined by the position's technical content. Here too we must know the value of the wage goods (as well as the composition of the basket of wage goods) which are required by a certain position in order to create an agent capable of filling that position. When an agent occupies a position, the value of his labour power adapts itself to the value required, i.e. the very fact of filling that position determines the *social* value of the agent's labour power. But since labour power is a commodity, there can be a discrepancy between its social value on the one hand and (a) the individual value of an agent's labour power and (b) the wages actually paid, on the other.(32) We can thus say that the determination of the value of an agent's labour power and of the value required by a certain position filled by that agent are not the same in the sense that, while the social value of an agent's labour power and the value required by a position filled by that agent always coincide, there can be a discrepancy between value required (and thus social value of labour power) on the one hand and either individual value or value actually paid (wages) on the other. However, even if the value required and the social value of the agent's labour power always coincide, the *ways* these two values change do not. We will see that while there is no chronological discrepancy between a change in these two values, the study of which one changes first *logically* will lead us to important conclusions for an analysis of the reproduction of social classes.

Let us start from the change in the value of labour power. We will deal here with the most important, and most general aspects of the problem, i.e. with the devaluation of labour power. In this connection, we should distinguish between two types of devaluation of labour power. (a) The first type, analysed in detail by Marx, is due to the increased productivity in the sectors of the economy producing — either directly or indirectly — wagegoods.(33) (b) The second type is due to the fact that some agents, whose labour power has a certain value, must fill positions with a lower value required. We will see soon how and why this might happen. At this juncture I only want to point out that the 'dequalification of labour' is in reality a dequalification of the technical require-ments; of the technical content of a function and thus of a posi-tion. In short, it is a dequalification of an operation. The de-qualification of an operation and thus of a position (a position can be dequalified for other reasons also, e.g. if the weight of the global function of capital decreases vis-à-vis the function of the collective worker) determines the dequalification of the con-crete labour of the agent who continues to occupy the same position after it has been dequalified. The agent, then, is more skilled than is necessary in the new circumstances. As a result his labour power has a value higher than the *new* value required. He will receive, in the new circumstances, a value tendentially equal to the new value required. Thus, his labour power has been devalued. Let us call this type of devaluation of labour power *devaluation through dequalification*. This type of devaluation of labour power is due to the fact that agents with certain qualifications, whose labour power has a certain value, must — for whatever reasons — fill positions which require lower qualifications and thus a lower value required. This is what seems to have happened in the field of chemistry in the last 10-15 years: what used to be the job of a chemist with a university degree has now become the job of a tech-nician with only a high school diploma. True, the technicians might make more mistakes than the university graduates, but evi-dently, the loss due to these mistakes is more than offset by the saving on variable capital due to the lower value of the labour power now employed. This lower value, this devaluation, has been achieved by introducing into the labour process new instruments which can now be handled by a technician. The operation changes, the technical requirements decrease, and new agents (the techni-cians) now occupy the dequalified positions. What about the old agents, the university graduates? They can stay in the now dequali-fied position and thus accept a devaluation of their labour power (which is thus brought into line with the new value required).(34) If they were also performing some managerial function (global func-tion of capital) this devaluation of their labour power and thus the dequalification of the operations to be performed might imply also the disappearance (or reduction) of the global function of capital and thus a further (i.e. social) dequalification of the position. Or, they can try to escape to other positions, perhaps more managerial in nature. But this is, in any case, an individual escape open only to a few. A much more common alternative 'solu-tion' is the unemployment of highly qualified personnel; 'academic' unemployment.(35) On the other hand, let us assume that a certain category of positions is dequalified, due to technical change, and that only the agents with the old, higher qualifications (and thus whose labour power is also higher) are available. For some time, the value paid will still be equal to the old social value and thus higher than the new social value (wages higher than value of labour power), although, over the time, new agents will be produced at lower costs, i.e. with lower qualifications, at the new social value. There are also other reasons for a discrepancy between the new social value (new value required) and the agents' wages. For example, the latter may be higher than the former due to the action of the trade unions. H. Braverman provides the example of the skilled machinist in the metal cutting industry whose position is fragmented into three positions (the programmer, the coder, and the new, unskilled machine operator of a numerically controlled machine). The extent of the devaluation undergone by the position can be seen from the fact that 'while it takes four years to give a machinist his basic training, an operator of the sort required by numerically controlled machine tools may be trained in four months' (1974: 200-3). But sometimes the unions retard the adjustment of the machine operator's wages to the new value required:

> This is not to say that, in unionised situations, the pay of machinists is immediately reduced to operator levels the moment numerical control is introduced. In some exceptional instances where few numerically controlled machine tools have been brought into a shop, the union has been able successfully to insist that the entire job, including programming and coding, be handled by the machinist. In many other cases the pay scale of the machinist has been maintained or even increased by the union after the introduction of numerical control, even though he has become no more than an operator. But such pay maintenance is bound to have a temporary character, and is really an agreement, whether formal or not, to 'red circle' these jobs as this is known in negotiating language; that is, to safeguard the pay of the incumbents. Management is thus sometimes forced to be content to wait until the historical process of devaluation of the worker's skill takes effect over the long run, and the relative pay scale falls to its expected level, since the only alternative to such patience is, in many cases, a bitter battle with the union (1974: 203).

Moreover, as long as new agents, whose labour power has a value in line with the new social value, are not produced, there are other possibilities of replacing the old agents or making them accept a wage equal to the new value. For example, new agents can be drawn into the labour force whose labour power is lower (females) or new agents can be drawn into the national labour force from abroad (migration).(36) This illustrates once more the determinant role of the reproduction of positions vis-à-vis the reproduction of agents.

Devaluation through dequalification is another aspect which points to the fact that there is no identity but only determination between positions and agents, in this case as far as the value of labour power (i.e. on the economic level) is concerned. This type of devaluation means that there is now a discrepancy between the *old social value* of the agent's labour power and the *new social value,* value which is fixed by the new value required. The agent is paid, tendentially, the full value of his labour power, which is now lower than the old value. In this case, then, we have normal exploitation. In order to clear away possible misunderstandings let us also

mention two other cases which have to do with the discrepancy between the individual and the social value of labour power. First
of all an agent's individual labour power and qualifications may be
in agreement with the qualifications and value required, and yet
there might be a discrepancy between the value actually paid
(wages) and the value required due to the policy of the capitalists
to fragment the working class, i.e. there are also political and
ideological wage determinants. As E. Mingione puts it:

> the barriers and distances between positions and between categ-
> ories of employees and technicians become increasingly ficti-
> tious and serve to create the impression of the possibility of
> career-making in order to divide the labourers who are doing
> work which is no longer so different (1973: 92).

The same author points out that the more diffuse the position, the
wider is the range of wage differentials for the same position.
But this of course is a reflection of the particular Italian situation. Here the system of wage differentials becomes a political
and ideological weapon dividing the working class. In other countries where the working class is less combative such a method might
not be necessary. In any case, when there is non-correspondence
between the value paid (wages) and the social value, we can distinguish between the following two subcases. Either the value paid
is lower than the social value (and value required), and this case
can be a consequence of keen competition among the workers. In
this case there will be extra-exploitation. Or, conversely, wages
are higher than the social value (the example of labour aristocracies). In this case there will be less than normal exploitation.

The other case concerning a discrepancy between the individual
value of an agent's labour power and the social value is that of an
agent who, for example, studies seven instead of the normal five
years. The moment this agent enters the labour market his individual value is reduced, through competition, to the social (lower)
value and is tendentially paid that value. This is also the case
of someone who has qualifications higher than the normally necessary ones because of the traditional lag between the school system
and the capitalist needs in terms of labour power. He too finds out
that his labour power is immediately devalued as soon as he enters
the labour market.

But let us go back to devaluation through dequalification. In
order to better understand its nature, let us compare it with
another type of devaluation of labour power, the devaluation due
to the cheaper production of the commodities making up the culturally determined subsistence minimum (either directly or indirectly).
Let us call this type of devaluation of labour power *wage goods
devaluation* in order to distinguish it from what I have called
devaluation through dequalification.

Labour power is a commodity and, like all other commodities, its
value decreases when the value of its component parts (in this case
wage goods) is lowered. The reduction of the value of the wage
goods is mostly due to the introduction of new technologies (at
least in the advanced capitalist countries) which in turn is due to
the constant need the capitalist has to increase the relative surplus value. Now, we can distinguish two subcases. First, one or
more wage goods, common to the whole of the working class, are

produced more cheaply. We have in this case a devaluation of the labour power of the whole working class which we call *general wage goods devaluation*. This would be the case, if, for example, there was a reduction of the production costs of primary education in the developed capitalist countries. Second, one or more wage goods are produced more cheaply and enter the basket of goods making up the labour power's value of a sector of the working class. This would be the case, e.g. of a certain type of training for some categories of skilled workers or a certain type of higher education for university graduates. Such an example is raised by Marx in his discussion of the commercial worker where he considers the reduction in the value of this worker's labour power due to the fact that the state produces training, knowledge, etc. more cheaply than the individual capitalists ('Capital', vol. III, 300 and ff.). We call this type of devaluation of labour power *partial wage goods devaluation*. The distinction between partial and general wage goods devaluation is important because *only the former explains the tendency for sectors of the working class which are higher than the average in terms of value of labour power to approach that average*. This reduction, however, relates to the value of labour power only and not to the concrete character of the labour provided by the agent. The skilled agent still has the same education, training, etc. as before, i.e. *in terms of skills there is still the same difference between this agent and the average worker* but that education and training cost less and thus in terms of value of labour power the difference tends to be bridged. A certain type of commercial worker, for example, must be able to speak foreign languages, as part of the operation he has to perform. Whether it takes X hours of social labour time to provide him with that knowledge or X/2 hours (partial wage goods devaluation) makes no difference as far as the operation is concerned. The difference between the value of his labour power and the average is reduced but the difference in skills (between him and the average, unskilled worker) remains. Thus, partial wage goods devaluation explains the reduction of the higher value of the labour power for certain categories of agents to the average value. More concisely, *partial wage goods devaluation explains the reduction of higher to average value of labour power*. General wage goods devaluation on the other hand explains the tendential decrease of the value of the labour power of the working class as a whole.(37)

We have seen that in his discussion of the commercial workers Marx considers what we have called partial wage goods devaluation. But, the first reason Marx mentions for the devaluation of the commercial worker's labour power is 'the division of labour within the office' and thus 'the one sided development of the labour capacity' ('Capital', vol. III). Clearly, then, Marx established a connection between increasing technical division of labour (which is basically a consequence of the introduction of new techniques within the production process) and the reduction of the worker's skills. *This is, then, the reduction of skilled to average labour, a reduction which takes place through what I have called devaluation through dequalification*. To explain this point, let us begin by mentioning that labour power can be subjected to technical devaluation, just like other commodities can be subjected to technical depreciation.

Take a certain commodity, A. Let us assume that its social value
is 50. If, after the introduction of new technologies, commodity A
can be produced more cheaply, at a value of 40, then the old commodities A still existing will be depreciated to 40 (since 40 is the
new social value). Take now labour power. Assume that an agent's
labour power has a value of 50. Assume also that he fills a position the value required of which is also 50. If, following technical changes, the level of skill required by that position falls so
that the new value required is 40, then the value of the labour
power of the agent filling that position will also be devalued to
40. What we have now is a change in the composition of the basket
of wage goods, either quantitatively (e.g. less of a certain type of
education) or qualitatively (e.g. a different type of education
which can be produced at lower costs). This is one of the differences between wage goods devaluation (both general and partial) and
devaluation through dequalification. The former devalues labour
power by lowering the value of wage goods: here we do not have to
assume a change in the composition of the basket of goods making up
the culturally determined subsistence minimum. The latter devalues
labour power by changing this composition: here we do not have to
assume a change in the value of the wage goods.

What we have to do, then, is to provide an explicit analysis of
devaluation through dequalification, i.e. of the links connecting
the introduction of technological changes in the production process,
the reduction of skilled to average labour and thus the reduction of
higher to average value of labour power. We know that the way to
increase relative surplus value is by introducing technical changes
in the production process. Technical changes mean, to begin with,
increased productivity in the sectors producing wage goods thus
leading to what has been called wage goods devaluation. But technical change also means a new technical division of labour within the
production process and thus a change in the nature and structure of
the operations making up that process. For example, some operations
will be fragmented others will require less training and knowledge,
etc. This implies a dequalification of positions, dequalification
which can be either only technical or both technical and social.
Technical dequalification means that less skill, etc. is required to
perform the new, simpler operations and thus means that the value
required has fallen. The value of the labour power of the agents
having to fill this dequalified position will have to adapt itself
to the new, lower value required. In other words, the new social
value of the agents labour power will have fallen. This is what
we have called devaluation through dequalification.

But a technical dequalification of positions can lead also to a
social dequalification. A particularly important example of social
dequalification is the one relating to positions whose social content (i.e. the content in terms of production relations) involves
performing both the function of the collective worker and the global
function of capital. In fact, technical dequalification means
fragmentation of tasks, etc., accompanied by less responsibility and
a consequent tendency to lose control and surveillance (the global
function of capital) over other agents. In short, changes in the
technical division of labour and thus in the technical content of
positions can also bring about changes in the social content of

positions.(38) *It is this technical and social dequalification of
positions which is at the basis of the proletarianization of the new
middle class. It is devaluation through dequalification, then,
which must be used to explain this process of proletarianization.*(39)
We know that both types of devaluation of labour power are a consequence of capital's inner need to increase relative surplus value.
What we have to do now is to examine the specific effects of devaluation through dequalification on relative surplus value, i.e. the
specific way this type of devaluation increases relative surplus
value when it causes not only a technical but also a social dequalification of positions. Let us consider the example of those agents
of production who, in terms of the function performed, carry out
both the global function of capital and the function of the collective worker (in terms of the functional element, these agents are a
part of the new middle class). The example of 40,000 agents performing both functions in a varying balance is depicted in Graph 1.
To understand the specific way devaluation through dequalification
acts on the creation of surplus value, let us consider the following
three situations.

Situation A. This is the initial situation in which 40,000
agents perform both functions. For the sake of simplicity let us
assume that all the time spent in performing the function of the
collective worker is also productive labour and let us also assume
a rate of surplus value of 100 per cent. The total surplus value
created by these 40,000 agents will then be equal to
$40,000 \times 4 \times 1/2 = 80,000$.

Situation B. Here we introduce the first effect of devaluation
through dequalification on the creation of surplus value, i.e. the
devaluation of the labour power of those agents who already perform
the function of the collective worker, the tendential reduction of
the value of their labour power to the average value. Let us assume
a reduction of the necessary labour time to 1/3 of the working day.
Now the rate of surplus value is equal to 200 per cent and the total
surplus value produced is equal to $40,000 \times 4 \times 2/3 = 106,666$. The
increase in the total surplus value is 26,666. The reduction in the
value of labour power has been achieved through a technical dequalification of the positions and thus through a reduction in the value
required.

Situation C. We introduce now also the other element of devaluation through dequalification, i.e. the possibility that a technical
dequalification of a position might cause also a social dequalification, i.e. the reduction of the global function of capital vis-à-vis
the function of the collective worker. Assume that 10,000 agents
have been proletarianized, i.e. in terms of production relations,
they do not own the means of production; perform only the function
of the collective worker, and are the exploited. Their production
of surplus value is, at the new rate of surplus value, equal to
$10,000 \times 8 \times 2/3 = 53,333$. Moreover, let us assume that the new
social division of labour within the enterprise requires the creation of one supervisor for each ten labourers. Thus, 1,000 agents
now perform only the global function of capital. Therefore, there
remain 29,000 agents whose total production of surplus value is
equal to $29,000 \times 4 \times 2/3 = 77,333$. Thus, the total surplus value
created under the new conditions (proletarianization) is

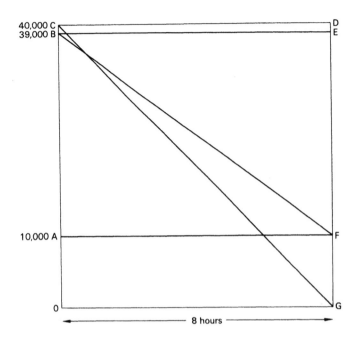

Graph 1

53,333 + 77,333 = 130,666. The increase in total surplus value
compared to the initial situation A is thus 50,666.
      It is now easy to see the specific effects of this type of deval-
uation of labour power on the creation of surplus value. First, all
the time previously spent in performing the function of the collective worker (in the example, productive labour) is paid proportionally less due to the devaluation of labour power. Secondly, of the
time previously divided between the two functions (where the time
devoted to performing the global function of capital is unproductive, even though of a different nature than that of the unproductive
worker) more time goes to performing the function of the collective
worker (and thus becomes time spent in productive activity) and less
time is spent in performing the global function of capital. The
extra time spent in performing the function of the collective worker
is also paid proportionally less than under the initial circumstances. Thirdly, of the time previously spent on performing both
functions, one small fraction is now devoted only to the global
function of capital, thus becoming unproductive time. The final
effect, however, is an increase in surplus value greater than would
be the case in the absence of a social dequalification of positions.
To conclude, it must be pointed out that in the example above the
disappearance of the global function of capital takes place only at
the bottom of the hierarchical scale, where agents are already
largely performing the function of the collective worker. This need
not be so. It can also happen that technical innovations within the
production process result in the disappearance of positions the
social content of which is heavily determined by the global function

of capital. For example, as long ago as 1958 T.L. Whisler and H.J.
Leavitt pointed out that the introduction of the computer tends to
cause the disappearance of the middle managers (p. 44).

Since the concept of positions is essential for an understanding
of devaluation through dequalification, let us use a scheme relating
the elements characterizing a position to the type of devaluation
under consideration and thus to the proletarianization of the new
middle class. Arrow 1 in scheme 1, indicates the first aspect of
the mechanism of devaluation through dequalification, i.e. the technical devaluation of a position (due to the introduction of new
techniques within the production process) reduces the value required
and thus the value of the agent's labour power. Arrow 2, indicates
the second aspect of devaluation through dequalification, which
serves to explain the proletarianization of the new middle class,
i.e. the disappearance of the global function of capital (social
dequalification) as a consequence of technical devaluation. Thus,
more time can go to productive labour. Arrow 1 then refers to situation B, in Graph 1 (devaluation through technical dequalification
of positions) and arrow 2 refers to situation C (disappearance of
the global function of capital).

Scheme 1

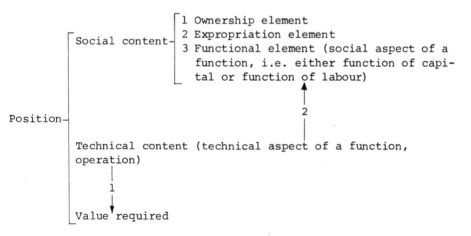

Let us now use a two-by-two table to list all possible examples
of devaluation through dequalification. Only cases 1, 2 and 3 are
examples of devaluation through dequalification, since they imply
changes in the operation. Cases 1 and 2 depict a change in the
operation such that comparison between the operation before and
after the change is impossible (given that we have here a qualitative change). *The only way to compare the two operations is to compare the value of the labour power required before and after the
change.* That is why, as long as one restricts one's analysis to the
technical aspects of a function (as bourgeois sociology does), the
discussion of proletarianization becomes confused to such an extent
that no sensible word can any longer be uttered. This is one of the
reasons why the whole discussion of the social effects of automation
often got stuck in insoluble (because not correctly posed) problems.

Table 1

		Operation	
		Fragmentation	No fragmentation
Knowledge	Qualitative change in type of knowledge (at lesser costs) required by a position	1	2
	No qualitative change in type of knowledge required by a position	3	4

Case 3 appears to be easier to handle because, 1, the technical contents of the position before and after the change are comparable and thus, 2, one does not feel the need to go deeper than this type of comparison, thus resting content with a partial (at the level of the operation) analysis. In fact, here too a comparison between the value required before and after the change is a necessary premise for a real analysis.

If we now compare cases 1, 2 and 3 on the one hand and case 4 on the other, we see that in the latter case there is no change in the operation. Then, *here the only way to achieve a devaluation of labour power is by reducing the cost of producing wage goods (wage goods devaluation).* If a certain category of skilled labourers is considered and if we assume case 4, the only way to reduce the value of their labour power is to produce more cheaply those commodities which enter their culturally determined subsistence minimum (e.g. a certain type of education, of training, etc.).

Before proceeding in our exposition, let us open a brief parenthesis. The reduction of skilled to average labour is neither the same as the lowering of relative wages nor the same as the absolute impoverishment of the working class. Under capitalism, relative wages (the proportion of the new value created going to wages rather than to profits) tend to decrease while absolute wages (the value of labour power) tend to increase, at least in the developed capitalist countries.(40) The average value of labour power is computed also in terms of education, training, etc. and tends to increase in the long run in absolute terms. As I have pointed out in chapter 1, the lowering of skilled labour to an average and the tendential increase of this average in absolute terms are just two aspects of the same phenomenon. Moreover, relative wages tend to decrease. When we consider statistical data, however, we might not see a fall in 'dependent income' (which, by the way, includes not only the wages of the skilled and unskilled labourers but also directors' salaries). As Blackburn points out, 'Rises in the *absolute* level of wages have obscured the remarkable fact that the relative shares of profits and wages have displayed a "historical constancy" since the end of the nineteenth century (though periods of depression necessarily involve low profits)' (1973: 183). This constancy is explained by the combination of the tendency capital has to appropriate an increasing share of the new value produced and by the contrary effects of a number of counter-tendencies such as the role of the trade unions. This absolute increase means not only more material commodities but also more services including education, knowledge, training, etc. Therefore, the knowledge and skills characteristic of today's unskilled worker are much greater than those of the industrial revolution's unskilled worker, for example. Thus, unless one holds to a view of a constant (and not culturally determined) subsistence minimum (which also includes knowledge, etc.), it makes no sense to talk about a working class becoming a class of skilled labourers. 'The educational qualifications normally required at any given point of the occupational scale have simply been raised.'(41) To close this section, we can now deal with the following two points. First, on the basis of what said so far, we will compare similarities and differences between the two types of devaluation of labour power. Secondly, we will try to provide a few, tentative guidelines to determine in what circumstances which type of devaluation of labour power can be dominant vis-à-vis the other.

From the analysis provided above, it should be clear that both the value required and the value of labour power can change either through wage goods devaluation or through devaluation through dequalification (and, of course, also when both types of devaluation take place at the same time). In fact, we have seen how a technical dequalification affects the value required of a position and thus the value of the labour power of the agent filling that position. It is also clear that the value required is automatically changed when one or more wage goods entering the computation of that value required are devalued. As far as the value of labour power is concerned, we have seen how a devaluation of one or more wage goods affects the value of labour power (either total or partial wage goods devaluation). But the value of labour power can also be devalued through a technical dequalification and thus a change in the value required, as we have seen. To say that both value required and value of labour power can change either through wage goods devaluation or through devaluation through dequalification also means, very simply, that the value of labour power can change either through a devaluation of wage goods, the composition of the basket of wage goods remaining the same (wage goods devaluation), or due to a change in this basket, the value of the wage goods remaining constant (devaluation through dequalification).

Why then use such a cumbersome way of expressing something which at first sight looks as though it could be said in far simpler terms? This question actually raises the issue of why we should distinguish between wage goods devaluation and devaluation through dequalification; why should we try to distinguish changes in the value of wage goods and changes in the composition of the basket of wage goods? To begin with we can point out that both the underlying logic and the concepts relating to the two sorts of devaluation of labour power are different; in short, the routes followed by these two types of devaluation of labour power are different. In fact,

from a *logical* and not from a *chronological* point of view, wage
goods devaluation changes first the value of labour power (through
devaluation of the wage goods' value) and then the value required
by certain positions. Here the study of positions and thus of
value required is not necessary. Devaluation through dequalification, on the other hand, changes first the value required by certain
positions and then the value of the labour power of those agents
filling those positions. Logically, only after the position has
been technically dequalified, and thus the value required reduced,
does the value of labour power change. This is one important reason
why an analysis of positions, both in their technical and in their
social content; of the changes undergone by them (e.g. dequalification); of their relation to the value required and to the value of
the agents' labour power, etc. is important. Whether the change in
the technical content (operation) is due to a quantitative change
(e.g. fragmentation) or to a qualitative change (see Table 1 above,
cases 1 , 2 and 3) the fact remains that we have here a change in
the operation and that this operational change, this technical dequalification, causes a reduction of the value required and thus of
the agent's labour power. In other words the new social value
(fixed by the new value required once the value of the wage goods
is known) is now lower than the old social value (which we can now
assume to be equal to the individual value for any particular agent)
and is lower just because that is now the cost the labour power
needed to fill that particular position should have.

Secondly, and this follows logically from what just said, only
devaluation through dequalification explains the reduction of
skilled to unskilled labour (42) through the technical dequalification of positions. Such an explanation cannot be provided by wage
goods devaluation (either partial or total) because here we only
consider changes in the value of labour power, its approximation to
an average (in the case of partial wage goods devaluation) without
considering the degrees of skill of various types of labour.
Thirdly, only devaluation through dequalification can serve as a
basis for an explanation of the proletarianization of the new middle
class. In fact, only through a study of the position, of its technical and social dequalification, and of the type of devaluation of
labour power connected with this dequalification, is it possible to
explain the meaning and mechanism of the proletarianization of the
new middle class.(43) *It is because of this, because it serves to
explain the proletarianization of a class which is typical of monopoly capitalism, that devaluation through dequalification is of
particular importance in the present stage of capitalist development.(44)*

It should be clear that the two types of devaluation of labour
power do not exclude each other. The possibility is always open for
those agents who are exposed to devaluation through dequalification
(e.g. technicians whose operation is fragmented and who thus lose
part of the global function of capital) to be subjected also to wage
goods devaluation (when, e.g. their technical training and education
can be produced more cheaply). Often a distinction is only possible
analytically. However, it is important to find out — and with this
point we will conclude this section — under what conditions one type
of devaluation becomes dominant vis-à-vis the other. I will mention

here only a couple of examples of how and in which direction analysis should be carried out. First of all, given that the process of
reproduction of capital can be viewed from a long-term, a short-
term, and a conjunctural point of view, I will consider briefly the
effects of the long term elements on devaluation through dequalification.(45) Undoubtedly, among these elements, one of the most significant is what has been called the permanent technological revolution and its connection with the long cycles. According to Mandel,
(46) one of the characteristics of capitalist development is a continuous succession of long (about 25 years) cycles basically either
of an expansive or of a stagnating nature. The expansive cycles are
characterized by the application to the production process of technological inventions produced during the long recession. The stagnating cycles are, on the other hand, characterized by inventions
but not their application; they are thus characterized by an absence
of massive technological changes.(47) Given the relationship outlined above between technological changes, technical division of
labour, dequalification of positions, and devaluation through dequalification, the hypothesis can be submitted that devaluation
through dequalification assumes a far greater importance during long
upswing than during long downswings.(48) Now, an expansive long
cycle began with the Second World War and seems to have lasted up to
the end of the 1960s.(49) Therefore, during this period, great technological changes and thus devaluation through dequalification have
been major features. This fact explains the great attention paid
to the phenomenon of 'dequalification of labour' by social scientists, both Marxists and others. The analysis of this phenomenon has
been further complicated by the introduction into the production
process of new technologies (the computer, and its effects on the
social structure, is one of the most glaring examples) which have
created local and time-bounded countertendencies to the general
trend towards the devaluation of labour power (and especially the
reduction of skilled to average labour).

But there is also another factor that seems to indicate that
devaluation through dequalification will continue to play an important role in the future relatively independently from the succession
of long cycles. I refer to the arms race and to the effects it has
on technical innovations within the production process. Since the
Second World War an enormous amount of such innovations has been due
to the spillover of new discoveries originating in the field of
military research into the civilian, economic sphere: the computer,
atomic energy, the laser, automation, etc. are only some of the most
eye-catching examples. Since military research is much more loosely
related to the economic cycle than civilian research, and since the
application of these new discoveries is bound to take place sooner
or later, due to oligopolistic competition, we have here the basis
of the *permanent technological revolution*.(50) If this is so, we
can safely expect devaluation through dequalification to continue
to play an important role in the years to come.

Secondly, aside from cyclical considerations, one should always
distinguish between the several parts of the capitalist class and
therefore one should consider which type of devaluation of labour
power is liable to play an important role for each one of these
parts. Let us consider the present Italian situation. The advanced,

monopolistic sector of the capitalist class will tend to compete
(i.e. will try to offset the rise in the organic composition of capital by raising the rate of surplus value) by introducing new technologies. New, qualified positions (i.e. skilled agents) will be
created, old positions will be dequalified, and also the new positions will be soon subjected to the tendency to dequalification.(51)
This sector of the dominant block can, very generally speaking,
afford a rise in the culturally determined subsistence minimum (the
'social' reforms, such as those relating to transportation, education, health, etc. which are demanded with increasing force by the
proletariat) due to its capacity to offset this rise by a greater
rise in the productivity of labour thanks to the introduction of new
technologies. For this sector, then, and quite aside from conjunctural considerations, devaluation through dequalification will be much
more important than for the backward part of the Italian capitalist
class.(52)   This latter part will not be willing to accept a rise in
the culturally determined subsistence minimum because its backward
technologies will not allow them to offset this rise with an increase in the rate of surplus value. For this part of the Italian
capitalist class it is much more vital to ensure a constant devaluation of the proletariat's labour power through a cheapening of the
value of the wage goods and, in particular conjunctural situations
as the present one (end of 1974, beginning of 1975), even through a
reduction of the *physical* quantity of some basic items of the subsistence minimum.

IV   THE PROLETARIANIZATION OF THE EMPLOYEES

In the previous three sections we have examined, within the framework of the problems concerning the reproduction of social classes,
two types of devaluation of labour power and the specific effects
the devaluation through dequalification has concerning the proletarianization of the new middle class. We have established a relation between devaluation through dequalification and the tendential
disappearance, for the greatest part of the agents performing both
the function of the collective worker and the global function of
capital, of the latter function. The rest of this chapter will be
more descriptive than analytical in nature and will use the conceptual framework worked out so far in order to interpret the changes
undergone by the Italian new middle class since its origins,(53)
even though the same general trends are applicable, mutatis mutandis,
to all other developed capitalist economies. This will provide the
opportunity to relate changes in the economic to changes in the ideological and the political. Let us start with the employees. We can
subdivide the process of devaluation of the employee's labour power,
the dequalification of their functions and positions, into three
phases which roughly correspond to the advent of the industrial
revolution (i.e. the stage of individual capitalism dominated by
real subordination of labour to capital), the advent of monopoly
capitalism until the Second World War, and the stage of monopoly
capitalism following the Second World War up to present. In the
first phase the function of capital is still basically carried out
by the individual entrepreneur. The employee is a sort of extension

of the entrepreneur. For example, he substitutes for the entrepreneur when the latter has to be absent. In this respect he performs the function of capital which is not yet a global function of
capital because the work of control and overseeing has not yet been
delegated to a hierarchically organized structure but is still the
task of the entrepreneur (and of the few who help him). Usually,
he also performs the function of the collective worker (if, for
example, he takes care of bookkeeping) because he then takes part in
the labour process as a whole. The fact that the employee is here a
sort of extension of the entrepreneur (54) is the basis for the
explanation of a whole series of phenomena. First of all, as there
are only few entrepreneurs compared to the total industrial population, so there are also few employees: the ratio of the employees to
the total industrial population is very wmall. Secondly, the relation between entrepreneur and employee is personal and direct, with
no in-between links. Thirdly, his place in the capitalist production process (partial performance of the function of capital)
ensures him a position of privilege and thus a salary much higher
than the workers' wages. Finally, this place in the capitalist production process requires a legal and economic education which means,
given the elitist character of the school system, that usually his
social origin is either petty bourgeois or bourgeois. For all these
reasons the employee, during this phase, belongs politically and
ideologically to the petty bourgeoisie.

   During the second phase, the number of employees increases. As
we know, the joint-stock company leads to the appearance of that
complex organization, both bureaucratic and hierarchical, within
which the function of capital is carried out globally. The transformation of the function of capital into the global function of
capital implies that many of those who perform the global function
of capital also perform the function of the collective worker.
That is to say, the position of the employee moves further and further away from that of the entrepreneur and thus the personal relation between the two is broken. The increased complexity of the
production process and the performance of the function of capital
by a complex structure of agents, the steadily increasing articula-
tion of the technical division of labour, are all causes of the
increase in the number of employees. Although he is no longer an
extension of the entrepreneur and his labour power has been devalued, he is still far from being proletarianized. He still performs
both the function of the collective worker and the global function
of capital, even though the former tends to become increasingly
important. His position of relative privilege expresses itself in a
whole series of characteristics proper to his position: he does not
work in unhealthy environments; he has a certain degree of autonomy
in performing his functions (even though the first forms of specialization, leading to a reduction of that autonomy, already start
appearing); he has a degree of freedom to determine when he should
be at the office (because his presence is not strictly checked by
the entrepreneur or managers); he still requires a broad culture for
the performance of his function (a fact which makes his replacement
difficult); he has a higher salary and has the possibility, individually speaking, of making career. That is, he can, at the end of
a long career, reach the highest levels of the enterprise's

hierarchy or at least the lower reaches of those levels. It is
during this phase that the ideology of career-making is born; an
ideology which becomes the centre of the employee's life, and which
ties him strictly to the enterprise's interests. Not only is his
level of salary much higher than the worker's level of wages but he
also receives much better treatment as far as the non-monetary elements of his income are concerned, such as the length of holidays,
the quality of health care, etc. For these reasons, the employee
has a privileged position which explains his identifying his
interests with those of the dominant classes. During this period
the stratum of the employee is, politically speaking, very conserv-
ative and, ideologically speaking (while no longer completely integrated with the entrepreneurial class) still has the entrepreneur as
his reference group, to the extent of attempting to imitate the life
style and the consumption pattern of the entrepreneur. Ingredients
of the employee's ideology are individualism, career-making, defence
of his higher socio-economic status (already threatened, however, by
the creeping devaluation of his labour-power), defence of the enterprise as the guarantor of his higher status and, therefore, defence
of the concept of private ownership of the means of production.
These remarks should be enough to explain why during this period the
employees never sided with the working class; neither in industrial
disputes nor on general political questions. Of course, during this
phase we witness not only the tendency to dequalify the employee's
functions and positions, but also the creation of new functions
(just think of the managers of big corporations) which ensure for
some the possibility of climbing the organizational structure. We
notice here, for the first time, a phenomenon which we will observe
again and again: the constant tendency to devalue the labour power
of many and to create higher positions for a few.
     During the third phase the number of employees increases not only
absolutely, as during the second phase, but also relatively to the
total industrial population. At the same time there is an accelera-
tion of the process of dequalification of the employee's functions;
of devaluation of his labour power, i.e. of the knowledge and training necessary to carry out functions which become more and more
fragmentated, more and more specialized, more and more repetitive in
nature. Not only the size but also the composition of the employee
stratum changes: the female part becomes increasingly important
(typists, lower-level secretaries, card-punchers, etc.) and the
average age drops due to the technological changes introduced by
monopoly capitalism and the new division of labour.(55) The separation between the entrepreneur and the employee reaches now its
highest degree. While on the one side positions of privilege are
constantly and increasingly eroded with the decline of the global
function of capital, on the other side it is important for the
entrepreneurial class to retain the ideological support of the
employee. Thus, the employee finds himself in an increasingly contradictory situation: his condition approaches more and more the
proletarian one, while he is asked to stick to an ideology and political practice which is based on a lost position of privilege.
     The process of devaluation of the employee's labour power and
thus the progressive disappearance, in his position, of the global
function of capital, has deep-going effects, which tend to bridge

the gap originally existing between the worker (as member of the proletariat) and the employee (as member of the petty bourgeoisie). First of all, from the economic point of view, the progressive dis-apperance of the global function of capital and the tendential red-uction of the employees' labour power to simple labour power (due to the technical dequalification of positions, itself a consequence of automation) imply not only the progressive disappearance, in the in-come of the employee, of the revenue part (i.e. of the part connec-ted with his position of privilege) but also a reduction in the wage part due to the dequalification of his functions.(56)   Therefore, for many strata of the employees, the difference between the employ-ee's salary and the worker's wage tends to be bridged and it is now-adays not unusual for a skilled worker to earn more than the lowest strata of the employees.(57)   The fact is that for these layers, i.e. for those strata which have been proletarianized, the distinc-tion between 'worker' and 'employee' is no longer relevant, at least as far as the economic aspect is concerned, when identifying their place in the social structure.   The only difference between a girl punching cards and a worker on the conveyor-belt, is that the former works on a 'paper conveyor-belt'.   Any sociological distinction, of the type that the former performs manual labour while the latter perform intellectual labour, is simply absurd.(58)   Both meet the requirements needed to be classified within the working class, i.e. neither own the means of production, both perform the function of the collective worker, are economically oppressed (or exploited) and are paid a wage the extent of which is determined by the value of their labour power.   It is therefore perfectly logical that a skil-led 'worker' earns more than an unskilled 'employee' (logical, that is, from the viewpoint of capital).   Secondly, this loss of his position of privilege is reflected in a variety of phenomena, all symbolizing the fact that the employees, or at least a large section of them, become, from the subject of the work of control and sur-veillance, its object.   For example, his private room has been sub-stituted by a large area where he works with tens of his colleagues. The private desk is increasingly substituted by a counter, a symbol of the loss of individuality, of his approaching the stage of the 'paper conveyor-belt'.   Now he does not take care of the whole dos-sier but only of a few specialized aspects of it.   For example, one employee computes the basic wages and then passes on the dossier to another employee who computes the piecework points, etc.   Even those elements of the job which give it the personal touch, such as per-sonal answers to letters, are eliminated by the introduction of standard forms.   Thirdly, the employee's changed status is also reflected in the variables so dear to the sociologist: alienation (the employee, who used to be able to place his activity in the wider context of the production process, whose work gave him a global view of this process, is now, with the proletarian, just a small cog in a complex machine: the purpose of his activity escapes him completely), status (his status drops with the dequalification of his functions even though there might be lags), etc.   In this connection, it should be mentioned that terms such as 'white collar' only serve to confuse the issue because they are not scientific but ideological in nature.   White collar jobs, in terms of production relations, encompass both sections of the new middle class and

sections of the working class, including both the technician who
also carries out work of supervision and management and the typist.
(59)   Since the process of rationalization and mechanization tra-
ditionally applied to the 'blue collar' jobs has been applied,
especially after the Second World War, to 'white collar' as well,
devaluation through dequalification plays an important part in the
devaluation of these agents' labour power.   Sometimes specific sectors of the 'white collar' (e.g. clerical) workers have their labour
power devalued to such an extent that their average income falls
below the average income of the 'blue collar' production workers.
In the USA, in 1969, the former's income was $105.00 per week while
the latter's weekly income was $130.000 (Braverman: 1974, 34).   How-
ever, it can happen that, because of the traditional lag between
school system and production requirements — as well as a host of
other reasons — the dequalified positions are filled by agents with
the same or even higher educational qualifications.   These higher
qualifications not only do not command higher wages (which are determined by the value required) but represent spilled social labour
(i.e. labour which went into the production of the unused skills of
those agents).   Hence the discontent to be found not only among
'blue collar' but also among 'white collar' workers and the application of job enrichment schemes to 'white collar' workers even more
than to 'blue collar' workers.   Let us quote H. Braverman:

> Traditionally, lower-level white collar jobs in both government
> and industry were held by high school graduates.   Today, an
> increasing number of these jobs go to those who have attended
> college.   But the demand for higher academic credentials has not
> increased the prestige, status, pay, or difficulty of the job.
> For example, the average weekly pay for clerical workers in 1969
> was $105.00 per week, while blue-collar production workers were
> taking home an average of $130.00 per week.   It is not surprising,
> then, that the Survey of Working Conditions found much of the
> greatest work dissatisfaction in the country among young, well-
> educated workers who were in low-paying, dull, routine, and
> fractioned clerical positions (1974:34).   It is interesting to
> note that although the discussion of job enrichment, job enlarge-
> ment, and the like began in connection with factory work, most
> actual applications have taken place in offices (1974:36).

Fourthly, and contrary to the trends depicted so far, the official
ideology tries to foster the employee's loyalty to the enterprise by
attempting to create or perpetuate the image of the employee as the
hard worker who never strikes.   The process of proletarianization
that the employee perceives or feels, rather than understands, is
the objective basis for his fear for social change; a fear that
creates a common view with the members of the old middle class and
which is of course amplified by the mass media.   But the contrast
between the reality of the social process unfolding itself and the
ideological view which denies it (just think of the atmosphere of
harmony and co-operation propagated by the enterprises' internal
bulletins and papers) is too big and this ideology is doomed to
loosen its hold even more.   Years of this accelerated process have
led to a situation in which the traditional hostility of the employees towards the workers is being replaced, at least in the lowest
strata already proletarianized, by a new consciousness of a

community of interests between workers and employees. It is not by
chance that, starting from the May 1968 events in France and the
'hot' autumn of 1969 in Italy, the workers and employees have often
formed a united front in industrial disputes. The ultimate cause
must be sought in the process of devaluation of labour power in many
employee strata and finally in their proletarianization. This is not
to suggest, of course, that proletarianization necessarily brings
about proletarian class consciousness. This was recently the case in
Italy because of a host of political and ideological factors, both
international (the influence of the Vietnam War, of the Chinese Cultural Revolution, of the May 1968 events in France and the crisis in
the bourgeois ideology brought about by these events) and internal
(the combativeness of the working class which becomes a point of reference for the employees, the direct and indirect influence of the
student movement, the so-called 'crisis of representation' of the
traditional left-wing parties, therefore the rise of strata of the
working class not politically and ideologically hegemonized by these
parties, etc) ('I Comitati Unitaru di Base': 1973).
     What has been said so far could lead one to think that technical
innovations, the change in the technical and social content of positions, etc. only lead unilinearly to a devaluation (even though in
various degrees) of the employees' labour power. In effect, if this
is true for a great part of the employees, there is also a small
part for whom positions of privilege connected with an increase in
the global function of capital within their functions, are created.
(60) In other words, the process of devaluation of labour power
splits the stratum of the employees into two parts, the largest of
which is pushed towards the bottom of the organizational chart where
the work of control and surveillance is greatly reduced and tends to
disappear, while a minority is pushed closer to higher management
positions. At least two important consequences are detectable.
First of all, the middle management section — those who decide
through experience — becomes increasingly thinner because increasingly substituted by the computer. Secondly, and this is a direct
consequence of the first point, the employee gets closer to the
worker also with respect to the ever decreasing vertical mobility,
since the intermediate steps tend to disappear (Whisler and Leavitt:
1958).

V   THE PROLETARIANIZATION OF THE TECHNICIANS

Let us now examine the specific changes undergone by the technicians.
Following Lelli (1973) and Martinoli (1968) we will consider three
sub-phases of the production process. This process can be subdivided
into (A) design of the product, (B) production proper, and (C) control and maintenance. Since, in talking about the production process, attention is usually focused on sub-phase (B), i.e. on the
production proper, it might be useful to examine the changes undergone by the technicians in the other two sub-phases of the production process. Let us start with the phase of the product's design.
The changes undergone within this phase provide a very good example
of the process of devaluation through dequalification (basically
achieved through fragmentation of tasks) undergone by the

technicians. The design of a new product used to be an activity
only limited by either the generic indications of the entrepreneur
himself or the intuition of the designer. Nowadays the phase of
planning a new product becomes more and more a standardized activity
The planner is not given any more a generic task which he can carry
out with an ample degree of freedom: his work becomes more and more
similar to the putting together of already available elements in
order to come up with a prototype which must have certain strictly
determined technical characteristics, must satisfy certain quality
requirements determined by market research, etc. At the same time,
what used to be an individual task, splits into several operations.
Thus, we can distinguish between, 1, the head-planner who gets the
task from the management and must deliver the completed prototype;
2, his assistants, who help him, 3, technical designers, 4, the
experts on the materials to be used in making the product, 5, the
business experts who determine the price of the product once the
costs of production and the results of market research are known,
6, the mathematicians who, by using various operation research
techniques, plan the new production cycle, 7, the computer programmers and analysts who help the mathematicians, 8, the legal experts
who deal with the patents of the new product, etc. Of all those
position, only nos 5 and 8 are still the traditional tasks of the
old-type employee. The others are new positions some of which (see
no. 1, for example) almost exclusively, in their functional (social)
content, carry out the global function of capital while most of the
other are made up of a balance between this function and the function of the collective worker (in which the latter element either
predominates or is already the exclusive element). Even though the
level of education and technical training necessary to perform
these tasks are still higher than those necessary to perform average
labour, they are increasingly becoming standardized and fragmented
and, as such, liable to be in the future substituted by the computer. (61) A typical example is given by category 3 above, the technical designers or draughtsmen. A recent research in four major
metalworking enterprises in Italy, (62) shows that the work is
extremely heavy; the pay low; the possibility of making a career
almost non-existent; the subordination to the computer increasing in
the sense that (a) the computer gives all the initial data, (b) the
computer determined the ever increasing fragmentation of the work,
(c) the computer, when the fragmentation has reached a sufficient
degree, tends to take over that function; the possibility of creati-
vity and invention has disappeared.

The same phenomena can be observed also in the third sub-phase,
that of quality control and maintenance. Quality control used to be
carried out after production was completed. Over the years it has
developed into a complex of operations taking place during production in order to be sure that a finished product meets certain
quality requirements. Statistical techniques allow the technician
to constantly keep track of the deviations from the standrad and
thus to suggest the necessary modifications in the machinery and
production process when these deviations become too large. The
équipe carrying out this complex task is made up of two groups: one
dealing with the mathematical, theoretical aspects and the other
dealing with the mechanical and technical aspects of quality control.

The same can be repeated for maintenance, which has also developed
into something which takes place during production. It is important
to note that the same phenomenon already observed above can be
observed for all three sub-phases, i.e. the tendency toward the
formation of two strata among the technicians. The higher stratum,
is close to management, retains positions of privilege (in terms of
salary, etc.), and, by carrying out the function of capital, is also
the carrier of the meritocratic ideology of the technicians as neutral production agents, etc. The lower stratum is made up of those
whose labour power is constantly devalued, whose work becomes more
repetitive and fragmented, who in short are getting closer to a
condition of actual proletarianization (or have already reached that
condition).

VI   AN EXAMPLE: THE COMPUTER FACTORY

As a practical example, let us consider these two different strata
in a computer factory. The lower stratum, in its turn, can be subdivided into two parts: those who have already been proletarianized
and those who are in the process of being proletarianized. The
former part is made up of those employees (e.g. typists, card-
punchers, etc.), who are actually working on what has been called
the 'paper conveyor belt'. Their activity is completely determined
by the needs of the computer. Here we find a confirmation of capital's constant drive to decrease costs (value of labour power and
thus wages) in order to increase profits: when the employee has been
completely proletarianized, i.e. his labour power devalued, his
function fragmented and simplified to the extent that he becomes
easily replaceable and extremely vulnerable to the threat of unemployment (a threat which can enforce the low salary corresponding to
the decreased value of labour power and sometimes even less), then
capital has finally a completely free-hand in dictating its conditions. In the case of the card-punchers there is already detectable
a tendency to hire them on a fixed contract basis which is close to
a piecework system. The higher level of the stratum is made up of
semi-professional technicians (e.g. the programmer, the maintenance
personnel, etc.) who are in the process of being proletarianized,
i.e. undergoing a rapid devaluation of their labour power. Their
technical knowledge becomes rapidly obsolete, due to the extremely
rapid technological change in the computer field. The frequent
courses, seminars etc, they have to follow in order to update their
knowledge makes them more specialized; more tied to a certain type
of machine and thus, rather than increasing their bargaining power
vis-a-vis the employer, weakens their position and makes them more
dependent.
   The higher stratum is made up of those who either carry out the
global function of capital exclusively (i.e. the top-managers), or
of those who combine this function with that of the collective
worker, the so-called 'political' technicians (Lelli: 1973, 71).
The work of the latter consists of researching concrete applications
of the computer for prospective clients (e.g. the computerization of
the bookkeeping system in a certain enterprise) as well as super-
vizing its installation and operation. From the point of view of

the social content of this position, as far as the first function is
concerned, this type of technician is to be compared to a highly
qualified commercial worker. His function is to sell a certain type
of service for which he needs knowledge directly related to the computer field (mathematics, the various types of computer 'languages',
etc.), as well as knowledge of organization systems, management,
etc. He thus performs the function of the collective worker, even
though at a very high level of specialization. The second type of
function (the supervision of computerization in a certain enterprise)
is work of supervision and management encompassing both the work of
control and surveillance (global function of capital) and the work
of co-ordination and unity of the labour process (function of the
collective worker). It is thus possible that this type of technician's position is a balance of the two functions in which the
global function of capital does not play the dominant role. Yet he
is in a position very close to the management in the organizational
chart and gets a relatively high income (perhaps not entirely
explained by the role that the global function of capital plays in
his functions). How can we explain this and other similar 'anomal-
ies'? Actually this is not an anomaly at all. FIrst of all, this
technician has a particularly important place in the production process, as determined by the technical division of labour and by the
particular characteristics of the production process under examination. The technician under consideration is a particular type of
salesman not only because of the qualifications needed to perform
his function but also because the production of computers is the
production of a commodity which, 1, is very expensive and, 2, is
produced on a fairly limited scale compared to most other commodities. This means that the sale of the *individual* computer (or sale
of its services, i.e. the rent of the computer) becomes extremely
important: an unsold computer means something quite different for
the computer enterprise than an unsold box of matches means for the
match-making factory. I.e. the proportion of the total value contained in a computer is much higher than the proportion of the total
value contained in one commodity produced in many other factories.
This is why the realization of the value contained in one computer
is much more important (for the computer factory) than is the realization of the value contained in a car for the car factory. As a
general rule, the smaller the number of the commodities produced
the higher their value (e.g., a new type of commercial aeroplane
such as the 'Concorde'), and the more strategic the function, within
the technical division of labour, of this particular type of 'salesman'. This means that even if this technician only performed the
function of the collective worker, his strategic position within the
production process would ensure that ideologically speaking, there
would be no difference between him and the manager tout-court. He
must have a knowledge of the managerial world and mentality; he
must himself be a carrier of a certain ideology; he must be convin-
ced of the 'rationality' of what he is doing (and thus of the
'rationality' of the system based on profit-making). He is, then,
an extreme example of labour aristocracies; of someone who is,
objectively speaking, a member of the proletariat but who, ideologically and politically speaking, and through a very high income on
which this ideological and political practices rest, has been won

over the the bourgeoisie or petty bourgeoisie.(63)
   But this is not all. The interesting thing is that since he performs the function of the collective worker (either totally or partially) he can be subjected to a devaluation of his labour power, a
process which is already detectable. His job used to entail real
craftsmanship. Computers were custom-built following a thorough
study of the organization of the client's enterprise in order to
improve its efficiency.(64) He was autonomous and made decisions
largely on the basis of his experience. It was he who, by introducing the computer into the enterprise, was the channel through which
many functions were fragmented and subordinated to the computer. In
a relatively short period, however, he himself becomes a victim of
this process. He is 'rented' to the customer on an hourly basis
(which means that this time too is now controlled by the management),
does no longer invent the application of the computer to the specific situation but must apply standardized methods and procedures
handed down to him by specialized offices, he does not take care of
the computerization of the whole system but of only a part of it.
In short, he becomes a sort of mobile library: 'he receives a few
kilograms of paper every month; he substitutes pages, studies the
substituted pages'.(65) Thus, these higher technicians also start
experiencing a process of devaluation of labour power through the
dequalification of their positions.
   We can now summarize what we have said so far about the modifications brought about by proletarianization and the process of devaluation of labour power. First of all, both employees and technicians can be divided into two groups (of which only one, the
lower and by far the biggest) has already undergone, to some extent,
a process of devaluation of labour power. Secondly, within these
two groups, a system of stratification is possible according to the
degree to which this process of devaluation of labour power has
advanced. For certain positions within the lower group, this process has gone so far that we can safely classify the agents performing those functions as having been proletarianized. This is so
in the case of the card-puncher and certain technical designers
(draughtsmen).(66) At the higher level of this lower group we find
semi-professional technicians who, even though in a better position
than the others (i.e. even though not yet proletarianized) are
experiencing a continuous and rapid devaluation in their labour
power. An internal stratification is also possible within the
higher stratum, although here the process of devaluation of labour
power, of fragmentation of positions, etc., is much less advanced
and, therefore, much less visible.

VII SOME GENERAL CONCLUDING REMARKS

What is the practical relevance of the theory submitted? To put the
same question in other words: how does this theory collocate itself
in the ideological struggle which is today taking place in Italy?
And, more specifically, how does this theory differ in its conclusions, and thus in the possibilities it offers to draw correct lines
of political action, from the policies of the Italian left-wing
forces, especially the trade unions and the left-wing parties?

From 1968 — the year in which employees and technicians started participating in a massive and organized way in the class struggle side by side the Italian proletariat — onward, the policy of the trade unions has been characterized by their inability to understand the new, proletarianized condition of large strata of employees and technicians (one of the fundamental cause of these agents' combativeness).(67) The unions perceive this combativeness as the expression of a desire to stop the process of professional down-grading and for more co-management. The revolutionary potential of employee combativeness is completely overlooked by the unions who consider the vanguards of this movement as radicalized petit-bourgeois groups. Employees and technicians are seen as elements of the middle class only interested in retaining a non-proletarian condition. The policy that follows automatically from this mistaken analysis is simply a generalization of corporative demands, which are of course still present in large sectors of employees and technicians. The effect on the class struggle and on the consciousness of these agents is therefore a depoliticization of the masses.

In 1970 the capitalist class, which had been caught by surprise by the explosion of the employees and technicians' movement, launched a counter-offensive in order to check this movement by resuming on the one hand a policy of wage differentials — in order to break the unity of the movement — and by encouraging on the other hand these agents to participate more actively in union activities at the factory level. The unions not only failed to combat but encouraged this policy by changing their organization, creating a new body: the Factory Councils (Consigli di Fabbrica). The aim of the Factory Councils is three-fold:

(a) To make up for the credibility lost by the Internal Commissions (Commissioni Interne) which were reduced by the 1953 agreement (between the major employers' association and the major confederations of Italian unions) to plant grievance committees.(68)

(b) To curb the growth of autonomous grass-roots organizations which are waging the class truggle (especially on the economic level) on platforms alternative to those of the unions.(69)

(c) To achieve a better control, at the grass-roots level, of the factory.

Since 1972 two types of policy are clearly discernible. On the one hand the unions' policy which, on the basis of a mistaken and reformist analysis, proposes, also through the Factory Councils, job rotation schemes in order to counter the ever increasing fragmentation of positions. On the other hand the policy of the autonomous organizations which proposes promotions and wage increases by seniority, i.e. automatically. At present, which of these two policies is accepted, depends upon the strength of the unions vis-à-vis the autonomous organizations at the plant level.

The policy of the unions and of the left-wing parties then, has curbed rather than stimulated the development of the proletarian class consciousness among employees and technicians, in spite of their proletarian condition. By considering these agents as members of the middle class, both unions and left-wing parties only emphasize corporative demands. In reality, large sections of these agents have already become part of the proletariat, at the level of production relations, and other sectors are approaching this situation. The problem, then, when correctly approached, becomes one of alliance among several sectors of the working class rather than one of alliance between the proletariat and the petty bourgeoisie. A correct strategy for the proletariat, not only in Italy but also in other developed capitalist countries, depends upon a clear understanding of this question. It is in this light that the theory submitted above should be considered.

NOTES

1 First published in Economy and Society, vol. 4, no. 4, pp. 361-417. Only technical changes have been made.
2 On the concept of determination, overdetermination, domination etc., see chapter 3.
3 The production relations are determinant within the economic structure; the latter, in turn, is determinant vis-à-vis the other instances of society. We will see below that the production relations are also a structure in the sense that, of the three constitutive elements, only one is determinant vis-à-vis the others. Thus, what is determinant at one level of abstraction becomes determined at another level. As H. Lefebvre puts it: 'To the dialectical method of analysis and exposition ... form at a certain level becomes content at a higher level.' 'The Sociology of Marx', Vintage Books, 1969, p. 119.
4 Althusser is right in emphasizing that the means of production are an element of the production relations. See 'Reading Capital', London, 1970.
5 A superficial reading might convey the impression that the frame of analysis, given the introduction of the functional element within the production relations, can be charged with 'functionalist, structuralist deviations'. The determinant role of the economic and within the economic of the ownership element is, as we will see, already sufficient to reject this charge.
6 For the concept of collective worker see e.g. K. Marx, 'Capital', vol. I, International Publishers, New York, 1967, p. 508, and chapter 1 of this book.
7 This analysis differs greatly from that of Balibar, 'Reading Capital', pp. 215 and ff., and of Poulantzas, 'Les Classes sociales...', Paris, 1974, as will be seen below. C. Bettelheim applies the concepts of ownership and possession to the analysis of a system in transition between capitalism and socialism. See, for example, 'Calcule economique et formes de propriete', Italian translation: 'Calcolo economico e forme di proprieta', Jaca Books, Milan, 1970.
8 Since we have not dealt with the functional element yet, we disregard those agents who are expropriated of surplus labour themselves and whose function is that of expropriating surplus value (e.g. the foreman, the supervisor, etc.).
9 For a more detailed analysis of this point see chapters 1 and 2.
10 The literature on productive and unproductive labour is vast. Besides Marx' own writings, I will mention only a review by Ian Gough, Productive and Unproductive Labour in Marx, 'New Left Review', no. 76, November-December 1972, and as a precise and

detailed study of the concept of productive labour in Marx,
J. Bischoff et al., Produktieve en Onproduktieve Arbeid als
Kategorieën in de Klassenanalyse, in 'Karl Marx, Over Produktieve en Onproduktieve Arbeid', SUNschrift 26, Nijmegen, 1970.
Many authors misunderstand the concept of productive labour.
For example, O. Lange, in his 'Political Economy', Italian
translation, vol. I, p. 20, identifies productive labour and
material production. For Marx, on the other hand, whether a
capitalist 'has laid out his capital in a teaching factory,
instead of a sausage factory' ('Capital', vol. I, p. 509), does
not make any difference as far as the production of surplus
value is concerned. Non-material production, e.g. production
of services, can be both productive and non-productive. The
sales effort is an example of capital employed in the non-
productive sphere. The fact that this branch of the economy has
become much more important under monopoly capitalism does not
change its nature as being an unproductive activity, in spite of
baran and Sweezy's contention to the contrary (see 'Monopoly
Capital', New York, 1968, p. 126). Marx, in 'Capital', vol. II,
p. 149, is quite clear on this point. Moreover, the concept of
productive labour has nothing to do with luxury production, i.e.
has nothing to do with the use value of a commodity, with the
type of concrete labour which went into the production of that
particular use value. The fact that many products are luxury
products is not a problem from the point of view of the capitalist production process. The important point is that this production process brings in surplus value, either through the production of luxury goods or through the production of wage goods.
Luxury production can be condemned, from the point of view of
capitalist production, only when too many means of production
and too much labour power are devoted to this type of production
so as to endanger the reproduction of capital. Luxury products
are non-reproductive items, i.e. commodities which cannot be
consumed productively, since they are neither means of production nor wage goods. If too much labour goes to the production
of luxuries, not enough labour will be devoted to the production of those goods with which to start a new production cycle
(the same holds for the production of weapons). On the other
hand, 'for a mode of production which creates wealth for the
non-producer and thus must give wealth forms which allow its
appropriation by wealth devoted only to enjoyment, luxury is an
absolute necessity' (Marx, 'Resultate...', p. 81[484]).
Finally, productive labour has nothing to do with labour necessary for the production process. This is the mistake made by
Mandel, in his 'Marxist Economic Theory', New York, 1968, p.
204. As shown in chapter 2 public services, such as the provision of water, gas and electricity, can be either a productive (of surplus value) activity if provided by a capitalist or
by a capitalist state activity, or non productive if provided
by a non-capitalist state activity. The difference between
these two types of state activities is explained in chapter 2.

11   As I say in chapter 1, section III (k), 'To perform the function of the collective worker means to take part in the capitalist production process as a whole (i.e. in all its three

phases) from the point of view of the labour process and thus
of the surplus labour producing process. Conversely, to perform
the global function of capital means to take part in the capitalist production process as a whole exclusively from the point
of view of the surplus labour producing process.' The notion of
function of capital has to do with performing what Marx calls
the function of control and surveillance (not to be confused
with the work of supervision and management which encompasses
both the work of control and surveillance and the work of co-
ordination and unity of the labour process). Under monopoly
capitalism, '(a) the global function of capital is separated
from the legal ownership of capital; (b) the global function of
capital is performed by a structure, a first part of which only
performs this function and has the real ownership of capital, a
second part of which performs this function without having the
real ownership of capital, and a third part of which does not
economically own capital and performs both the function of the
collective worker and the global function of capital (in a
variable balance).'

12 See chapter 1, section VI, and further down in this chapter.
Many Marxist authors perceive the tendential disappearance of
the global function of capital as a 'loss of responsibility'.
This point is discussed, as far as the West German scene is
concerned, by A. Lange, L. Peter, and F. Deppe in De technies-
wetenschappelijke revolutie en de theorie van be 'nieuwe arbeidersklasse' in 'Sunschrift 14', Nijmegen, 1970, pp. 13-28. See
especially pp.22-3.

13 That the possession reverts to the collective labourer is shown
by the innumerable examples of workers occupying a factory and
managing the factory themselves without needing the direction of
the capitalist. The case of the French watch-making factory LIP
is only one of the last instances. See F.H. de Virieu, 'LIP,
100,000 montres sans patron', Calmann-Levy, 1973.

14 That the collective labourer is now becoming an international
entity is shown by the (still not very frequent) instances of
strikes co-ordinated on an international level.

15 The coincidence of the rise of monopoly capitalism and of the
global function of capital (of which scientific management is
one form) can be detected also in the following passage: 'It
will already have been noticed that the crucial developments in
the process of production date from precisely the same period as
monopoly capitalism. Scientific management and the whole "movement" for the organization of production on its modern basis
have their beginnings in the last two decades of the last century'. See H. Braverman, 'Labor and Monopoly Capitalism', New
York, 1974, p. 252.

16 But, as I have shown in chapter 1, section 4, the function of
capital always outweighs the function of labour. This is one of
the differences between the individual capitalist, i.e. the old
middle class, and the new middle class, parts of which perform
both functions in a ratio, in which the function of labour dominates the function of capital.

17 Marx, in the unfinished chapter on classes ('Capital', vol. III,
chapter LII), distinguished between wage-labourers, capitalists

and land-owners. This seems to indicate that the concept of
productive labour, while essential for an analysis of the capitalist productive process, is not *the* dividing line separating
one class from another. The industrial and the commercial capitalists are not two classes because, (aside from the fact that they
both own the means of production and perform the function of
capital) they both expropriate surplus labour. However, they
are two parts of the same class because the former expropriate
surplus labour in the form of surplus value (exploitation) while
the latter expropriates directly surplus labour (economic
oppression).

18   H. Braverman, in his 'Labour and Monopoly Capital', fails to
make this distinction as well even though at times he gets very
close to it. His starting point is correct: 'The complexity of
the class structure of modern monopoly capitalism arises from
the ... consideration ... that *almost all of the population has
been transformed into employees of capital*' (p. 404). However,
'the form of hired employment gives expression to two totally
different realities: in one case, capital hires a "labor force"
whose duty it is to work, under external direction, to increase
capital; in the other, by a process of selection within the capitalist class and chiefly from its own ranks, capital chooses a
management staff to represent it on the spot, and in represent-
ing it to supervise and organize the labors of the working
population' (p. 405). But to supervise and to organize are two
different things: the former implies the performing of the function of capital, the latter of the function of labour. Thus,
inasmuch as management 'organizes' (the labour process) and thus
performs the function of the collective worker, it too 'increases capital'. Let us assume, however, in order to follow Braverman's argument, that management performs only the global
function of capital. 'Thus far the difference is clear, but
between these two extremes there is a range of intermediate
categories, sharing the characteristic of worker on the one side
and manager on the other in varying degrees. The gradations of
positions in the line of management may be seen chiefly in terms
of authority, while gradations in staff positions are indicated
by the levels of technical expertise' (p. 405). Thus Braverman
comes considerably close to identifying the new middle class, in
terms of the functional aspect of the production relations, as
those agents who perform both functions. Authority implies, in
this context, control and surveillance (i.e. global function of
capital) while technical expertise implies co-ordination and
unity of the labour process (function of the collective worker).
Moreover, further down, he touches upon the other segment of the
new middle class (to be discussed below), those agents who do
not own the means of production and perform only the global
function of capital, i.e. the 'subalterns and noncommissioned
officers of the industrial army, the foremen, the petty "managers", etc.' (p. 406). However, Braverman's analysis, instead
of going further in this direction, stops at this point thus
failing to identify the new middle class in terms of contradiction between the determinant element of the production relations, the ownership element, and the determined elements, of

which the function performed is one. Moreover, what Braverman
calls 'the middle levels of administrative and technical employment' and which 'embraces in the United States today perhaps
over 15 but less than 20 per cent of total employemnt' (p. 404)
is a spurious category since it encompasses agents employed both
in the capitalist production process (both pure and unproductive) and agents in 'hospitals, schools, government administration, and so forth' (p. 404). Since there is no analysis, in
Braverman's book, of the various production processes (besides
the capitalist one) and of the production relations which support them, his analysis cannot go much further.

19 This is so because the class identification of an agent depends
on all three aspects of the capitalist production relations.
Disregard of one of them leads to grave mistakes. For example,
both the commercial worker and his supervisor, 1, do not have
the real ownership of the means of production and, 2, are expropriated of surplus labour. Yet there is a basic difference
between the expropriation of surplus labour of these two agents.
The former is expropriated while performing the function of
labour, while the latter is expropriated while performing the
function of capital. To disregard the functional element means
giving both agents (at the level of production relations, i.e.
disregarding ideological and political practices) the same class
collocation. In order to avoid doing this, Poulantzas must
define the working class as the productive labourers and the
middle class as the unproductive labourers. Under the middle
class he must then lump together the unproductive labourer and
the non-labourer, both the commercial worker and his supervisor,
at whatever level in the hierarchy. The same approach is followed by P. Walton and A. Gamble (London, 1972) whose disregard
of the functional element leads to the lumping together in the
same class of agents whose labour has an opposite social significance.

20 There are a number of theoretical constructions — besides the
'managerial revolution' — which are the ideological reflection
of the advent of the global capitalist. Let me mention just one
of them; organization theory. 'In economic theory, it is the
individual, the entrepreneur, who makes the decision; organisation theory has the organization or the firm as the decision-
maker. In other words, in the latter approach, decisions are
organisational, not individual one.' (K. Dunkerley, 'The Study
of Organizations', London, 1972, p. 49). The concept of the
firm as the decision-maker is the distorted, mythical way in
which the bourgeois sociologist perceives, 1, the fragmentation
of economic ownership among a restricted number of top managers
and, 2, the delegation of parts of the global function of capital to agents who do not own the means of production and who
either perform only this function or perform this function
together with the function of the collective worker. Whenever
attempts are made (as in 'job satisfaction' schemes) to involve
the agents who perform exclusively the function of the collective worker in the decision making process, all that happens is
the delegation of a (small) part of the global function of capital to those agents without giving them any real economic power,

any real ownership of the means of production. On this latter point, see below, section II.

21   In spite of these critical remarks, I do not wish to diminish the considerable theoretical importance of Poulantzas' work.

22   We disregard the legal ownership of the means of production, an element which does not belong to the capitalist *production* relation.

23   As we will see below, a position is also characterized by a third element (besides the technical and social content), i.e. by the value required. By this latter concept I mean that each position must be filled by an agent and that the position *requires* (but *does not determine*) that the agent's labour power must have a certain value.

24   For the difference between the old and the new middle class, at the level of production relations, see chapter 1, section 4. The concept of middle classes is a very precise one and is far from being 'one of the spongiest catchalls in the Marxist vocabulary'. (P. Worsley, 'The Third World', London, 1964, p. 140).

25   Why Management is Pushing 'Job Enrichment', 'International Socialist Review', December 1974, p. 25. Academic sociology is not unaware, of course, of the real reason behind job satisfaction schemes. A report under the title 'Work in America' prepared by a Special Task Force selected by the Secretary of Health, Education and Welfare and published in 1973, found that 'significant numbers of American workers are dissatisfied with the quality of their working lives....As a result, the productivity of the worker is low....Moreover, a growing body of research indicates that, as work problems increase, there may be a consequent decline in 'balanced socio-political attitudes.' Quoted by Braverman, op.cit., p. 31. As to the nature and extent of the various job enrichment, job enlargement, work participation etc. schemes, let us quote Braverman again. 'The reforms that are being proposed today are by no means new ones, and have been popular with certain corporations (IBM for instance) and certain management theorists for a generation. They represent a style of management rather than a genuine change in the position of the worker. They are characterised by a studied pretence of worker "participation", a gracious liberality in allowing the worker to adjust a machine, replace a light bulb, move from a fractional job to another, and to have the illusion of making decisions by changing among fixed and limited alternatives designed by a management which deliberately leaves insignificant matters open to choice.' (Emphasis added.) See Braverman, op.cit., pp. 38-9.

26   Op.cit., p. 44. I make a similar point in chapter 1, section III, where I mention the double function performed by the project leader who carries out a feasibility study.

27   J.P. Windmuller, 'Labor Relations in the Netherlands', Cornell University Press, 1969, pp. 259-60. The social nature of a function does not change whether it is performed within the enterprise (see the above-given example of all those agents engaged in 'job enrichment' schemes and who thus perform the global function of capital) or outside it (thus, all those working in an employers association perform the global function of

capital even if they do not 'work' within an enterprise; the
fact that a group of agents, previously performing the global
function of capital, becomes separated from the enterprise does
not change the nature of their function).

28 It should be borne in mind that we are here dealing with only
the capitalist production process proper, i.e. with the production process which produces surplus value. This restriction of
my field of inquiry should not be interpreted to mean that I
regard the capitalist structure as made up exclusively of the
pure capitalist production process and of the production (and
distribution) relations upon which this process rests. An indication of the complexity of the economic structure is provided
in the Introduction.

29 What just said should not be interpreted as if the determinant
role reverts to the technical rather than to the social division
of labour.

30 We can use the terms vertical and horizontal mobility provided
we give them a specific content, provided we refer to the social
content of positions, i.e., at this level of abstraction, to the
three aspects of the capitalist production relations. Thus,
vertical mobility describes the movement of an agent from one
position to another, the social content of which is different.
If the social content of the two positions is the same, then we
can talk of horizontal mobility.

31 This theoretical operation is justified by the fact that under
capitalism there is a real tendency to reduce all skilled labour
to average labour. See K. Marx, 'Capital', vol. I, p. 198.

32 I am anticipating points to be worked out in more detail below.

33 See e.g. 'Capital', vol. I, pp. 520 and ff., 'Theories of Surplus Value', vol. I, p. 216. This type of devaluation, which
we will examine in detail shortly, will be called wage goods
devaluation.

34 From the point of view of qualifications, and if we consider
those skilled labourers who are not far from the unskilled
labourers, this process can mean for them a change from skilled
to unskilled labour. Yet, intellectually, they will still be
able to perform skilled labour. A study by Kuylaars in Holland
(werk en leven van de industriële loonarbeider als object van
een sociale ondernemingspolitiek, Leiden, 1951, quoted in J.
Berting and L.U. de Sitter, 'Arbeidssatisfactie', Van Gorcum,
1971, p. 23) shows that half of the unskilled labourers are in
fact intellectually able to perform skilled jobs. The usual
explanation for this phenomenon is provided in terms of discrepancy between the school system and the requirements of production, where the former keeps, for some time, providing a type of
labour force with higher than necessary qualifications. However,
another element of the explanation is the dequalification of
labour undergone (for the reasons and in the fashion to be explained shortly) by many agents, their becoming unskilled labourers. We will see below that this phenomenon is not at all in
contradiction with the trend for the general level of skills of
the labour power to increase.

35 According to N. Poulantzas, nowadays we can talk about a verit-
able reserve army of intellectual labour. See 'Les Classes
sociales...', p. 333.

36   Thus the migrant worker must be considered as a member of the
collective worker. For a good analysis of migrant labour, see
S. Castles and G. Kosack, The Function of Labour Immigration in
Western European Capitalism, in 'New Left Review', no. 73, May-
June 1972, pp. 3-21. See also F. Corbillé, Homage et réserves
de main-d'oeuvre: une gestion impérialiste des excédents?,
'Critique de l'économie politique', no. 10, Jan.-March 1973, pp.
4-29; for the psychological aspects, see J. Berger, Directions
in Hell, 'New Left Review', no. 87-88, Sept.-Dec. 1974, pp. 49-
60.

37   Tendential decrease, because of the various counteracting tendencies. Thus, in terms of value, the value of labour power
can display a constant trend. Labour power is a special commodity because in its value determination there enters a culturally determined element. Thus, as the level of productive
forces increases, the absolute amount of wage goods making up
the culturally determined subsistence minimum also increases and
new wage goods enter into this minimum.

38   Of course, there can also be a social *requalification* for a
minority of positions (and thus of agents) in which the global
function of capital increases vis-à-vis the function of the
collective worker.

39   Much confusion has arisen, in discussing the proletarianization
of the new middle class, from the lack of distinction between
positions and agents. Take the foreman, for example, This
position encompassed originally both the function of capital and
the function of the collective worker. The foreman, in fact,
was performing not only the work of control and surveillance
but was also the master craftsman, as C.W. Mills rightly points
out in 'White Collar' (pp. 87 and ff.). With the coming of big
industry and thus under monopoly capitalism, this position is
deprived of the function of collective worker aspect. As Mills
puts it: 'Even though foremen are no longer master craftsmen
and work-guides as of old, they are still seen by management as
key men, not so much in their technical roles in the work process as in their roles in the social organisation of the factory. It is in keeping with the managerial demiurge and the
changed nature of the foreman's role that he is led into ways of
manipulation. He is to develop discipline and loyalty among the
workers by using his own personality as the main tool of per-
suasion. (p. 90) We have here a devaluation of labour power and
thus a dequalification of position. *However, we cannot speak of
proletarianization in this case because one of the three elements of the production relations (the functional one) changes in
the opposite direction.* The proletarianization of the foreman
takes place when his position, due to reationalization, is
abolished and he, as an agent, must occupy a new position, thus
becoming a worker.

40   As E. Mandel says, 'the conclusion regarding the tendency of
average wages to fall needs to be qualified by two observations.
It applies only to capitalist society taken as a whole, that is,
on the *world*scale; and it may well find concrete expression in
a tendency for average wages in industrialized countries to
rise, since there the accumulation of capital takes place on

such a scale that employment constantly expands, in comparison
with the growth of population, *because the abolition of jobs
implied in this movement takes place not so much inside these
countries as outside them, in the countries of the "Third
World"*. It may be tempered, too, by the fact that alongside
the increasing use of machinery, there is also an increase in
the number of jobs in the service sector, and a "new middle
class" develops which prevents continual growth in the industrial reserve army — phenomena which Marx had foreseen long
before they occurred, in two passages in "Theories of Surplus
Value". And large scale migratory movements such as the emigra-
tion of some 70 million Europeans to America and overseas
regions during the nineteenth century, may eventually profoundly
alter the tendencies in the evolution of supply and demand of
labour'. 'The formation of the Economic Thought of Karl Marx',
Monthly Review Press, 1971, pp. 149-50. See also S. Amin:
'...in the European model, capitalist industry employs more
workers than it ruins craftsmen....In the colonial model,
industry employs *fewer* workers than it ruins craftsmen. The
effect of competition by overseas industry is obvious.'
'Accumulation On A World Scale', Monthly Review Press, New York,
1974, p. 153.

41 Westergaard: 1973, 131. What I have said does not imply, of
course, the acceptance of the 'upgrading theory' which has been
correctly criticized by Braverman, op.cit., chapter 20. F.
Pollock discusses the effects of automation on the upgrading
and downgrading of jobs in 'The Economic and Social Consequences
of Automation', Oxford, 1957, especially pp. 49, 80, 88, 90-2,
210-12. An extreme version of the upgrading theory can be found
in S. Mallet, 'La Nouvelle Classe Ouvrière', Editions du Seuil,
1969. For a criticism of Mallet's theory, see N. Poulantzas,
1974, op.cit., pp. 258-61. According to Mandel (Workers Under
Neo-Capitalism, 'International Socialist Review', vol. 29, no.
6, pp. 1-16), the effects of automation on the working class are
both a reduction of industrial labour in the factory and a great
increase of industrial labour in agriculture, distribution, the
service industries, and administration. Thus, automation 'tends
to integrate a constantly growing part of the mass of wage and
salary earners into an increasingly homogeneous proletariat'
(p. 7). There is therefore no qualitative difference between
old and modern labour. The latter is characterized, just as the
former, by 'its key role in the productive process, its basic
alienation, its economic exploitation' (p. 6). Mandel cites
some indicators of this increased homogeneity of the proletariat: 'reduced wage differentials between white-collar and manual
workers, which is a universal trend in the West; increased
unionisation and union militancy of these "new" layers, which is
equally universal;...rising similarities of consumption, of
social status and environment of these layers; growing similarities of working conditions, i.e. growing similarity of monoto-
nous, mechanised, uncreative, nerve-racking and stultifying
work in factory, bank, bus, public administration, department
stores and airplanes' (p. 8). These phenomena are explained in
terms of 'equalisation of the conditions of reproduction of

labour-power, especially of skilled and semi-skilled labour-
power'. (p. 8). Thus, 'the third industrial revolution is
repeating in the whole society what the first industrial revolution achieved inside the factory system' (p. 8). Mandel
focuses, correctly, on the devaluation of skilled labour power,
within the frame of rising absolute wages, and on its economic
and social consequences (e.g. growing homogeneity of wages and
salaries, of labour itself, of status, etc.). However, the devaluation of labour power is not a new phenomenon and cannot be
a characteristic of neo-capitalism. What is missing in Mandel's
analysis is the non-labourer, i.e. the agents performing the
function of capital. Therefore, Mandel does not see that the
advent of monopoly capitalism is characterized by the global
capitalist, i.e. by all those agents who perform collectively
and hierarchically the function of capital. Thus, the proletarianization of the new middle class, of which the increased
union militancy (especially under neo-capitalism) is an effect,
is to be explained not only in terms of devaluation of labour
power (something which is characteristic also of individual
capitalism) but also in terms of the tendential disappearance
of the global function of capital through a technical dequalification of positions. I.e. this process must be explained in
terms of devaluation through dequalification. Moreover, there
are also other factors which characterize the agents of production under neo-capitalism, e.g., the internationalization both
of the collective worker and of the global capitalist.

42 Keeping in mind what has been said above, i.e. that the rise
    in absolute wages implies also a rise in the minimum level of
    education and skills.

43 It is these changes at the economic level which are the origin
    of the phenomena which are usually associated with the prolet-
    arianization of the new middle class: lowering conditions of
    life, loss of independence and of positions of privilege,
    liability to unemployment or to disguised unemployment, loss of
    prestige, etc. Also the decrease (relative to the average) of
    wages has to be explained in terms of devaluation of labour
    power (and thus also, in the case of devaluation through de-
    qualification, in terms of the tendential disappearance of the
    global function of capital). But political and ideological
    considerations play also a role in wage determination. This
    point has already been mentioned above. This is one of the
    factors explaining why the levelling of the proletarianized
    sectors' wages around the average can be observed in recent
    years in Germany and England but not in France. See Poulantzas,
    'Les Classes sociales...', p. 329. This is an example of over-
    determination as defined in chapter 3.

44 The point that the proletarianization of the new middle class
    is explained by the concept of devaluation through dequalifica-
    tion rather than that of wage goods devaluation is not suffi-
    ciently clearly formulated in chapter 1. Moreover, it should
    be clear that this type of devaluation is also important under
    individual capitalism (but not in the first stage of capitalist
    development, the stage of formal subordination of labour to
    capital, because in this stage there is practically no technical

division of labour and thus there can be no devaluation through dequalification). However, its importance is amplified under monopoly capitalism because it is the mechanism which makes possible the proletarianization of the new middle class, i.e. the disappearance of the global function of capital. The economic rationale behind such a disappearance is made clear in graph 1 above and in the following numerical examples.

45   Usually, Marxist analysis has been focused only on the connection between long term elements (e.g. higher level of productive forces) and wage goods devaluation (e.g. cheaper production of wage goods).

46   See E. Mandel, 'Wat is Neokapitalisme?', Nijmegen, 1970, pp. 9-12 and 'Inleiding in de Marxistiese Ekonomie', Nijmegen, 1970, pp. 63-73. In these two books Mandel mentions only the work of N.D. Kondratieff who 'discovered' in 1920-1 the existence of long waves of an average length of about 50 years. I use the term 'discovered' in quotation marks because, as Mandel shows in his 'Der Spatkapitalismus', Suhrkamp Verlag, Frankfurt-am-Main, 1972, ch. 4, other authors before Kondratieff studied the problem of long waves, e.g., the Russian Marxist Parvus, the Dutch J. van Gelderen, and Kautsky. According to Kondratieff 'During the rise of the long waves years of prosperity are more numerous, whereas years of depression predominate during the downswing....Moreover, during the recession of the long waves an especially large number of important discoveries and inventions in the technique of production and communication are made, which, however, are usually applied on a large scale only at the beginning of the next long upswing'. N.D. Kondratieff, The Long Waves in Economic Life, 'Review of Economic Statistics', vol. XVII, November 1935, no. 5, pp. 105-15. For a critical view of Kondratieff's analysis see G. Garvy, Kondratieff's Theory of Long Cycles. 'Review of Economic Statistics', November 1943, pp. 203-20. However, by far the best treatment of the long waves (including not only a criticism of Kondratieff's work but also an explanation of the phenomenon) is to be found in E. Mandel, 'Der Spätkapitalismus'.

47   A discussion of the nature of economic cycle is obviously beyond the scope of this paper. It should however be pointed out that the massive periodical introduction of technological innovations should not be considered as the cause of the cycle. This point was already made in 1935 by N. Mozkowska, in her 'Zur Kritik Moderner Krisentheorien', Italian translation, 'Per la critica delle teorie moderne della crisi', Turin, 1974, p. 50. See also Kondratieff, op.cit., p. 112, and E. Mandel, 'Der Spatkapitalismus'. According to Kondratieff both the direction and intensity of inventions and their application are determined by the condition of the economy, i.e. by the cycle. We will see in a moment that this relation is somewhat weakened after the Second World War by the effects of the arms industry on the discovery and application of new techniques.

48   We disregard here a host of other factors.

49   'It seems that the type of growth that the capitalist world has known since 1945, based on the Americanisation of Western Europe, is tending in its turn to exhaust its possibilities.

The world monetary crisis and the reappearance of chronic
"deflationary tendencies" are perhaps symptoms of this. What
may take over the role on ensuring the growth of capitalism?
     'I see three possibilities. First, progressive integration
of the countries of Eastern Europe (Russia and its satellites)
in the world market, and *their* modernisation. Second, the contemporary scientific and technical revolution which, along with
automation, the conquest of the atom, and the conquest of space,
may open up substantial possibilities for deepening the market.
Third and last, a new wave of extension of capitalism to the
Third World, based on a new type of international specialisa-
tion made possible by the technical revolution of our time. In
this context, the countries of the centre would "specialize" in
ultramodern activities, while forms of classical industry hith-
erto reserved for them would be transferred to the periphery.
S. Amin, 'Accumulation on a World Scale', p. 532. E. Mandel
locates the end of the expansive long cycle at around 1966-7
('Der Spätkapitalismus', p. 115). He gives schematically the
following reasons at p. 125: 'Das langsame Aufsaugen der
"industriellen Reservearmee" der imperialistischen länder
blockiert trotz wachsender Automatisierung ein weiteres Steigen
der Mehrwertrate. Der Klassenkampf greift die Profitrate an.
Verschärfte internationale Konkurrenz und Weltwährunsskrise
wirken im selben Sinne. Expansion des Welthandels verlang samt.

50   See note 45 above. See also Mandel, 'Der Spätkapitalismus',
     chapter 6.
51   The fact that the introduction of new technologies in the pro-
     duction process both introduces 'simplification of tasks' and
     increases 'technical competence' is also perceived by bourgeois
     sociologists. See, e.g. S.R. Parker, R.K. Brown, J. Child,
     M.A. Smith, 'The Sociology of Industry', London, 1967, p. 30.
52   By backward capitalists I understand, for the purpose of the
     present discussion, the small and medium entrepreneurs. But it
     should be kept in mind that this concept is in reality much
     wider and that it encompasses also other elements: e.g. the
     state bureaucracy.
53   A great part of the following is based on material to be found
     in M. Lelli, 'Technici e lotta di classe', Bari, 1973; C. Bag-
     lioni, 'Il conflitto industriale a l'azione del sindacato',
     Bologna, 1966; G. Martinoli, I. laureati nell'industria in
     'I Laureati in Italia', Bologna, 1968; my interpretation of the
     material and the perspective are of course quite different.
     Occasionally I will refer to other countries as well. As the
     reader will notice, the material presented in this and the
     following sections sketches only the basic trends, thus disre-
     garding cyclical fluctuations. For example, in the following
     pages I will focus on the steady process of devaluation of the
     technicians and employees' labour power, and on the loss, for a
     great part of them, of the global function of capital. This
     process is of course reflected — even though not automatically —
     in the narrowing of the wage gap between working class and new
     middle class. However, this process is not unilinear, but cyc-
     lical and a more comprehensive historical analysis than the one
     provided here must take this into consideration. We might find

an indication, as far as the USA is concerned, in C.W. Mills:
'In 1890, the average income of white-collar occupational
groups was about double of wage workers. Before World War I,
salaries were not so adversely affected by slumps as wages were
but, on the contrary, they rather steadily advanced. Since
World War I, however, salaries have been reacting to turns in
the economic cycles more and more like wages, although still to
a lesser extent. If wars help wages more because of the greater
flexibility of wages, slumps help salaries because of their
greater inflexibility. Yet after each war era, salaries have
never regained their previous advantage over wages. Each phase
of the cycle, as well as the progressive rise of all income
groups, has resulted in a narrowing of the income gap between
wage-workers and white-collar employees.' ('White Collar',
Oxford University Press, 1961, p. 72. For a more detailed analysis, see pp. 279-80.)

54   See also Braverman, 'Labor and Monopoly Capital', pp. 259-60 and
293-5.

55   See 'I Comitati Unitari di Base', Quaderni di Avanguardia
Operaia, no. 6, Sapere Edizioni, Milan, 1973, pp. 36-7.

56   The reader will recall that the income of those agents performing both functions is made up both of a wage component and of a
revenue component.

57   These are, usually, employees who have been already proletarian-
ised.

58   See also Braverman, 'Labor and Monopoly Capital', pp. 293-358.

59   'The industrial managers range from the production engineer and
designer at the top to the foremen immediately above the workmen
at the bottom.' C.W. Mills, 'White Collar', p. 82. White collar
people are, for Mills, a residual category: 'Their position is
more definable in terms of their relative differences from other
strata than in any absolute terms.' See ibid., p. 75.

60   'In its early stages, a new division of labour may specialise
men in such a way as to increase their levels of skill; but
later, especially when whole operations are split and mechanised,
such division develops certain faculties at the expense of
others and narrows all of them. And as it comes more fully
under mechanisation and centralised management, it levels men
off again as automatons. Then there are a few specialists and a
mass of automatons.' Mills, op.cit., p. 227. See also p. 245.

61   Concerning the American scene, Braverman mentions the example of
the engineer. 'The engineer's job is chiefly one of design, but
even design, where a project has grown large enough, may be subjected to the traditional rules of the division of labour...At
the same time, so-called computer-aided design and computer-aided
engineering encourage the translation of the traditional graphic
language of the engineer into numerical form so that it may be
handled by computers and numerical control instrumentation.' As
a result of the fragmentation and the routinisation of tasks,
and thus of devaluation of labour power through dequalification,
the engineers' wages display a long-run tendency to decline.
The 'index of the ratio of median engineering salaries to those
of the full time manufacturing wage earner shows that, if the
1929 ratio is taken as 100, by 1954 the ratio was only 66·6.'

See Braverman, 'Labor and Monopoly Capital', pp. 243-4. It is clear that this long-run tendency for these salaries to approach the average wage cannot be explained in terms of excess of supply over demand, as D.M. Blank and G.J. Stigler do in their 'The Demand and Supply of Scientific Personnel' (quoted in Braverman, op.cit.). Any such 'explanation' is nothing more than an ideological device to avoid the study of production relations.

62   See FIM-FIOM-UILM, 'Impiegati 1972'.

63   This is also an example of how the *determinant* role always reverts to the economic while the *dominant* role can revert to either the ideological (as in this case) or the political. In this case, the economic has the determinant role because it is the position this technician has within the production process which determines his importance, his strategic position. But it is the ideological which has the dominant role because the performance of this strategic (economic) function is ensured by the role played by the ideological. Therefore, his place in the social structure is determined (in the last instance) by the economic, while the dominant element is the ideological. In other words, it is the conditions determined by the economic which assign the ideological its dominant role. What I have called in chapter 1, *direct overdetermination* is nothing more than the reflection, in placing the agents in the social structure, of this non-correspondence between the determinant and dominant role. For an extended discussion of these concepts, see chapter 3.

64   Let us be clear on this point. In his role as a highly qualified salesman, this technician takes part in a certain labour process (to sell or to rent a computer), i.e. the production of a commodity, which in this case is a non-material commodity, a service. He is unproductive, yet performs the function of the collective worker. His work is totally different (from the social content point of view) from the work of those whose task is to make sure that he is an 'efficient ' salesman. This is his function *within the enterprise in which he works*, within the production process in which he takes part. On the other hand, when he counsels the prospective client on how to arrange the labour process, he helps the manager as a co-ordinator of the labour process and thus as performing the function of the collective worker. But the function of the collective worker this technician performs within the computer factory has nothing to do with the fact that he helps the client in carrying out the work of co-ordination and unity of the labour process and thus the function of the collective worker. If this technician would only counsel the client on how to carry out a better system of control and surveillance, he would still be performing within the computer factory the function of the collective worker. In other words, the social content of the function he performs in the creation of a certain commodity (in this case a service) within the enterprise where he works is independent of whether that commodity helps the purchaser to perform the function of the collective worker or the global function of capital.

65   FIM, FIOM, UILM, op.cit., p. 265.

66   Most are ex-workers who, with great sacrifices, have followed
     courses in order to become draughtsman and have escaped one
     proletarian condition only to fall into another.
67   Much of what follows has been taken from E. Bonavitacola,
     G. D'Arrigo, G.C. Majorino, D. Roma, 'Sulla collocazione di
     classe degli impiegati', Calusca Editrice, Milan, 1975. I do
     not agree, however, with the analysis provided in this book,
     analysis which collocates employees and technicians within the
     proletariat simply by denying the existence of the middle class
     in terms of capitalist production relations.
68   See Seyfarth, Shaw, Fairweather and Geraldson, 'Labor Relations
     and the Law in Italy and The United States', University of
     Michigan, 1970, p. 41 and passim.
69   See G. Carchedi, Socio-economic Development, Unitary Committees
     of the Base, and Industrial Relations in Italy Since 1968,
     paper presented to the Third World Congress of the International
     Industrial Relations Association, London, 3-7 September 1973.

REFERENCES

ALTHUSSER, L., 'For Marx', Vintage Books, New York, 1970.
ALTHUSSER, L., Reply to John Lewis (Self Criticism) Part 1, in 'Marxism Today', October 1972.
ALTHUSSER, L., Reply to John Lewis (Self Criticism) Part 2, in 'Marxism Today', November 1972.
ALTHUSSER, L. and BALIBAR, E., 'Reading Capital', Allen Lane, London, 1970.
AMIN, S., 'Accumulation on a World Scale', Monthly Review Press, New York and London, 1974.
ANDERSON, C.H. 'The Political Economy of Social Class', Prentice-Hall, Englewood Cliffs, 1974.
ARMANSKI, G., Staatliche Lohnarbeiter - Teil der Lohnarbeiter-klasse oder neue Mittelklasse? Zum Verhältnis von Akkumulation des Kapitals und unproduktiver Arbeit, in 'Probleme des Klassenkampfs', no. 14, 1974.
ARTHUR, C.J., Introduction to K. Marx and F. Engels, 'The German Ideology', New York, 1970.
BAGLIONI, C., 'Il conflitto industriale e l'azione del sindacato', Bologna, 1966.
BARAN, P.A. and SWEEZY, P.M., 'Monopoly Capital', New York, 1968.
BAUMAN, Z., 'Lineamenti di una Sociologia Marxista', Editori Riuniti, Rome, 1971.
BECKER, J.F., Class Structure and Conflict in the Managerial Phase, 'Science and Society', Fall 1973, pp. 259-77 and Winter 1973-4, pp. 437-53.
BERGER, J., Directions in Hell, 'New Left Review', no. 87-88, September-December 1974, pp. 49-60.
BERTING, J. and de SITTER, L:U., 'Arbeidssatisfactie', Assen, 1971.
BETTELHEIM, C., 'La Transition vers l'économie socialiste', Italian translation, 'La transizione all'economia socialista', Jaca Books, Milan, 1969.
BETTELHEIM, C., On the Transition between Capitalism and Socialism, in 'Monthly Review', March 1969.
BETTELHEIM, C., 'Calcule économique et formes de propriété', Italian translation 'Calcolo economico e forme di proprieta', Jaca Books, Milan, 1970.
BETTELHEIM, C., More on the Society of Transition, in 'Monthly

Review', December 1970.

BETTELHEIM, C., 'Révolution culturelle et organisation industrielle en Chine', Maspero, 1973.

BISCHOFF, J., et al., Produktieve en onproduktieve arbeid als kategorieën in de klassenanalyse, in 'Karl Marx over produktieve en onproduktieve arbeid', Sunschrift 26, Nijmegen, 1970.

BLACKBURN, R., The New Capitalism, in R. Blackburn (ed.), 'Ideology in Social Science', Fontana, London, 1973, pp. 164-86.

BLACKBURN, R., STEDMAN-JONES, G., Louis Althusser and the Struggle for Marxism, in Howard, D. and Klase, K.E. (eds), 'The Unknown Dimension', Basic Books, New York, 1972.

BONAVITACOLA, E., D'ARRIGO, G., MAJORINO, G.C., ROMA, D., 'Sulla collocazione di classe degli impiegati', Calusca Editrice, Milan, 1975.

BRAVERMAN, H., 'Labor and Monopoly Capital', Monthly Review Press, New York, 1974.

CARCHEDI, G., 'Socio-economic Development, Unitary Committees of the Base, and Industrial Relations in Italy since 1968', paper presented to the Third World Congress of the International Industrial Relations Association, London, 3-7 September 1973.

CASTLES, S. and KOSACK, G., The Function of Labour Immigration in Western European Capitalism, 'New Left Review', no. 73, May-June 1972, pp.3-21.

COLLETTI, L., Marxism and the Dialectic, 'New Left Review', September-October 1975, pp. 3-29.

COLLIOT-THÉLÈNE, C., Contribution à une analyse des classes sociales, 'Critiques de l'économie politique', no. 19, pp. 27-47 and no. 21, pp. 93-126.

CORBETTA, P., 'Tecnici, disoccupazione e coscienza di classe', Bologna, 1975.

CORBILLÉ, F., Chômage et réserves de main-d'œuvre: une gestion imperialiste des excédents? 'Critique de l'Economie Politique', no. 10, January-March 1974, pp. 9-29.

CORNFORTH, M., Some Comments on Louis Althusser's Reply to John Lewis, in 'Marxism Today', May 1973.

DAHRENDORF, R., 'Class and Class Conflict in Industrial Society', Stanford University Press, 1959.

DAVIES, Robert, The White Working Class in South Africa, 'New Left Review', no. 82, pp. 40-59.

DOS SANTOS, T., The Concept of Social Classes, 'Science and Society', Summer 1970, pp. 166-93.

DUNKERLEY, D., 'The Study of Organizations', Routledge & Kegan Paul, London, 1972.

ENGELS, F., 'Anti-Dühring', New York, 1970.

FAIRBROTHER, P., Consciousness and Collective Action: A Study of the Social Organization of Unionized White Collar Workers, first draft of a D Phil thesis, to be submitted at the University of Oxford.

FIM, FIOM, UILM, 'Impiegati 1972'.

GARVY, G., Kondratieff's Theory of Long Cycles, 'Review of Economic Statistics', November 1943, pp. 203-20.

GERAS, N., Althusser's Marxism: An Account and Assessment, 'New Left Review', January-February 1972, no. 71.

GERAS, N., Marx and the Critique of Political Economy, in R. Blackburn (ed.), 'Ideology in Social Science', Fontana, London, 1973.

GIDDENS, A., 'The Class Structure of the Advanced Societies', London, 1973.

GLUCKSMANN, A., A Ventriloquist Structuralism, in 'New Left Review', March-April 1972, no. 72

GODELIER, M., 'Rationality and Irrationality in Economics' (English translation of 'Rationalite et irrationalite en economie'), New Left Books, London, 1972.

GORZ, A., Their Factories and Our People, 'Telos', Winter 1973-4, pp. 150-6.

GORZ, A., Technical Intelligence and the Capitalist Division of Labor, 'Telos', 12, Summer 1972, pp. 27-41.

GOUGH, Ian, Produktive and Unproductive Labor in Marx, 'New Left Review', no. 76, November-December 1972.

GRANT, D.D., The Althusser Debate, in 'Marxism Today', August 1973.

GRAY, G., The Althusser Debate, in 'Marxism Today', July 1973.

GRUPPO DI STUDIO IBM, 'Capitale Imperialistico e Proletariato Moderno', Milan, 1973.

GURLEY, J.G., Capitalist and Maoist Economic Development, in 'America's Asia', New York, 1971.

HARNECKER, M., 'Los Conceptos elementales del materialismo histórico', Siglo XXI Editores, Mexico, 1971.

HARRIS, A.B., Pure Capitalism and the Middle Class, in 'Journal of Political Economy', June 1939, pp. 328-56.

HOBSBAWN, E.J., Karl Marx Contribution to Historiography, in R. Blackburn (ed.), 'Ideology in Social Science', Fontana, London, 1973.

ILLUMINATI, A., 'Sociologia e classi sociali', Turin, 1967.

I QUADERNI DI AVANGUARDIA OPERAIA, 'I comitati unitare di base', no. 6, Sapere Edizioni, Milan, 1973.

I QUADERNI DI AVANGUARDIA OPERAIA, 'La Concezione del Partito in Lenin', Sapere Edizioni, Milan, 1970.

JANCO, M. and FURJOT, D., 'Informatique et Capitalisme', Maspero, Paris, 1972.

JOHNSON, T., 'Professions and Power', Macmillan, London, 1972.

JOHNSON, T., 'The Professions in the Class Structure', to be published in the Proceedings of the British Sociological Association, Annual Conference, 1975.

KAY, G., 'Development and Underdevelopment', Macmillan, 1975.

KEMP, T., 'Theories of Revolution', Dobson, London, 1967.

KOGA, E., Problèmes théorique de l'organisation des classes et du travail productif, 'Critique de l'Économie Politique', January-March 1973, pp. 54-75.

KONDRATIEFF, N.D., The Long Waves in Economic Life, 'Review of Economic Statistics', vol. XVII, November 1935, no. 6, pp. 105-15.

LANGE, H., PETER, L. and DEPPE, F., De technies-wetenschappelijke revolutie en de theorie van de 'nieuwe arbeidersklasse' in 'Sunschrift 14', Nijmegen, 1970, pp. 13-28.

LANGE, O., 'Political Economy', Italian translation: 'Economia Politica', vol. 1, Rome, 1970.

LEAVITT, H.J. and WHISLER, T.L., Management in the 1980's. in 'Harvard Business Review', November-December 1958.

LEFEBVRE, H., 'The Sociology of Marx', Vintage Books, New York, 1969.

LELLI, M., 'Tecnici e lotta di classe', Bari, 1973.

LENIN, V.I., 'A Great Beginning', Collected Works, vol. 29, Moscow.

LENIN, V.I., Report on the Tax in Kind delivered at the Meeting of

Secretaries and Responsible Representatives of R.C.B. (B) Cells of
Moscow and Moscow Gubernia, 9 April 1921, Collected Works, no. 32,
Moscow, 1965, pp. 286-98.
LENIN, V.I., 'The Development of Capitalism in Russia', Moscow, 1967.
LENIN, V.I., 'A Note on the Question of the Market Theory', Collected
Works, no. 4.
LENIN, V.I., 'What the "Friends of the people" are and how they fight
the Social-Democrats', Collected Works, no. 1, Moscow, 1963, pp. 129-
332.
LEWIS, J., The Althusser Case, Part 1: Marxist Humanism, in 'Marxism
Today', January 1972.
LEWIS, J., The Althusser Case, Part 2, in 'Marxism Today', February
1972.
LOCK, G., Louis Althusser: Philosophy and Leninism, in 'Marxism
Today', June 1972.
'Lotta di classe nella scuola e movimento studentesco', I Quaderni
di Avanguardia Operaia, Milan, 1971.
LUXEMBURG, R., 'The Accumulation of Capital', New York, 1968.
MALLET, S., 'La Nouvelle Classe ouvrière', Paris, 1969.
MANDEL, E., 'Marxist Economic Theory', New York, 1968.
MANDEL, E., 'Inleiding in de marxistiese ekonomie', Nijmegen, 1970.
MANDEL, E., 'Lenin en het probleem van het proletaries klassebewust-
zijn', SUN, Nijmegen, 1970.
MANDEL, E., 'Wat is neokapitalisme', Nijmegen, 1970.
MANDEL, E., 'The Formation of the Economic Thought of Karl Marx',
Monthly Review Press, 1971.
MANDEL, E., 'Der Spätkapitalismus', Frankfurt am Main, 1972.
MANDEL, E., Workers Under Neo-Capitalism, 'International Socialist
Review', vol. 29, no. 6, pp. 1-16.
MAO TSE-TUNG, On Contradiction, 'Four Essays on Philosophy', Foreign
Languages Press, Peking, 1966.
MARTINOLI, G., I laureati nell'industria, in 'I laureati in Italia',
Bologna, 1968.
MARX, K., 'Capital', vol. I, International Publishers, New York,
1967.
MARX, K., 'Capital', vol. II, International Publishers, New York,
1967.
MARX, K., 'Capital', vol. III, International Publishers, New York,
1967.
MARX, K., 'Grundrisse der Kritik der politischen Ökonomie', English
translation by M. Nicolaus, London, 1973.
MARX, K., 'Theories of Surplus Value', vol. I, Progress Publishers,
Moscow, 1968.
MARX, K., 'Theories of Surplus Value', vol. II, Progress Publishers,
Moscow, 1968.
MARX, K., 'Wage-Labour and Capital', International Publishers, New
York, 1969 edn.
MARX, K., 'Resultate des unmittelbaren Produktionsprozesses', Italian
translation 'Il Capitale, Libro 1, Capitolo VI inedito', Florence,
1968.
MARX, K. and ENGELS, F., 'The German Ideology', New York, 1970.
MAUKE, M., 'Die Klassentheorie von Marx und Engels', Italian trans-
lation 'La teòria delle classi nel pensiero di Marx e Engels', Milan,
1971.

MILIBAND, R., 'The State in Capitalist Society', Weidenfeld & Nicolson, London, 1969.

MILLS, C.W., 'White Collar', Oxford University Press, 1951.

MINGIONE, E., 'Impiegati, sviluppo capitalistico e lotta di classe', Rome, 1973.

MOK, A.L. and DE JAGER, H., 'Grondbeginselen der sociologie', Leiden, 1971.

MOSZKOWSKA, N., 'Zur Kritik moderner Krisentheorien', Italian translation 'Per la critica delle teorie modene della crisi', Turin, 1974.

MYRDAL, G., 'Asian Drama', vol. III, New York, 1968.

NAIRN, T., The English Working Class, in R. Blackburn (ed.), 'Ideology in Social Sciences', Fontana, London, 1973.

NICOLAUS, M., Foreword, in K. Marx, 'Grundrisse', Penguin edn, 1973.

NICOLAUS, M., The Unknown Marx, in R. Blackburn (ed.), 'Ideology in Social Science', Fontana, London, 1973.

NURKSE, R., 'Problems of Capital Formation in Underdeveloped Countries', Oxford University Press, 1967.

OAKLY, J., Marxism and Ideology, II Althusser and Ideology, in 'Marxism Today', September 1972.

PARKER, S.R., BROWN, R.K., CHILD, J. and SMITH, M.A., 'The Sociology of Industry', London, 1967.

PICCONE-STELLA, S., 'Intellettuali e Capitale', Bari, 1972.

POLLOCK, F., 'The Economic and Social Consequences of Automation', Blackwell, Oxford, 1957.

POULANTZAS, N., On Social Classes, 'New Left Review', no. 78 March-April 1973.

POULANTZAS, N., 'Political Power and Social Classes', London, 1973.

POULANTZAS, N., The Problems of the Capitalist State, in R. Blackburn (ed.),'Ideology in Social Sciences', Fontana, London, 1973.

POULANTZAS, N., 'Les Classes sociales dans le capitalisme aujourd' hui', Paris, 1974.

RASMUS, J., Why Management is Pushing 'Job Enrichment', 'International Socialist Review', December 1974.

ROLLE, P., 'Introduction à la sociologie du travail', Italian translation 'Sociologia del lavoro', Bologna, 1973.

SEYFARTH, SHAW, FAIRWEATHER and GERALDSON, 'Labor Relations and the Law in Italy and the United States', University of Michigan, 1970. 'Sunschrift 14', Nijmegen, 1970.

SWEEZY, P.M., 'The Theory of Capitalist Development', New York, 1968.

SWEEZY, P.M., Czechoslovakia, Capitalism and Socialism, in 'Monthly Review', October 1968.

SWEEZY, P.M., Reply, in 'Monthly Review', March 1969.

SWEEZY, P.M., Reply, in 'Monthly Review', December 1970.

SWINGEWOOD, A., 'Marx and Modern Social Theory', Macmillan, 1975.

THOMPSON, E.P., 'The Making of the English Working Class', Penguin edn, 1963.

TUMIN, M.M. (ed.), 'Readings on Social Stratification', Prentice-Hall, Englewood Cliffs, 1970.

URRY, J., Towards a Structural Theory of the Middle Class, 'Acta Sociologica', 16, 175-87.

URRY, J., New Theories of the New Middle Class, 'Amsterdam Sociologisch Tijdschrift', forthcoming.

VALLIER, J., Les théories de l'impérialisme de Lenine et Rosa Luxemburg, in 'Critique de l'économie politique', nos 4-5, July and December 1971.

VELTMEYER, H., Towards an Assessment of the Structuralist Interrogation of Marx: Claude Lévi-Strauss and Louis Althusser, 'Science and Society', vol. 38, no. 4, Winter 1974-5, pp. 385-421.

VINCENT, Jean-Marie, Etat et classes sociales, 'Critiques de l'économie politique', no. 19, pp. 4-26.

VIRIEU, F.H. de 'LIP, 100.000 montres sans patron', Calmann-Lévy, 1973.

WALTON, P. and GAMBLE, A., 'From Alienation to Surplus Value', Sheed & Ward, London, 1972.

WESTERGAARD, J.H., Sociology, The Myth of Classlessness, in R. Blackburn (ed.), 'Ideology in Social Science', Fontana, London, 1973.

WHEELWRIGHT, E.L. and McFARLANE, B., 'The Chinese Road to Socialism', New York, 1970.

WHISLER, T.L. and LEAVITT, H.J., Management in the 1980's, 'Harvard Business Review', November-December 1958.

WINDMULLER, J.P., 'Labor Relations in the Netherlands', Cornell University Press, 1969.

WORSLEY, P., 'The Third World', Weidenfeld & Nicolson, London, 1971.

WRIGLEY, J., The Althusser Debate, in 'Marxism Today', September 1973.

WYGODSKY, W., 'De ontwikkeling van het ekonomies denken van Marx', SUN, Nijmegen, 1974.

INDEX

For Product Safety Concerns and Information please contact our EU
representative GPSR@taylorandfrancis.com
Taylor & Francis Verlag GmbH, Kaufingerstraße 24, 80331 München, Germany

www.ingramcontent.com/pod-product-compliance
Ingram Content Group UK Ltd.
Pitfield, Milton Keynes, MK11 3LW, UK
UKHW021829240425
457818UK00006B/135